# PLAIN

# LETTERS

## Mona Sheppard

THE SECRET
OF SUCCESSFUL BUSINESS WRITING

SIMON AND
SCHUSTER
NEW YORK
1960

*TO BETTY AND EMMETT LEAHY*
*in appreciation*

ACKNOWLEDGMENTS

The author wishes to thank the following authors, publishers and representatives for their courtesy in granting permission to reprint selections in this book:

The Atlantic Monthly Press for the letter from C. E. Perkins to Henry Lee Higginson, from *Life and Letters of Henry Lee Higginson* by Bliss Perry, © 1921 by The Atlantic Monthly Press; and the letter from William James to his pupils, from *The Letters of William James*, edited by Henry James, © 1920 by The Atlantic Monthly Press.

Estate of James Gibbons Huneker for the letter from James Gibbons Huneker to David Munro, from *Intimate Letters of James Gibbons Huneker*, edited by Josephine Huneker, published by Liveright Publishing Company, 1936.

Harper & Brothers for the list of verbs and adverbs for idiomatic phrasing, from *The Art of Readable Writing* by Rudolf Flesch, published by Harper & Brothers, 1949.

Ives Henrick, M.D., for the letters from Walter Hines Page to Ralph W. Page, Sir Edward Grey, Woodrow Wilson and Edward M. House; and the letter from Theodore Roosevelt to Walter Hines Page, from *The Life and Letters of Walter H. Page* by Burton J. Hendrick, published 1922 by Doubleday, Page & Company.

Houghton Mifflin Company for the letter from Henry Adams to Whitelaw Reid, from *Henry Adams and His Friends*, edited by Harold Dean Cater, published by Houghton Mifflin Company, 1947.

Mrs. Anne Wintermute Lane for the letters from Franklin K. Lane to Woodrow Wilson, from *The Letters of Franklin K. Lane*, edited by Anne Wintermute Lane and Louise Herrick Wall, published by Houghton Mifflin Company, 1922.

McGraw-Hill Company, Inc., for the selection from *Copy Capsules* by Hal Stebbins, © 1957 by McGraw-Hill Company, Inc.

*National Review* for the selection "Before You Say No . . ." by Mrs. Benjamin Heath, © 1958 by *National Review*.

National Underwriter Company for selections from *Better Life Insurance Letters* by Mildred F. Stone, © 1950 by National Underwriter Company.

# Contents

*Letters are the literature of business. Your personal stake in letters may be greater than you think. The 4-S virtues of plain letters: shortness, simplicity, strength and sincerity. How to get the most out of this book in the shortest length of time.*

Part One

## HOW TO WRITE A PLAIN LETTER

*Say only what needs to be said, and use only the words needed to say it. Six ways to keep from saying too much. Eight ways to economize on words.*

*Simplicity in words, sentences and paragraphs. Seven suggestions on how to make letters easy to read.*

*Right words move others to work and think with you. Five ways to make better use of your word power.*

Part Two

## THE PRACTICAL APPROACH TO GRAMMAR AND PUNCTUATION

Part Three

## PRODUCTION AIDS

*appropriate? How to design printed letters. How to personalize forms.*

## Part Four

# EXAMPLES

*Sixty plain letters exemplifying some common purposes of business writing.*

# APPENDIX

# Foreword

WHILE browsing through a correspondence file in a large bank several years ago, I noticed that one man's letters always attracted my attention. One by one, perhaps a dozen in all, these letters impressed me as the kind anybody might enjoy reading. I found myself reading them not simply because I had a job to do as a correspondence consultant but because I wanted to.

As an experiment I shuffled six of those letters into a deck with forty-six others selected at random. I then asked eight people of diverse backgrounds—including a Harvard-trained vice-president, a messenger with an eighth-grade education and a professional writer—to read the entire deck and answer one simple question: Which letter do you like best?

The result? Five of the readers chose one of the letters I had planted in the deck. Although the other three passed up these particular letters, it is worth noting that their selections were just as readable. As it happened, not one of the winning letters concerned anything other than a routine business matter. In each case the writer had won his reader not by what he had to say but by the way he said it.

Was the five-time winner a professional writer? A born writer? Had he taken a college course in letter writing? The answer to these questions as I was later to learn from him is No. What he told me is so much to the point of this book that I am sure that he—a vice-president of the Bank of America—will not mind my repeating it.

"If I can write good letters, anybody can," he said modestly. "I discovered my letters were not the kind that people like to read, so I decided to do something about it. Here's my secret."

Reaching into his desk drawer he pulled out the fifty-page handbook Plain Letters that I had written for the United States government a year earlier. "The principles of Plain Letters have helped me more than anything else," he said. "But you should write another book."

"Another book?"

"Yes, a book for business people."

I understood what he meant. The original Plain Letters was written especially for government letter writers, with scarcely any thought of the problems of men and women in business, industry and professional fields. He had discovered for himself how the same principles can be applied to business letters. But how much easier that discovery might be for others if the principles were restated in the terms of business problems!

In the years since I wrote the original Plain Letters I have been conducting correspondence studies and letter-writing courses in practically every line of business—fast-moving courses for busy people who have no time for academic meanderings. College graduates and grade-school graduates, vice-presidents and clerks, business and professional men alike have taken this training. I, too, have been in training. In banks, investment houses, airlines, railroads, insurance companies, retail houses and manufacturing firms, I have been gathering firsthand information about business letters. All told I have read, tested, edited or rewritten more than a quarter of a million letters.

My assistants have run up this score to a million odd. In each case we tried to show how the principles of plain letters can be applied in every line of business. At the same time we have worked hard to add to the training courses any practical ideas overlooked in the original Plain Letters.

Many of those enrolled in my courses have asked for a plain-letter book so that they might pass it on to friends. Scores of others—individuals and companies that have not had the opportunity for training—have written me to ask if such a book was available. Here it is. I hope you will find it helpful.

CHAPTER 1 | A
Quick Look
at the Subject

ONCE, when Franklin K. Lane was U.S. Secretary of the Interior, he happened to see an ornate letter from a lawyer to an Indian. That letter, in Mr. Lane's own words, was "so involved and elaborately beaded and braided and fringed" that he himself could not understand it. So he sent it back to the legal department with these three words of good advice: "*Use straightaway English.*"

If the lawyer who wrote that Indian letter took Mr. Lane's advice I can easily imagine how he slashed through the trappings that hid the meaning of his message. He cut out lazy words and cut down big ones. He woke up passive verbs and made them active, straightened out roundabout phrases and shortened long sentences. Then he tied all his sentences together. When he had done slashing and straightening, I can imagine that the Indian letter was transformed. From beginning to end its meaning shone clearly in every single word. It may not have been a literary masterpiece, but it was easy to read and easy to understand. It was a *plain letter.*

## THE READER'S VIEWPOINT

Franklin Lane was a writing craftsman. He had been a journalist long before joining Woodrow Wilson's cabinet. In the writing trade he is bound to have discovered that plain writing is by no means the plain fare of unsophisticated readers. Everybody—whether an untutored Indian or a Ph.D.—prefers good plain English.

The trouble is, the reader may have no choice when it comes to a letter. He reads a book by choice, he reads his favorite newspaper by choice, he subscribes to his favorite magazine by choice. But when he looks at the morning mail he may do so only because it is put before him in the manner of *Here, read this.* Expecting good news— a new order for business or a favorable reply—he may open a letter eagerly. Otherwise, he may open it with a sense of cold compulsion: *What now?* To be sure, the prosaic affairs of everyday business are hardly calculated to offer him exciting reading. But when he is trapped he certainly has the right to expect a letter that is easy to read.

## MR. COWPER SETS AN EXAMPLE

It was just such an easy-to-read letter that William Cowper, the English poet, wrote nearly two hundred years ago about a shipment of meat. A more prosaic subject is difficult to imagine. Yet thousands of people have read Mr. Cowper's letter by choice; and it has been held up to generations of English-speaking rhetoric students as an outstanding example of a good plain letter.

*Olney, Jan. 1, 1771*

DEAR JOSEPH,—*You will receive two parcels of venison, a haunch and a shoulder. The first was intended for you, the other comes to you by mistake. Some hours after the basket was sent to the wagon we discovered the shoulder had been packed up instead of the haunch. All imaginable endeavors were made to recover it, but without success. The wagon could not be unloaded again, and it was impossible otherwise to get at it. You may, therefore, thank a blundering servant for a venison*

pasty which, if she had minded her own business better, would
have been eaten at Olney.

Yours, my dear friend,
WM. COWPER

Let us compare the way a modern businessman might "bead and
braid and fringe" a letter on the same subject.

DEAR SIR,—This is in reference to a shipment of meat forwarded by this company to your firm under date of September
12, 1959, invoice number N–54901, in accordance with your
order number 7327, dated September 10, 1959, for one haunch of
venison in the amount of $15.60.

Undoubtedly, you have received as of this date another shipment under separate cover which was also made on September
12, containing a shoulder of venison to which you are not
entitled inasmuch as this company has no record of receiving
your order for same. We would like to explain that this shipment was inadvertently packed by a new shipping clerk and
forwarded under the above-mentioned invoice number. Inasmuch as discovery of the inadvertency was not made until
after the package was delivered to the carrier for delivery to
you, we regret to say that it was impossible to rectify the error.

It would therefore be appreciated, in the event that the
necessary steps have not been taken to return the shoulder,
carrying charges collect and shipment moving under refrigera-
tion to prevent spoilage, that you remit your check payable
to the order of this company in the amount of $18.12 to cover
the net cost less 2 per cent discount under our 30-day payment
terms.

Hoping that you have in no way been inconvenienced and
anticipating your continued patronage,

Very truly yours,
THE X PROVISION COMPANY

This modern version of the Cowper haunch-and-shoulder letter may be exaggerated. Yet it sounds much like many other business letters you and I have read. Wordy. Dull. Pompous. *Unreadable.* The wonder of it is that the people who write these letters—if they would try—could make them just as readable as Mr. Cowper's.


## OUR STAKE IN LETTERS

When you come right down to it, letters are just about all the sentence writing that most of us in business ever do. But the volume of this writing and its role in our economy and personal business affairs combine to make it a vast and influential literature of business.

There are now nearly 29 billion pieces of first-class mail each year. Three quarters of these letters, according to the Postmaster General, originate in commercial firms. Of course, much of it carries checks, bills, statements and other miscellaneous items. Even so, at least 60 per cent—a whopping 12 billion pieces a year—are what we would call business letters. Can you imagine such a fantastic quantity of mail? Piled one on the other ready for mailing these letters would reach 4,500 miles into the stratosphere. The total word count is easily 2,000 times that of the more than 10,000 books published in this country each year. And still we have not included memorandums, those members of the letter family that never enter the mails.

Can anyone doubt the colossal role that letters play in the affairs of business? Or that the letters most likely to succeed are the ones that people like to read? As I write this chapter I have just seen the report that one big steel company has increased responses to a form letter 140 per cent by making it a little more readable. There are dozens of similar examples from business and government that I have collected through the years. Human-interest stories from companies that have received heartfelt thanks from readers. Dollar-mindful reports of how better letters have increased sales and of how shorter letters have reduced administrative costs. Reports of the railroad that saved $100,000 during the first year of its better-letter program, of the life insurance company that is saving $85,000 a year, of one district office of Internal Revenue Service that cut office cost by $157,000 a year while making life a bit more pleasant for taxpayers with readable letters. As reported by *Time* and *Newsweek*, here's how one Internal Revenue letter used to start:

> *Reference is made to your income tax return Form 1040 or 1040a for the year 1952. The return was received in this office without the required form(s) W-2 attached to substantiate your claim as to amount(s) withheld by your employer(s) from your wages.*

And this is how the new letter begins:

> *Your withholding statements, Form W-2, are missing from your income tax return.*

Each of these stories is an example of better business such as would lead you to think that every company, every government department would cultivate the art of writing good letters. To find this is the exception rather than the rule, that's the surprise! Two surveys made a few years ago in the Los Angeles area by the National Office Management Association revealed that only 26 companies out of 200 provided any instruction in letter writing, while only 20 had taken the trouble to study letter-writing costs.

## THE MAN BEHIND THE LETTER

Your personal stake in letters may be greater than you think. For in the business world the ability to express ideas clearly and convincingly shows up in letters more than in any other form of written communication.

Speaking of a junior executive trainee, the president of one company said to me, "We had high hopes for this man. He's a graduate in business administration, personable, energetic. But he's not getting across. His reports and letters are so wordy and confusing that some of my staff have grave doubts about his ability to think straight. Now, it's my theory that his trouble is not so much a matter of *straight thinking* as of *straight writing*. Yet I must be sure before we spend another dime grooming him for a key job in this company."

The president's theory was right. In the letter-writing course that followed, his junior executive learned how to apply a few simple principles of plain writing to those confusing, haltering reports to give them logic, lucidity and march. When, a few months later, I again spoke to the company's president he told me, "Our man is licking his problem, and we have him slated for a manager's job."

I then told him the story of an older man who once enrolled in a letter-writing course. For twenty years this man had been an assistant credit manager while a succession of managers came and left. The company's controller admitted that this loyal worker knew more about their accounts and credit policy than anyone else in the company. "But," he said, "the poor guy can't write a letter. Those unfortunate letters of his are always bouncing back on the president of our company."

For this man, breaking writing habits of so many years was hard. But he tried. And he succeeded. At the age of fifty-eight he won the job he coveted. When he reported the good news he told how a customer had recently called at his office and planked down a letter. "It was one of my collection letters," he said. "Did I get bawled out? No! The customer just wanted to congratulate me on the best letter he had ever received from this department. And we've written him dozens. What's more, he paid off—in full."

Like these men you may be judged by your letters for the ability to communicate effectively. And if your letters are falling short of the mark, you can improve your chances for advancement by learning to apply a few simple principles of plain writing. For the same principles that help us write plain letters also help us become better thinkers and spokesmen. It is not surprising that executives as a rule are among our best letter writers.

## THE 4-S VIRTUES

The principles that help us most are not the rules of grammar.
There's nothing wrong with the grammar of most business letters. It may not pass the standards of the purist, but if we can win the sympathy and understanding of our readers, who cares a fig about a split infinitive or a dangling participle? One short chapter on grammar has been included in this book with the hope of giving confidence to those who feel unsure about a few controversial points, and with no thought of setting businessmen straight on matters learned in the eighth grade.

Neither need we be concerned about vocabulary. Concern for vocabulary can actually inhibit the writing of plain letters. Some of us spend a lot of time searching for words we never use in everyday speech. Out they come, unnatural and pretentious, when words on the tip of the tongue might be more effective. So we find an engineer referring to an airbump as a "sudden vertical acceleration of an aircraft." Had he thought of his words as a stimulus for getting a prompt response, what better word could he have chosen than "airbump"? The little words we use when we talk—the common everyday speech of Americans—these are all the vocabulary we need for business letters. The only problem is making better use of it.

Finally, let us not be concerned about that mysterious thing called style. Whatever it is, each of us has his own. Quiller-Couch says, "Essentially style resembles good manners. It comes of endeavoring to understand others, of thinking of them rather than of yourself. . . ." On this same subject Matthew Arnold once remarked, "Have something to say and say it as clearly as you can. That is the secret of style." The advice of both Quiller-Couch and Arnold is perfect for business letters. Those who follow it can achieve good style in their own way.

What, then, is the secret of letters that everybody likes to read? The secret lies in just four words, each of them beginning with the letter S. These words stand for those 4-S virtues that you will hear about in this book:

Shortness
Simplicity
Strength
Sincerity

The principles that guide us in writing letters with these virtues are the basis of effective communication. They have been followed consciously or unconsciously by great writers of all ages. You can follow them, too. If you do, you are certain to improve your own art of self-expression, even though you never become a "great writer."

From the golden rule of business writing in the next chapter you will see how to *shorten* letters to clarify their meaning and improve their tone. In the chapters that follow you will discover why *simplicity* is the supreme excellence and how the *strength* that moves others to work and think with us flows from the power of right words. Tips on how to get yourself on paper show how naturalness serves to convince the reader of your *sincerity*. There are suggestions, too, on how to improve the appearance of letters and on how to cut letter-writing costs.

These principles are not arbitrary rules. They are guides to help you help yourself in handling what may be the most important tool of your business career—*language*.

SHORT CUT TO PLAIN LETTERS

Here are seven suggestions on how to get the most out of this book in the shortest time:

1. *Be sure that you have the right attitude toward writing.* This is the first and an indispensable requirement.

Do you dislike writing letters? Do you find writing of any kind a laborious task for which you have no more taste than you had for those themes in school? If the answer is Yes, don't get the idea there's anything wrong with you. Thousands of other business writers feel the same way, mostly because they have been poorly conditioned for writing of any kind. Somehow our schools, as if by design, manage to make the business of writing seem highly complicated. Teachers set before us the best examples of literature and at the same time convince us that these examples are shrouded in mystery. Our own attempts to emulate them—those occasional themes—came back to us with little notes about metaphors and similes, periodic sentences, allusions, and so on. All very necessary, no doubt; but how discouraging for most students! If this is what it takes to write, you may have concluded, I'll stick to reading and let the other fellow do the writing.

Don't let your thinking be distorted by false analogy. The people who read our business letters don't look to us for their literary masterpieces. Don't think for a minute that it is a complicated task to write the kind of letter people like to read. If you think it is, begin now to change your attitude. Think of letter writing as an enjoyable hobby—as indeed it can be—rather than a distasteful task. Think in terms of the word *simple* rather than in terms of the word *complicated.* If you think of writing as complicated, it is very likely to turn out that way.

Above all, beware of a false pride of authorship. Even those of us who consider letter writing a sort of necessary evil sometimes tend to cherish our poorest efforts. Our pride is pricked by the merest suggestion that our letters fall short of the mark. We fly to the defense of our letters as we would to the defense of our own flesh and blood.

Pride of authorship need not be frustrating. We can be richly rewarded when our pride is derived from the feeling that our letters are satisfying our readers.

Unless you have the right attitude, nothing this book has to say can help you. But with the right attitude there is no obstacle in your way.

2. *Have confidence in your own manner of self-expression.* The problem of "freezing" before a stenographer has nothing to do with that young woman who takes your dictation! This problem, if it is yours, is a lack of confidence in your own manner of self-expression. If your natural manner of expressing yourself seems to be not good enough, you may strive for pretentious words. Letter clichés, seemingly so safe, rush to your rescue in filling up those awkward gaps. As a result, you are not doing your best in satisfying one of your reader's principal requirements—naturalness. *Be yourself.*

3. *Collect copies of some letters you wrote before you began reading this book.* Try to get at least twenty-five samples, fifty if possible.

4. *Read carefully and slowly to the Appendix.* If you come to a passage that isn't clear to you, please forgive me and read it again. I might even suggest that you get the enjoyment of saying to yourself, "Look, the writer has fallen into the same trap she warns us against."

Mark or underscore any passage in the book that will be helpful in overcoming your particular shortcomings. This book is not an adornment for an office bookshelf. It is a practical book that should be kept on your desk and referred to as often as need be.

5. *Test your L.Q.* (*Letter-writing Quotient*). When you come to the Appendix, take the letters you wrote before you started reading the book and look into them for answers to the questions in "Test Your L.Q." When the answer to a question is negative or when you do not recall the principle involved, turn back and

reread the part of the book in which the principle is discussed. You will find the page numbers referenced.

After a few weeks collect some more copies of your letters and again take the test. Note how much you have improved. Do this as often as necessary.

6. *Don't get discouraged.* In your first game of golf you probably shot as high as 140, unless you had beginner's luck. But if you kept at the game, you are probably now shooting an average of about 90. You may even have become an expert.

As you read the book, you will find many of the principles taking hold in your mind and altering your daily correspondence. You will be able to put some of these principles into practice without any special effort. Others may be forgotten. Never mind. The business of improving letters may take time, but if you go about it in the right way improvement will come more easily and sooner than you think.

7. *Make better use of edited letters.* When you begin to see how much you have improved, take the next big step—especially if you write a large number of letters. Predraft the letters on subjects you frequently write about. You can edit these letters with the care of a professional copywriter.

Chapter 10 has some practical suggestions on how to capture subject matter and predraft top-quality, personalized form and guide letters. Follow these suggestions and you will be amazed at the time you can save for yourself and at the profit to your business.

# Part One

# HOW
# TO WRITE
# A PLAIN
# LETTER

4-S
SHORT-SIMPLE-STRONG-SINCERE

# The
# 4-S
# Formula

*(in a nutshell)*

FOR SHORTNESS

1. The golden rule of business writing: *Say only what needs to be said, and use only the words needed to say it.*

FOR SIMPLICITY

2. *Know your subject so well you can discuss it confidently and naturally.*
3. *Use short words, short sentences and short paragraphs.*
4. *Keep closely related parts of sentences together.*
5. *Connect sentences so the reader can follow you from one to the other without getting lost.*

FOR STRENGTH: *Your Astonishing Word Power*

6. *Use words standing for things your reader can see or touch.*
7. *Use active verbs.*
8. *Approach your subject positively.*
9. *Attend to your reader's wants, especially his want for recognition.*
10. *For that big idea, use a periodic sentence: a "nonstop" sentence that must be read from beginning to end for a complete thought.*

FOR SINCERITY

11. *Get yourself on paper. Be natural.*
12. *Be human. Use words that stand for human beings, like the personal pronouns* you, he, they, *etc., and the names of people.*
13. *Be conversational. Avoid old-fashioned letter language. Use some contractions such as* couldn't *instead of* could not *and* isn't *instead of* is not.
14. *Admit mistakes. Don't try to hide them behind meaningless words.*
15. *Be businesslike yet friendly: dignified but not arrogant, forthright but not blunt.*

SHORTNESS

CHAPTER 2 | The Golden Rule

of Business Writing

THE FIRST and golden rule of business writing is: *Say only what needs to be said, and use only the words needed to say it.*

There are three reasons why I am suggesting this rule as the golden one.

1. My reading of some quarter of a million business and government letters has convinced me that brevity is the most abused principle of plain writing. As the title of a recent magazine article put it, *Wanted: A Reducing Diet for Business Letters.*

2. Wordiness is expensive. How staggering this toll can be has been proved again and again by cost measurements. One such study showed an excess verbiage of 38 per cent in the half-million letters a year rolling from the typewriters of a railroad—needless words (plainly squandered) that are adding $60,000 a year to typing costs alone.

3. *Shortness,* the first of the 4-S virtues, magically encourages the other three—simplicity, strength, sincerity. "We welcome your suggestions" is simpler and stronger than "Your suggestions are welcomed by this company." Also note how much more warmth and sincerity the shorter expression conveys. The right tone of a letter can be weakened or destroyed by meaningless words with which the writer strives to impress his reader.

One of the first letters in recorded history is striking proof of

the power of brevity. Here is David writing to Joab (II Samuel
11:15):

> Set ye Uriah in the forefront of the hottest battle, and retire
> ye from him, that he may be smitten, and die.

Imagine how a military strategist at the Pentagon might have
written that letter!

To be sure, it is harder to write orders that briefly today. Modern
technology, laws and organizational rules leave more to be said. But
matters are worsened by the writer's anxiety to give every possible
shred of information needed for the reader's or his own protection.
Too many letter writers feel that it is safer to say too much than
too little. Through this safety valve flow millions of needless words.

Actually, the complexity and diversity of modern life make brevity
more desirable, not less. All too often, harried readers are antagonized,
or their interest is deadened, by needless facts and words.

Consider, for example, the plain man who comes from work
to find several pieces of mail on his living-room table. He may have
had a difficult day at office or factory or farm. Maybe his wife has
not returned from an afternoon bridge game, and there are no signs
of dinner under way. One of the letters is from an insurance company replying to his inquiry about cash-surrender of a policy. It
is a prompt reply, neatly typed on an attractive letterhead. So far,
so good. But as he wades into the letter, his interest begins to fade.
It is too long. There is too much about options of borrowing and
changing plans. The information he really wants is hidden somewhere in the letter—but where?

I have seen many letters like this returned with angry words like
these scrawled across the face: "I asked one question. Please
answer it."

Executives plagued by long-winded reports are undoubtedly
tempted to send back the reports with the same reply. A common
failing of business report writers is to try to tell all they know rather
than all the executive needs to know. In one big oil company, the

internal reports going to the president's desk each year were found to constitute reading matter three times as long as the King James Bible. When boiled down, these reports lost 60 per cent of their volume and not a single essential fact.

Some top executives employ an assistant just to condense long-winded reports. Others, pressed by committee meetings, phone calls and interviews during office hours, drag heavy brief cases everywhere they go, for snatched moments of reading in barber chairs, taxis, and commuter trains. How much they could save by insisting on shorter reports!

But brevity can be overdone too.

Sam Levenson tells the yarn of the husband who phoned his wife and asked, "What are we having for dinner? And how are the children?" The wife answered, "Chicken. And chicken pox."

That would be going a little far in a letter. Fragmentary sentences are all right now and then. Like this one! But most sentences should be complete with subject and verb. Words that clarify meaning and improve tone should not be sacrificed, and information that will genuinely aid the reader should be offered freely even if he hasn't asked for it.

The right length for a letter can be measured only by comparing it with how much longer—or shorter—the same message might have been for best results.

A number of years ago a major magazine wrote its readers a five-page letter offering them the opportunity to buy an important new book at discount. A casual observer might have thought that the five-page letter was too long. But before the letter was mailed, it and a four-page letter on the same subject were both tried out on 50,000 readers. The five-page letter brought 10 per cent more orders. On the full mailing to the magazine's five million readers it produced $250,000 more in orders than the four-page letter would have.

This didn't mean that the five-page letter was better because it was longer. In fact, it could be argued that the longer letter really was the shorter one because it had less padding.

Never measure the length of a letter with a ruler. Do it with a pencil. Count the words that don't contribute to the "sell" or "tell" in your letter. If your tally of unnecessary words is zero, that's a short letter—no matter whether it's one page or ten!

## SIX WAYS TO KEEP FROM SAYING TOO MUCH

Of course, we can only generalize about what needs to be said in a letter. Each one must be judged individually by what it takes to get the message across. But I can show you some of the reasons why two out of every three letter writers are trapped into saying too much; and here I shall have some specific suggestions to help you avoid what the German philosopher Schopenhauer called "tedious details that every man can supply for himself."

1. *Don't repeat what is said in a letter you are answering.* The most common type of the tedious detail is to be found in this example:

> This will acknowledge receipt of your letter of July 13 in which you state that you desire to have your party numbering about 30 travel from Hartsville to New York on Monday, August 15th, leaving Hartsville as close to 9:00 A.M. as possible.
> There is a train leaving Hartsville at 8:24 A.M. Daylight Saving Time. The next train is in the early afternoon.
> Will you please advise whether we should protect arrangements for your party on the train leaving Hartsville at 8:24 A.M.

See what happened? It took as many words to repeat the content of the reader's letter as it did to answer it.

Those who write this way may feel that the repetition is needed to build a bridge between the inquiry and the answer. But when we talk to people we don't ordinarily repeat their questions before answering them.

Give your reader credit for a better memory. You can then

frame your reply so he will know that you understand his question. Like this:

> Thank you for your letter outlining your party's travel plans. There is a train leaving Hartsville for New York at 8:24 A.M. Daylight Saving Time. Shall we make a reservation for 30 on it for August 15? There isn't another train until early afternoon.

In the following letter the writer took nearly 100 words to get started.

> We are in receipt of your recent letter requesting a review of your present stockholdings. We see you have additional funds to invest and that you have expressed an interest in various issues. You state you are primarily interested in income but it is noted that you also wish appreciation. You say that you would like to have not less than 4 per cent and preferably 5 per cent over-all. Your fund has been reviewed with this in mind, and our comments are noted below. It is a pleasure to have this opportunity to serve you.

Here again, fewer words could have made the reader aware that the writer understood his aims and questions:

> Thank you for coming to us for a review of your stockholdings and suggestions on the investment of additional funds. It is a pleasure to assist you. In making our suggestions we shall keep in mind the fact that you are interested in capital appreciation as well as good income.

The bridge building doesn't always end with the first paragraph. A second bridge is thrown up right in the middle of this short letter:

> This is in reply to your letter of April 7 in which you ask about the availability of the book entitled Practical Guides to

Mapmaking. *I regret to inform you that this book is out of print.*

*You also ask about the approximate publication date of Maps of Ten Centuries. This book is scheduled for release within the next month. Your local bookdealer will be pleased to take your order if he does not have it in stock.*

Even if no reference had been made to the inquiry, the information in the above reply would have come as no surprise to the reader. Imagine that you were the person who asked the questions that prompted this letter. Would you be at loss upon receiving a straight-to-the-point answer:

We are sorry that our book Practical Guides to Mapmaking is out of print. But Maps of Ten Centuries is coming off the press now, and should be available from your local bookdealer by the end of the month. If he does not have it in stock by then, he will be pleased to take your order.

I think it is not an exaggeration to say that American business and government are spending millions of dollars a year in the needless rehashing of inquiries. The baleful influence of this tedious detail has even spread into the business offices of houses engaged in the professional writing business. *The New Yorker* magazine wrote me:

*Acknowledging your letter of November 2nd requesting permission to reprint in a book on government and business letter writing that you are preparing for publication by Simon and Schuster, the item which appeared under the heading "The Welfare State in Action," in our issue of September 20, 1952:*

*Since this item did not originate with us, it is not within our province to authorize a use of it by others.*

In its year-in-year-out drive for effective letters the New York Life Insurance Company distributes blotters printed with helpful hints.

One tip is, "Don't bother to mention receiving a letter when you reply." When the reply goes to the individual, such as an individual policyholder, you can take this tip with the assurance that the reader will have no difficulty tying your answer to his inquiry. On the other hand, a company, especially a big one, may need to draw the file in which a copy of its inquiry is kept. If you have the file number, that's all you need. Type it where it will be noticed, preferably in the upper right corner of your letter. If you don't have the file number, give the company just enough information to identify the file.

Similar to the practice of rehashing the contents of an incoming letter is the practice of interpreting what the reader said or did. These interpretations are found in sentences beginning, "As we understand," or "We understand that."

*We understand that your application to us was occasioned through your desire to effect an income savings by having tax deductible charges added to the cost of your annual premium rather than having the premium increased as is required when monthly payments are made to the carrier.*

This complicated sentence has the ridiculous effect of telling the man who requested a loan why he had requested it. You may see it as an attempt to avoid misunderstanding. It was nothing of the sort. Many of us delight in going on record with our interpretations of what the other fellow says or does.

No doubt we are influenced by our lawyers, who are tediously explicit. But, except in rare instances, our letters are not contracts and don't need to be written that way. Those "as we understand" sentences are purposeful only when there is some doubt as to whether the reader's statement or action is correctly understood.

The next time such a sentence comes up in your dictation, pause a second. Ask yourself whether you actually need to give the reader a chance to set you straight. If you do, say so. If you don't, resist the sentence.

2. *Beware of sentences beginning with* "*As you know.*" The feeling that prompts you to give your reader credit for knowing as much as you do is commendable, but those sentences beginning "As you know" are not worthy of your generosity. They are extravagancies more likely to impress him as crude and silly attempts at flattery.

If the reader does know what you are about to say, why tell him? You might use "as you know" instead of "as you recall" when you want to remind him of something in the dim past without expressing doubts about his memory. You should not, however, rely on this clumsy way of making a point. If you get a letter saying "I am unable to meet your 30-day payment terms," avoid getting off on this track:

> *As you know, our terms call for payment net 30 days after invoice, and our merchandise is sold on an open account basis with the expectation that these payment terms will be observed. It will be appreciated that we cannot in fairness to our other customers make exception to the standard payment terms.*

Instead, ease the tension for the reader by going straight to the point:

> *As much as we would like to oblige you, we cannot—in fairness to our other customers—make an exception to our 30-day payment terms.*

3. *Don't give the reader information he has at hand.* Files readily available to the reader and enclosures with a letter are "information at hand." When the writer puts the same information in a letter, he is again supplying details the reader can supply for himself. If this is a convenience to the reader, there is no quarrel with the practice. The waste comes when he must in any event examine the file or the enclosure.

Take the widespread practice of quoting or paraphrasing the contents of an earlier letter: "On January 12 we wrote you as follows. . . ." The dictator then goes on to quote an earlier letter when it would be sufficient to say "Please refer to my letter of January 12." One company discovered that 30 per cent of its letters (equal to $45,000 a year typing costs) were tracers, follow-up letters repeating the contents of earlier ones.

Some practical advice on this subject comes to us in a memo from a vice-president to members of his staff:

> *Everybody knows that files get misplaced. But if that were not the exception rather than the rule we might be out of business. I think we can assume that the same thing is true in every other company.*
>
> *Let's keep this in mind when dictating memos and letters involving earlier correspondence. I find that we are quoting our earlier letters with the thought, perhaps, that these letters have been misplaced or lost. Yesterday I received two memos, each of them two pages long, that might have been written in a dozen lines had the dictators placed more reliance on my files. In less than a minute my secretary found the files containing the matter quoted in those memos.*
>
> *I recognize that there may be times when it is desirable to reproduce the contents of earlier communications. I am suggesting only that you use a little more judgment as to when this is necessary. When it is, why not use the copying machine in our Stenographic Department?*

Another example of information at hand—quite literally at hand— is the form (usually an application) enclosed with a letter. Most modern business forms are efficiently designed, with explicit instructions on how they should be completed. If the person who is to fill out one of these forms cannot follow the instructions on them, how can we assume that he would do better from the instructions in a letter?

> *In order to file a claim for loss of damage it is necessary that you complete the enclosed form in accordance with the*

*instructions thereon. Check the proper block at the upper right corner of the form to indicate whether the claim is for loss or damage. Fill in the rest of the form in the proper spaces, depending on whether you are claiming loss or damage on the shipment. The form should be signed in the space provided for the purpose and returned to the Claims Department at the address shown above.*

Perhaps the writer of this letter, having undertaken an answer, was seeking something to say. Indeed, I have had many dictators defend themselves, "But we must say something or the letter sounds abrupt!" If that is so, the reason is that the words are poorly managed, not that they are scarce. I doubt that any reader would find this letter abrupt:

*We shall be pleased to consider your claim for damages to the furniture delivered by our van. Simply complete and return the enclosed forms so we will have the information needed for the investigation. You can count on us to make an adjustment for any damages for which we are responsible.*

4. *Avoid the commonplace.* There is an old story of how a young man, the son of a boyhood friend of Abe Lincoln's, appealed to the President for an endorsement of an invention. The Rube Goldberg–like contraption of this young man's invention was hardly calculated to appeal to a practical man, but Lincoln is supposed to have come up with this unquestionable endorsement:

*I have carefully examined this young man's invention, and I am confident it would be a fine thing for anybody that could use it.*

There is no proof that Lincoln ever wrote such a letter, but this fanciful one brings out an interesting twist: the usefulness of a commonplace—an obvious fact—as a tool of evasion. Every writer at times finds the commonplace handy, but as a general practice, truisms are unbusinesslike, inflicting ideas on the reader that he can supply for himself. A sophisticated reader is certain to deride us for:

> Good management is desirable in every company.
> The most important thing is to be on the right side in stocks.
> Every honest man wants to pay his debts.

Even out of context one would suspect that sentences like these could have been dispensed with. The last sentence, of a type seen fairly frequently in collection letters, is intended to appeal to the reader's sense of fair dealing. The same idea, when implied as a compliment, would be more appealing. For example, "I am sure you want to pay this debt, Mr. Jones."

5. *Don't qualify statements with irrelevant ifs.* When we have said that something is so—or may be so—it is an easy matter to think of the *ifs* that stand in the way. "If" sentences and clauses are often essential to the reader's understanding or the writer's protection. Again, they are a welter of useless detail encouraged by eagerness to be on the safe side. This eagerness can even lead a dictator to confuse the conditional with the problematical as it did when the government writer ended his letter:

> You are advised that this information is furnished on the assumption that there will be no changes in the law prior to the time you become eligible for benefits.

The policyholder who wants to know only the present loan value of his policy need not be told what happens *if* an insured dies before a loan is repaid; the claimant for lost merchandise knows without being told that his claim will be invalid *if* it turns out that the merchandise is in his warehouse; and the executive who reads your report may not be interested in what you would have reported *if*.

One way to get around irrelevant "if" sentences is to avoid general statements beginning, "The law provides," or "Regulations provide," or "The plan provides," or "Our policy is." Once launched on this general approach, you may be forced into a conditional statement to be strictly accurate. Example:

> Section 2 of Part III of General Office Procedure requires each department to submit a work progress report on or before the 15th day of the month following the month covered by the report. If, however, the department is engaged in research projects, the section further provides. . . .

We might suppose that the dictator, having made the general statement in the first sentence, recognized that he hadn't told the whole story. He felt impelled to explain that Section 2 provided an exception, even though the exception did not apply to the department receiving the memo. He could have got around this difficulty by dealing with the specific case rather than with a generality.

> Your work progress reports under Section 2, Part III of General Procedures Manual are due on or before the 15th day of the month.

6. *Answer straightaway.* Then decide whether you need to back up your answer with an explanation.

The making of a case for ourselves before answering a question is responsible for no end of mumbo jumbo. The idea, it seems, is to prove how right we are, so the reader will be defenseless when he finally gets to the answer. The letters sometimes turn out like this one:

> This is in reply to your letter of July 17 about the minimum rental bill you recently received from us.
> Section 3, subsection (f) of a lease agreement with the company provides: "If in any minimum rental year the rental paid is less than $300 multiplied by the number of machines installed

hereunder, Operator shall at the end of such year pay to the Company the amount of such deficiency. . . ."

Under Section 3, subsection (f) of your lease agreement, the minimum rental for the four machines we installed on your premises is $1,200 a year. Your total rent paid for the year ended June 30 was $173.60 short of this amount. The minimum rental bill we sent you is for this shortage.

I hope this answers your question satisfactorily. If we can be of further help, just let us know.

Paragraph 3 is the answer. Had the dictator begun there, he would have recognized that was enough.

There is more to be said on this subject in the chapter on planning letters.


## EIGHT WAYS TO ECONOMIZE ON WORDS

So far, we have considered some ways to guard against details that do not add to the "tell" or "sell" of a letter. We can now turn to some suggestions on ways of saving words in what is said.

Underlying these suggestions is the realization that business can be (though I've seen no evidence that it *is*) penny-wise and pound-foolish in a word-economy drive. True word economy takes ruthless application of the blue pencil and that in itself is uneconomical. Look at the sentence I have just written. Look only at the adjectives *true, ruthless, blue*. My editor would not question *blue*, because it puts across the editing idea. But had I not made such a point of that sentence he probably would have struck out *true* or *ruthless*.

The editing of my sentence need not stop with the adjectives. You might boil it down to an unshaded meaning, "Word economy takes application of a pencil, etc." Although a good editor does not remove words he feels will shade or make more exact the meaning, his judgment on shading and exactness may differ from the writer's.

And here we can get into difficulties of a kind plentiful enough as it is—the differences of opinion between the man who writes a letter and the boss who signs it. These differences can lead to endless rewrites by which nothing of any real importance is gained.

For all practical purposes business letter writers must concentrate on words that are plainly squandered. These words don't fill piggy banks—they fill mints. Save on even a fraction of them and the cost of running your office will go down.

But to realize this saving you must try to keep from squandering words in your letters when they are first written. It costs more to take words out than it does to put them in.

To keep from squandering words is something of a game. First you learn what these misspent words are. Then you do your best to keep from spending them on your dictation. It's fair game to enlist your stenographer's help. She can learn to recognize the misspent word and help you to avoid it.

I promise you that the game will be lively. You won't always win. Nobody does. Your goal is to save as many words as you can without investing too heavily in editing.

Here are eight ways to go about it:

1. *Boil down roundabout prepositional phrases.* One of the most noticeable traits of business writers is the fondness for little groups of words beginning and usually ending with prepositions. These word groups, known as prepositional phrases, abound in business letters. Yet they are so easy to recognize and replace with single words that there is no reason why they should so often get the best of us. Here are the common ones, with replacements shown in parentheses.

> along the lines of (like)
> as of this date (today)
> as regards (on, about)
> at the present time (now)
> at the time of (when)
> as to (on, about)

by means of (by, with)
for the purpose of (to, for)
in accordance with (as, by, with)
in the amount of (for, of)
in the case where (when)
in the event of (if)
in the majority of instances (usually)
in the matter of (in)
in the month of (in)
in the near future (soon)
in the possession of (has, have)
in the time of (when)
in a number of cases (some)
in a position to (can, may)
in a satisfactory manner (satisfactorily)
in case of (if)
in connection with (on, for, of)
in order to (to)
in reference to (about)
in relation to (to, toward, for)
in respect to (to, toward)
in view of (because)
inasmuch as (as, because)
of even date (today)
on a few occasions (occasionally)
on behalf of (for)
on the basis of (by)
on the part of (by, among, for)
under date of (on)
with reference to (about, on)
with regard to (about, in)

All of these phrases are at times useful. Sir Ernest Gowers, author of *Plain Words, Their ABC*, points to the usefulness of the most abused of them all, *as to*. According to Sir Ernest, "*as to* serves a useful purpose at the beginning of a sentence by way of introducing a fresh subject." (Notice his own use of "by way of.")

"As to the terms of the contract, I have no question," is a good to-the-point sentence. But avoid a series of sentences with this phrase. They become monotonous. Usually you can rely on a new paragraph to serve notice of a fresh subject, without introductory phrases like *as to* or *as regards*.

Sometimes a roundabout phrase may be omitted as in the following sentences:

> *I shall expect you to inform me (as to) whether the plan meets your approval.*
>
> *Please tell me how many man-hours are spent (in connection with) auditing vouchers.*
>
> *You should have no difficulty (with respect to) meeting your quota.*

Let the phrase go if the sentence reads smoothly without it. When it doesn't, try to shorten and sharpen the sentence with a single-word replacement.

> *We mailed you a check in the amount of [for] $123.32 under date of [on] August 13 to cover the balance due in connection with [on] this transaction.*
>
> *On a few occasions [occasionally] in the past we have had difficulty getting raw material in the months of [in] January and February, but at this time [now] we have a stockpile for the purpose of [for] such an emergency.*
>
> *Your letter of August 17 in reference to [about] your continued availability for employment with this firm has been received. [Better: Thank you for letting us know that you are still interested in employment with our firm.]*
>
> *In reply to your letter of May 18 in regard to the $9.16 shipping charge on your April statement, you are advised that this sum was posted to your account in error. [Better: Thank*

you for calling our attention to the $9.16 erroneous shipping charge on your April statement.]

With reference to the credit balance shown on the statement for July, a check in the amount of $68.50 to cover same was forwarded to Mr. Jones under date of August 7. [Better: A check for $68.50 covering the credit balance on his July statement was forwarded to Mr. Jones on August 7.]

His suggestion as to [on] raising the interest rates was rejected.

Look suspiciously at any noun sandwiched between two prepositions. You can often substitute a verb or a single preposition, as in these examples:

You were given two weeks for completion of [to complete] the report.

There is a past-due balance in the amount of [of] $43.50 on the account.

A favorite circumlocution of the American business writer is *in the amount of*. There is no telling how many millions of typed words would be cut out if it were possible to ban this phrase for one single day. *In the amount of* need not be replaced by *for* or *of*, either. Why not hit the mark directly with a *$100 check* instead of a *check for $100*? That's the crisp executive style of writing.

Another favorite is *in a position to*. This phrase has gained its popularity with some because they believe *we are not in a position to* is less harsh than *we cannot*. Other writers fly to its defense with the explanation, "It's not a matter of *we cannot*. We *can* but we won't!" The point is well made. Still, I know at least one salesman who was convinced that *in a position to* is not the happy phrase many think it is. He once wrote an old and valued customer, "I regret that we are not in a position to fill your order in time to meet your requirements." Whereupon the irritated customer replied, "If you guys would get your feet off the desk, you'd be in a better position to take care of my order."

2. *Watch out for nouns and adjectives that derive from verbs. Use these words in their verb form more frequently.* Examine the stories in magazines like *Time* and *Newsweek*. You will find the writers leaning heavily on verbs. They do so because verbs are the action words of our language, giving force and movement to the sentence. Later on we shall see how active verbs star in this role. Just now let's consider the verb only for its efficiency.

Many words in our miraculous language have both a noun and verb form or both a verb and adjective form or all three forms. Often the words are identical in two forms. The words *profit* and *estimate*, for example. Say "I profit from Friday sales," and *profit* is a verb. But say "I made a profit from Friday sales," and *profit* becomes a noun. Say "Give me an estimate of the cost," and *estimate* is a noun; say "I estimate the cost at $500," and *estimate* becomes a verb.

Other words get their noun or adjective forms from endings like *-ing, -tion, -ment, -ence, -ency, -able, -ion,* and so on. Thus the verb *meet* becomes *meeting, state* becomes *statement,* and *tend* becomes *tendency. Examine* is the forebear of *examination, rule* becomes *ruling,* and *action* derives from *act.* Tack *-able* on *suit* and you get *suitable.* Without opening the pages of a dictionary you can name dozens of other examples.

Pit the verb form against the noun form, and the verb is always the first to strike the mark. Why? Because you must pick up another verb to introduce a noun into the sentence. Compare:

| Noun | Verb |
|---|---|
| He made a reply. | He replied. |
| Please give consideration to this question. | Please consider this question. |
| He has a tendency. | He tends. |

You work with words like these whenever you write a letter. If you favor nouns instead of verbs, your writing gets cluttered.

There are six verbs that snare letter writers, more than any others, into choosing nouns and adjectives. They are *make*, *take*, *give*, *hold*, *have*, and *be*. Watch them steal the place of the basic verbs that might have been used in these sentences.

| *Nouns and Adjectives* | *Verbs* |
|---|---|
| Please *give this your attention* at once. | Please *attend* to this at once. |
| Please *make an adjustment* on your records to show that a *reimbursement* of this difference in the amount of $6.50 *will be made* to us. | Please *adjust* your records so we can be *reimbursed* for this difference of $6.50. |
| Has your field representative *had any success in taking repossession* of the car? | Has your field representative *succeeded in repossessing* the car? |
| Please *make immediate replacement* of this thermometer, making sure that same is safely packed in order *to prevent breakage.* | Please *replace* this thermometer immediately, packing it for shipment so it will not *break.* |
| Mr. Smith phoned Henry Osgood in our office asking if *we had any objection to holding the meeting* in Chicago rather than Detroit. | Mr. Smith phoned Henry Osgood in our office asking if we *objected* to *meeting* in Chicago rather than Detroit. |
| He *is negligent in* the details of paperwork. | He *neglects* the details of paperwork. |
| Have you *taken any action* on this claim? | Have you *acted* on this claim? |
| We have *made arrangements* for a night force to *take inventory* of supplies. | We have *arranged* for a night force to *inventory* supplies. |

By the noun route the word count in the above sentences is 118. By the verb route it is only 82.

Nouns that derive from verbs are not the only ones that can be replaced by verbs. Many nouns and verbs with different roots express the same meaning. *He made a talk* may be expressed as *he spoke;* or *these results leave the impression that* may be expressed as *these results indicate that.* Similarly, *make, take, give, hold, have* and *be* are not the only pickup verbs that link nouns to a sentence. You may *put an end to a matter* that will be just as final if you *end it,* or *show an inclination* that will be just as perceptible if you *are inclined.* But if you have a heavy hand with nouns and adjectives, you can go a long way toward efficient writing by avoiding those that are linked to your sentences by the six little verbs: *make, take, give, hold, have* and *be.*

3. *Cut out superfluous adjectives and adverbs.* After serving as a major in the Union Army, Henry Lee Higginson tried several business ventures without success. Later, as partner of the investment firm Lee, Higginson and Company, he went on to become a successful businessman, philanthropist and music patron. Reading his biography, one is impressed by the importance he attached to letters throughout his life. In his boyhood correspondence he expressed a preference for the informal, direct and simple style of writing. Later he was to say to a young partner of his firm, "I would like to talk to you about letters; I talked to the president of Harvard College about them . . . Now my theory of a letter is this: you sit down and visualize the person you are addressing; you dictate exactly as if he were present; you watch the changes in his face and anticipate his replies. You put yourself into the letter exactly as if you were looking into his eyes. *You go through and cut out all adjectives and adverbs; then you probably have a good letter.*"

Of course, the suggestion that you cut out *all* adjectives and adverbs can't be taken literally. Walter Hines Page, whose editorial letters have been described as matchless, spoke of the need for taking away the superfluous and distracting. That seems to get at the heart of the matter. You will find some of those superfluous and distracting adjectives and adverbs in these sentences:

That was a very fine job you did straightening out that awful mess in the Cleveland branch. It is highly gratifying to know that our great company can rely on the good sound judgment and unquestionable leadership of men like you.

Thank you so much for coming to us with your questions on investment. It is always a real pleasure to serve you and we certainly hope that you will find the little booklet I am enclosing helpful.

Experimenting with sentences like these is fun. Remove an adjective or adverb here and there and keep an ear tuned for the effect. Although there are bound to be differences of opinion as to what is distracting, most of us will detect some degree of overdoing. In my opinion all the adjectives and adverbs in the above sentences might go, except "fine" in the first sentence and "helpful" in the last.

One word that is almost always superfluous is very. You might question how often you can do without this word in your letters, and you may conclude that "We are very pleased" is no more convincing that "We are pleased."

4. Boil down relative clauses beginning with that, which and who. Adjectives and adverbs can be efficient, especially in boiling down relative clauses:

The question that is in doubt [doubtful question] is whether we should rely on an upturn in fall business.

The delay in answering your question, which is to be regretted, calls for an explanation. [The regrettable delay in answering . . .]

He taught us some new methods that save our time and that can be used throughout the company. [He taught us some time-saving methods, useful throughout the company.]

Please inform us should there be any change in the plans that you have [your plans].

If you can do so without changing the meaning of the sentence, attach an adjective to the word it modifies instead of introducing it by that or which.

The only book that is recent on the subject was written by a partner of the firm. [The only recent book on the subject . . .]

If you have any information that will be helpful, please let us know. [If you have any helpful information, please . . .]

This short cut won't always work when a restrictive clause is needed.

The truck that was brand new was demolished in the accident.

Here the idea is that the truck was one of several. "The brand-new truck was demolished" may suggest that only one truck was involved.

Which and who can often be stricken from the sentence without rephrasing it. Omit these pronouns from the following sentences and nobody will miss them:

C. E. Abrams, (who is) our general agent in Carlisle, has reported his conversation with you.

We are enclosing the file (which) you requested.

The Committee (which was) established to study records problems meets on the second Tuesday of each month.

5. Guard against sentences beginning "It is" and "There is." "It's a" (it is a) and "there's a" (there is a) are as common in conversation as "yes" and "no." In writing, the inefficiency of sentences beginning with these words becomes readily apparent.

It is a good sign of a sounder economy when the number of persons employed increases. [Increased employment is a good sign . . .]

There are many problems which arise from the attempt to market out-of-season merchandise. [Many problems arise from the attempt to . . .]

(It was) about three weeks later (that)I discovered the error.

*(There is) a standard policy (that) is always followed in ac-
cepting returned merchandise.*

Spare "it is" and "there is" to introduce sentences in which you
want to create anticipation, as in this sentence beginning a *Reader's
Digest* story:

> *There is one point about that much disputed figure, Richard
> Milhaus Nixon, which neither his enemies nor his admirers
> can dispute: the Vice President is a most extraordinary man.*

6. *Don't double your trouble with words of overlapping meaning.*
Several years ago the Washington *Daily News* carried this editorial
about lawyers on the double:

*Cease and Desist*

> *The lawyer never lived who willingly would use one word
> when he could think of two.*
> *The wretch before the court is charged with breaking and
> entering, burglary and larceny, or with conduct lewd and
> lascivious, or perhaps simply with having been drunk and dis-
> orderly.*
> *Before arriving in the court room, he may have suffered
> abrasions and contusions, never one or the other. And even
> though law-abiding he probably once took a wife to have and
> to hold, and has thought to make a last will and testament.*
> *We outsiders long have suspected that most of these extra
> words were unnecessary, but maybe lawyers have the last laugh.
> In a British court recently a citizen was charged, as many a
> Washingtonian has been, with assault and battery. He had
> thrown a plate of sausages at his father-in-law. Two found their
> mark.*
> *The court clerk explained that "assault" could've been caused*

*by the seven sausages that were thrown, and the "battery" by the two which hit the target.*

*The ruling was good and sufficient.*

Taking a chance on one of a pair of words of similar meaning may be risky business in law. Yet how many letters get scrutiny in a court of law? I suspect writers couple words of overlapping meaning because they think thereby to gain emphasis or grace. Nonsense! The Victorian doublet is out of style, and redundancy is plain inefficiency.

Here are some words of overlapping meaning that I have seen frequently in letters:

| *Double* | *Single* |
| --- | --- |
| absolutely complete | complete |
| advance planning | planning |
| arrange to inform | inform |
| ask the question | ask |
| assembled together | assembled |
| basic fundamentals | fundamentals |
| carbon copy | copy |
| continue on | continue |
| cooperate together | cooperate |
| demand and insist | demand or insist—*not both* |
| each and everyone | each or everyone—*not both* |
| enclosed herewith (herein) | enclosed |
| exactly identical | identical |
| expired and terminated | expired or terminated—*not both* |
| first and foremost | first or foremost—*not both* |
| indorse on the back of the check | indorse |
| misposted in error | misposted |
| open up | open |
| profoundly and deeply | profoundly or deeply—*not both* |
| repeat again | repeat |
| return back | return |

| *Double* | *Single* |
|---|---|
| same identical | same |
| seldom ever | seldom |
| send in | send |
| still remains | remains |
| the reason is because | because |

Redundancy takes many different forms. Here, for example, is the redundant preposition:

> *The laboratory tested (out) the effect of acid on this fabric.*

In the next example the same trouble is found in an adverb attached to a word it cannot qualify with good sense:

> *This is a (very) unique situation.*

And here the trouble comes from introducing a word when the meaning is established without it:

> *We questioned everybody who was (present) in the room when the accident occurred.*

7. *Don't pad.* You may think of all superfluous words as padding, but I have in mind a special kind of cottony language rarely found anywhere except in letters. It comes in four distinguishable varieties. The first variety I would identify as *reference clauses.* Here are some of them for your black list:

> *I* [we] *refer to your letter*
> *receipt is acknowledged of your letter*
> *reference is made to your letter* [or *question*]
> *referring to your letter* [or *question*]
> *this is in reference to*
> *this is to acknowledge*

Any of the above expressions can be avoided simply by answering questions directly.

The second variety is the expression by which the writer calls attention to what he has to say. These obtrusive paddings will be recognized in a number of forms:

*an important consideration is*
*as a matter of information*
*attention is called to the fact*
*for your information*
*it will be noted*
*it is pointed out*
*kindly be advised [informed]*
*please be advised [informed]*
*this is to advise [inform] you*
*we [I] am inclined to say*
*we [I] take the liberty of*
*we [I] take this opportunity to*
*we [I] wish to say*
*we [I] should like to mention*
*we [I] would say*
*you are advised*
*your attention is called*

Occasionally you will want to call special attention to your statements. The point is, don't make a habit of it. Shorter phrases such as "note this" or "remember this" or "keep in mind" have more punch. Again, you can avoid the circuitous emphatic by rephrasing the sentence. Here is a trite emphatic:

> We call your attention to the fact that *you must have your report in this office by June 30 to meet the deadline.*

Why not turn the sentence around to place emphasis on important words?

*To meet the deadline, you must get your report into this office by June 30.*

The third variety of cottony expressions is a symptom of one of today's big problems—records.

*according to our records*
*examination of our records discloses*
*our records show*
*please review your records and inform us*
*search of our records fails to reveal*
*we have made a careful search of our records*

The concern with records is expressed in countless sentences like these:

*Our records indicate that a check for $45.25 was sent to you on August 4.*

*Upon checking our files it is observed that you furnished an accounting statement to support the claim for monetary loss.*

*A most careful search of our files fails to reveal any record of the receipt of the invoice mentioned in your letter. It is therefore necessary to request that you again furnish us a copy.*

In the first two examples any mention of records as a source of information should be omitted. Where else would the evidence supporting these statements be had? In the last example the reader might be told that the invoice was lost or misplaced, but he has no interest in the writer's problem of searching records. This should be sufficient:

*May I have a copy of the invoice mentioned in your letter? I am sorry to trouble you, but we can find no trace of it.*

I think we can be sure that the reader would not come back with the suggestion that the writer make a more careful search.

Finally, cottony words are used with the good intention of soften-
ing harsh, unpleasant or negative ones. You have seen how the expression *we are not in a position to* is used to soften the impact of
*cannot.* Similarly, *it will be appreciated* is used as a protective
covering for unpleasant facts.

> It will be appreciated that due to unforeseeable circumstances
> such as weather conditions it may not be possible at all times
> for our planes to depart on schedule.

Soft words turn away wrath? All right. We can speak softly yet
directly.

> The unexpected cancellation of your flight because of weather
> conditions probably caused you a great deal of inconvenience.
> Please accept our apology.

8. *Take the cure for rambling: Plan your letters.*

> Quite frankly, Mr. Smith, if this situation were reversed and
> you handled our account for us and we took in excess of 60
> days to make payment, we feel sure that you would feel the
> same way we do.

That's rambling. Thirty nine words used to express the simple idea:

> Wouldn't you feel the same way if you were in our shoes?

Again:

> We have a party interested in acquiring a truck scale for an
> installation in Raleigh, North Carolina. This party, C. A.
> Henderson, operates a masonry plant.
> Will you please advise me if we have any such scales that
> are not in use and which we would consider selling to this
> concern. Mr. Henderson has told us that they could convert

one of our truck scales to their use, if such a type of scale is available.

Will you please advise me if we have any such scales available in order that I may develop further with Mr. Henderson. I would also be interested in knowing what price we would expect to receive for any such scales that might be available.

With better planning the above letter would have been turned out in thirty or forty words instead of 120.

C. A. Henderson, operator of a masonry plant at Raleigh, is interested in buying one of our truck scales. Do we have any such scales for sale, and, if so, at what price?

A letter is—or should be—akin to conversation, but the notion that good letters are to be had by writing just as we talk is nonsense. Mark Twain reminds us, "Spoken speech is one thing, written speech is quite another. . . . The moment talk is put into print you realize that it is not what it was when you heard it." Haven't you experienced the bitter truth of those words when the letter you talked rolled off the typewriter?

A good plain letter is neither purely colloquial nor formal. It is some of both. It is like talk, because everyday words are its language ingredient. Everyday words, though, must be put together more pleasingly and efficiently than the average person's talk. Most people ramble naturally—and sometimes even entertainingly—when they talk. But it's much too inefficient to ramble on paper.

There's only one cure for rambling: Plan your letters. In Chapter 6 you will find some suggestions on how to go about it.


APPLYING THE BLUE PENCIL

Originally written in 235 words, this letter can be cut nearly in half simply by striking through the superfluous words (here put in parentheses):

(*I wish to acknowledge and*) thank you for your letter of October 27 requesting further information on the X Company.

Attached (*hereto*) are recent(*ly prepared*) statistical reports on the X debenture and preferred stock issues (*in accord with your desire for information relative to this company. It is interesting to take note that*) the company's record has been highly erratic in recent years, and the issues are generally regarded as (*somewhat*) lower than the better-grade investment status (*which one may*) ordinarily (*apply*) [*applied*] to senior issues. (*Further note is taken of the fact that*) earnings on the preferred stock have been on the deficit side for some time and an exchange offer is (*now in process of preparation*) [*being prepared*]. We trust (*that the information contained in*) the enclosed statistical reports will (*be of sufficient scope in order to*) help you formulate a confident investment appraisal (*relative to your personal holdings*).

(*We have not enclosed the Y report inasmuch as*) we do not have [*the Y reports*] (*available from this office*). It is suggested that you contact Mr. A. L. C. (*for your further information and*) possibly he (*will be able to*) [*can*] supply (*you with*) copies (*of these reports should they be available from that office*).

*It is a pleasure to serve you.* We (*will*) welcome the opportunity to (*be of further assistance*) [*assist you*] whenever you call on us (*at some future date*).

To the next letter we can apply six of the eight rules for word economy:

1. Avoid roundabout prepositional phrases.
2. Use words in the verb form rather than the noun form.
3. Cut out superfluous and distracting adjectives and adverbs.
4. Boil down relative clauses.
5. Don't double your trouble with words of overlapping meaning.
6. Don't pad.

In reference to your note on our statement regarding the charge to your account in the amount of $11.70, we wish to advise that this invoice was misposted to your account in error and the transfer is now being made to the proper account. Thank you for bringing this error, which is sincerely regretted, to our attention. The balance remaining due on your account at this time is $40.60 which was rendered on invoice A7–9043, February 10. Would you be so good as to check this transaction and, if your records are in agreement with ours, please arrange to forward us your check to cover this rather old transaction.

Here's how the person who wrote the above letter revised it in keeping with the golden rule:

> Thank you for calling our attention to the $11.70 charge posted to your account in error. And please forgive us for inconveniencing you in this way.
>
> The charge has been removed, leaving a balance owing of $40.60 for invoice A7–9043 of February 10. We would appreciate your check for this purchase within the next few days.

You may feel that the next letter is a pretty good one. The circumlocutions are not easily spotted, and it reads smoothly:

> We are advised by Mr. A. C., our sales representative in your area, that you have recently forwarded to us a check for approximately $200 in payment of your past-due account. Our records do not indicate the receipt of this check.
>
> We request, therefore, that you review your canceled checks to determine whether or not your check has cleared back to your bank. If it has not, it would be obvious that it has become lost in transmission to us and it would be in order for you to place a stop on the original check and to issue a substitute to us.

If you find that your check has in fact cleared to the bank, and that you now have a canceled check, we would appreciate it if you will examine the check to determine the date on which our bank, The First National of this city, placed its stamp of endorsement. With this information we will then see that your account is properly credited.

Because we are so anxious to clear this whole item from record, we would appreciate it if you could give it prompt attention.

Here is the same subject carefully distilled by another writer:

Mr. A. C., our sales representative in your area, tells me you recently sent us a check for $200. That is good news, and I am sorry to say that we did not receive the check.

If you have the canceled check, will you please give us the date it was endorsed by our bank, The First National of this city? On the other hand, if the check has not cleared your bank, we would appreciate your stopping payment and issuing us another for the same amount.

Thank you for your co-operation in helping us clear up this long-overdue item.

Distilled prose comes naturally with some people. If it doesn't come naturally with you, don't be concerned. Set about ridding your letters of the easily recognized superfluities. If you do only that, you will be ahead in your own game of writing.

## SUMMARY

The golden rule of business writing is: *Say only what needs to be said, and use only the words needed to say it.*

There are six practical ways to avoid needless information:

1. Don't repeat what is said in the letter you answer.

2. Beware of sentences beginning with "As you know."

3. Don't give the reader information he has at hand.

4. Avoid the commonplace that every reader can supply for himself, as "Honest men want to pay their debts."

5. Don't qualify your statements with irrelevant *ifs*.

6. Answer questions straightaway, then decide whether you need to explain the answer.

There are eight ways to avoid needless words in what has to be said:

1. Boil down roundabout prepositional phrases. For example, say *a check for $50* or *a $50 check*, instead of *a check in the amount of $50.*

2. Watch out for nouns and adjectives that derive from verbs. Use these words in their verb form more frequently. (*The committee met* instead of *the committee held a meeting.*)

3. Cut out superfluous adjectives and adverbs.

4. Boil down relative clauses beginning with *that, which* and *who*. (*Doubtful question* instead of *question that is in doubt; the file you requested* instead of *the file which you requested; Mr. Kane, the defendant's attorney* instead of *Mr. Kane, who is the defendant's attorney.*)

5. Guard against those little thieves of efficiency, *it is* and *there is.* (*Increased employment is a sign of sounder economy* instead of *it is a sign of sounder economy when employment increases.*)

6. Don't double your trouble with words of overlapping meaning. For example, say *fundamentals* instead of *basic fundamentals, co-operate* instead of *co-operate together.*

7. Don't pad sentences with phrases such as *reference is made, attention is called to the fact, according to our records,* and *it will be appreciated that.*

8. Take the cure for rambling: *Plan your letters.*

# SIMPLICITY

CHAPTER 3 | That Supreme Excellence

"THERE was a man in the land of Uz, whose name was Job." With these 13 one-syllable words begins the Book of Job.

"I would rather be right than President," cried Henry Clay in idiom so natural it is hard to imagine expressing the same idea in any other way.

"I feel how weak and fruitless must be any words of mine," goes Lincoln's letter to Mrs. Bixby on the loss of her five sons in the Civil War.

Each of these quotations is a perfect example of what Longfellow called the supreme excellence—*simplicity*.

In the last chapter we saw how it is possible to simplify letters as well as shorten them by following the golden rule of brevity. But simplicity, the second of our 4-S virtues, is not alone a matter of avoiding the needless word. It is also the choice and arrangement of words so our readers will know at once what we are saying, without being conscious of how we say it.

Suppose the Book of Job had begun, "An individual resided in the territory of Uz whose name was Job." Suppose Henry Clay had said, "I would prefer rectitude to the presidency." Or suppose Lincoln had written Mrs. Bixby, "I perceive that any expression of mine would be impotent and ineffectual." The average reader would understand perfectly well *what* was said, but he might be ill at ease in the consciousness of *how* it was said.

Misunderstanding caused by lack of simplicity is not the big problem in government and business writing. Those incomprehensible examples of government gobbledygook and business bafflegab are only the exceptions to remind us of our worst ineptitudes. The more pressing need for simplicity is the need to put our readers at ease, making reading so comfortable they will feel at home with our services and products.

And remember: Simplicity, like shortness, can be overdone. Never underestimate your reader or feel that you must write *down* to him. This-is-a-cow kindergarten prose is unnatural. It can make a reader just as conscious of *how you say* it as those pretentious words.

Express your ideas as quickly, clearly and *naturally* as you can. You then have a simple letter.

## SIMPLICITY FROM SURENESS

Two thousand years ago the Roman poet Horace said, "Knowledge is the source and foundation of good writing." This is obvious when we compare the letters we write on familiar subjects with our first attempt at those subjects we are not quite sure of. When ideas are vague the letter is certain to be vague, if not completely baffling.

The dictator who is unsure of his subject—or who fears it—is tempted to play safe by speaking in generalities; and it is amazing how those generalities complicate a matter that is downright simple under the specific treatment of a confident writer.

One might imagine the writer playing it safe, sticking to the general language of some government regulation, when dictating this letter:

> *Denial is premised upon the obvious proposition that a flight course is embarked upon with a view to its completion and*

consequent licensure of the applicant, and for no other legitimate reason, and when a course is not possible for completion
within a veteran's period of entitlement under the law, the
Veterans Administration has a right to determine that in the
absence of satisfactory evidence that payment for completion of
the course is arranged for, there can be no determination respecting the relationship of such a course to the veteran's oc-
cupation or his earning of a livelihood.

That sentence is the essence of gobbledygook—abstractions and
generalities cast from big words into a long sentence. Yet the
hapless veteran who received that letter a few years ago had a
specific problem. He didn't have enough GI benefits to complete
a course in flight training. The Veterans Administration's problem
was a little more complicated. It had to be sure that veterans completed this type of course so the training would be useful in earning
a living. Had the dictator been less wary of his problem, he most
certainly would have tackled that veteran's specific one, getting
some simple you into his letter. The forthright question might have
been: Can you show us that you intend to complete the course,
paying for the part not covered by your benefits?

Generalities and abstractions are the "infirmities of speech," to
borrow a phrase from Quiller-Couch. In the next chapter we'll
consider the abstract and concrete word in greater detail, showing
how the one weakens letters and the other strengthens them. The
present advice is: If you want to avoid gobbledygook and bafflegab,
don't fear your subject. Know it so well you will feel safe discussing
it in specific terms.

## SIMPLICITY IN WORDS AND PHRASES

Having thus cleared the decks, we can now turn to some of the
helps in simple writing. The best of these are those little and
informal words we use when we talk, the common everyday speech
of Americans.

Walter Hines Page, in a letter written in 1918, gave his eldest son, Ralph, this advice:

> If you have a long word, see if a native short one can be put in its place which will be more natural and stronger. Avoid a Latin vocabulary and use a plain English one—short words instead of long ones.
>
> Most of all, use idioms—English idioms of force. Say an agreement was "come to." Don't say it was "consummated." For the difference between idioms and Latin style, compare Lincoln and George Washington. One's interesting and convincing. The other is dull in spite of his good sense. How folks do misuse and waste words! . . .

What Page says about short words and idioms is excellent advice every business writer should take to heart.

## LITTLE FISHES AND WHALES

One of the charges brought against modern business writing is the use of oversized and showy words. For example: to do is to effectuate, to issue is to promulgate, and to try to find out is to endeavor to ascertain. After is subsequent; a first thought, a dominant consideration; an end, an expiration; a proof, a verification. A check, two times out of three, is termed a remittance, while the little word pay shows up as remuneration. As if there are not enough of the big words, the little ones are stretched. Lapse, as the lapse of an insurance policy, is sometimes stretched to lapsation; and the temptation to make a visitation out of field office visit is one the organization man can seldom resist.

Our everyday speech is full of little words. No matter how many big ones we know, most of us talk most of the time with little ones. If we don't—if we load our talk with big words—people are likely to say we are stuffy. You can be sure that they say the same things about letters loaded with big words.

Did you ever call at your bank and have your banker ask you to "affix your signature" to a paper? Of course you haven't! "Please sign it," he says, handing you the paper. But let him hand you the same paper by letter and see what happens!

If you want to make your customers comfortable in the feeling that you are a "regular guy," show little words the same respect in letters that you do in your speech. Don't let words like these invade your sentences:

> *We appreciate the confidence you have reposed in us.* [Talk: *We appreciate your trust.*]
> *After perusing your letter, I decided* . . . [Talk: *After reading your letter, I decided* . . .]
> *I am incorporating the letter in your files.* [Talk: *I'm filing your letter.*]
> *Mr. Smith presented his personal check to this office for encashment.* [Talk: *Mr. Smith asked us to cash his personal check.*]

Big words sometimes obscure the meaning:

> *Jurisdiction over your insurance records has now been established in this office.* [Talk: *Your insurance records are now kept here.*]

And sometimes just tire the reader:

> *The existence of the aforementioned relationship has been disclosed to stockholders intermittently.* [Talk: *This relationship has been made known to stockholders from time to time.*]
> *The letter is transmitted to you in duplicate, and if you find that these stipulations meet with your approval it will be*

*appreciated if you will* indicate *same by* affixing your signature *to one copy of the* document *and returning it for our records.* [Talk: *If you agree to these terms, please sign and return one copy of this letter.*]

This is not to say that you should black-list big familiar words. When a common word conveys your exact meaning or lends interest and rhythm to a sentence, don't feel you must cast it aside because it has several syllables. The average reader of business letters is familiar with as many words as the average dictator. Actually, the reader most likely to criticize a letter for pretentiousness is the one who has a better vocabulary than the writer.

The general rule is to prefer the little word when it expresses your meaning as well or better than the big one. Above all—if you would like to make life pleasant for your readers—avoid showy words. Let us not, as Oliver Goldsmith said, "make little fishes . . . talk like whales."

TRADE, TECHNICAL AND SCIENTIFIC LANGUAGE

Business writing is sometimes complicated by trade, technical or scientific language that is sheer jargon to the lay reader. In the investment field I run across big abstract words like "volatile reflection of unpredictable factors"—which I am told is the language of Wall Street. Defenders of these puzzling phrases earnestly believe that readers are impressed by them. But can you imagine Miss Sylvia Porter, the widely read columnist who has made a fine art of economic and investment language, "pontificating in polysyllabic" words?

Puzzling plain men is an old custom with scientists. Long before the current vogue for abstractions, doctors were baffling plain men with Greek and Latin. A patient might have the wits scared out of him upon being told that he had *pes planus,* only to learn that this is nothing more than flat feet. And what, we may wonder, did the insurance claimant make of this fairly recent letter about his multiple infirmities?

> This matter concerning the diagnosis has been previously explained to you and your wife on a number of occasions. However, in view of your request concerning this matter, we would again explain the diagnoses shown on the form dated September 1 are no different from those previously shown except as to terminology. Dr. X signed the reports prior to August 1 stating the diagnoses as "fracture, compression of cervical cyst vertebra, old; arthritis, spine, due to trauma; concussion of brain, old; and encephalopathy due to trauma, old," while Dr. Y who signed the form on and after that date stated them as "compression in fracture, cyst cervical vertebra, old; osteoarthritis, generalized, of spine; and concussion of the brain, old." Medically they add up to and are exactly the same thing.

As a technical or scientific writer, you may have a tough job getting your story across in easily understood words. No matter how hard you try to avoid the unfamiliar word, you will not always find an adequate synonym. Fortunately, most letters about scientific and technical matters are directed to fellow scientists and technicians. The only solution when writing to a layman is to define unfamiliar terms. For example, if you are writing about "installments certain" in insurance, explain what this term means to a lay reader who might not understand it.

## HONORING THE IDIOM

Three people out of four—if they have any idea at all on the subject—will tell you that an idiom is a local and not generally accepted peculiarity of speech. Southerners, for example, are supposed to say "you all" when addressing one person. (They don't, of course.) Or, in some parts of Pennsylvania, people are supposed to say, "Throw Mamma from the train a kiss." This may be idiom, all right, but it is not what Page meant when he advised his son to use English idioms of force. He was speaking of the generally accepted idioms that Porter G. Perrin calls "thoroughly respectable members of the language." *

There are thousands of these respectable idioms. They are the informal language of everyday speech as contrasted with formal, written English. Whitfield and Dixon list and define 4,500 of them in the *Handbook of American Idioms*, and I still find quite a few of my favorites missing. Whether or not you are aware of it, you probably use an idiom or two in every letter you write. The trouble with most business writers is that they don't use enough of them for the color and force, as well as the simplicity, that idioms add to letters.

Phrases that have taken on special meaning (*fly in the ointment, frame of mind, face the music, talking turkey,* and so on) are clichés easily recognized as idioms. But the most commonly used idioms are seldom recognized as such. They are Page's "idioms of force," formed as we need them by adding a preposition or adverb to a little verb, as *"line up* for inspection," *"draw up* an agreement," *"set down* rules," and *"set about to* learn."

Take the example Page gave his son. "Say an agreement was come to," he suggested. "Don't say it was consummated." *Come to* is good English idiom; consummate—from the Latin *consummatus*—is a formal latinism. Again, take the word *continue*—Latin *continuare*—and note the variety of ways it can be replaced by English idiom:

He continued [carried out] this argument for thirty minutes.
He continued [kept on] in this vein for thirty minutes.
After a pause he continued [went ahead with] his story.
Continue! [Keep it up!]

Analyze idioms and you will see how much they differ from formal English. "I would be right rather than be President," is what

* Porter G. Perrin, *Writer's Guide and Index to English*, Scott, Foresman and Company, 1950.

formal English would have us say. "I would rather be right than President," is the idiomatic way in which Clay expressed the same idea. Sometimes idiomatic English isn't even logical. But how idioms perk up our dull sentences!

We feel sure it was not your intention to let payments on your account become delinquent. [We feel sure you did not mean to let your payments fall behind.]

Upon discussing the matter with Mr. Cooper I ascertained that arrangement will be made for visiting your office for the purpose of reviewing his account. [I found out from Mr. Cooper that he plans to call at your office to go over his account.]

Incidentally, have you requested Jim O'Brien to give us the benefit of his suggestions regarding the establishment of an office in Sacramento? [By the way, have you asked Jim O'Brien for his idea on setting up a Sacramento office?]

You may find, as I have, that the Rudolf Flesch list of fifty verbs and twenty adverbs is especially handy for idiomatic phrasing.* Of his list Flesch says, "Not every verb can be combined with every adverb, of course; but what with different meanings in different contexts the list covers about a thousand abstract ideas." Here it is:

| Verbs | | | Adverbs | |
|-------|------|-------|---------|----------|
| bear  | go   | slip  | about   | forth    |
| blow  | hang | split | across  | in       |
| break | hold | stand | ahead   | off      |
| bring | keep | stay  | along   | on       |
| call  | lay  | stick | apart   | out      |
| carry | let  | strike| around  | over     |
| cast  | look | take  | aside   | through  |
| catch | make | talk  | away    | together |
| come  | pick | tear  | back    | under    |

* Rudolf Flesch, *The Art of Readable Writing*, Harper & Brothers, 1949.

| Verbs | | | Adverbs | |
|-------|------|-------|---------|-----|
| cut | pull | throw | down | up |
| do | push | tie | | |
| draw | put | touch | | |
| drive | run | turn | | |
| drop | set | walk | | |
| fall | shake | wear | | |
| get | show | work | | |
| give | skip | | | |

By combining verbs and adverbs from the Flesch list you come up with such phrases as *giving up* insurance instead of *surrendering* it; *talking it over* instead of *discussing the matter;* *going ahead* with plans instead of *proceeding* with them; *getting through with* the task instead of *completing* it; and *looking into* the matter instead of *investigating* it.

Try Mr. Flesch's suggestion. Better still, just be yourself when you dictate. The idiom will then show up in your letter as naturally as it does in your speech.

### WORD PRECISIONISTS

Everybody knows that words should express the intended meaning, but some of us are much too concerned with *proper* words.

Did you ever come to grips with a word precisionist? Every company has at least one. "But we can't say *check,*" objects the precise soul. "We'd just as soon have a money order or cash. *Remittance* is the proper word." So, to appease the precise soul, you might agree on *payment.*

To be sure, business writing demands cautious use of words. There's a chance—however slim—of liability from an injudicious word. The trouble is, in making a fetish of precision, we often sacrifice simplicity when the only risk involved is the disapproval of a precise manager or vice-president.

The word with the precise dictionary meaning is often not the familiar and colorful one. The professional writer seeks words for effect as well as precision. He might consider the precise word—an anglicized Latin one, perhaps—and reject it for a simpler and more effective one of similar meaning. If that were not so, those forceful and colorful idioms—often defying logic—would never be used in writing.

## ROUNDING UP BIG WORDS

In my letter-writing courses the students round up big words overworked in their business. The idea is to see how many of these long words can be replaced by shorter ones. Nine times out of ten somebody in the class comes up with a little synonym without even looking in a dictionary.

Here is a list that will help you get started on a similar project. It is my beginner's list, made up of the big words commonly used in practically every line of business. The little words suggested as replacements, though not always exact synonyms, will usually do the same job as well or better.

accompanied by (with)
accomplish (do)
accordingly (so)
acknowledge (reply)
acquire (get)
acquaint (tell)
additionally (also)
afford an opportunity (allow)
affix your signature (sign)
alternative (choice)
apprise (tell)
approximately (about, roughly)
ascertain (learn, find out)

beneficial (helpful)
cognizance (notice)
commence (start, begin)
commitment (promise)
communication (letter, wire, phone call)
concerning (about)
consequently (so)
consummate (bring about, come to)
contribute (give, add)
credit accommodation (credit)
currently prevailing (present)

delinquent (past-due)
demonstrate (show)
determine whether (find out)
disclose (show)
dispose of (sell)
effectuate (do, bring about)
employment—as of funds (use)
encourage (urge)
endeavor (try)
equivalent (equal)
eventualities (events)
evidence—as a verb (show)
expedite (hurry, hasten)
experience indicates (we learn)
expiration (end)
facilitate (make easy)
facilities (services)
finalize (complete, end, finish)
function—as a noun (work, act)
furthermore (then)
implement (carry on)
impression (idea)
inadvertency (mistake, error)
indicate (show)
initial (first)
initiate (begin)
instruments (papers)
liquidate (pay off)
locate (find)
maintain (keep)

materialize (happen, occur, come about)
minimum (least)
modification (change)
necessity (need)
negligible amount (little)
nevertheless (but)
notification (notice)
obligation (debt)
optimum (best)
participate (take part)
practically (nearly, almost)
procure (buy, get)
promulgate (issue, make known)
provided that (if)
purchase (buy)
pursuant to (as)
regarding (about)
remittance (check, payment)
remuneration (pay)
requirement (need)
stipulations (terms)
submitted (sent)
subsequently (later)
subsequent to (after)
sufficient (enough)
supplement (add to)
transmitted (sent with)
utilization (use)
verification (proof)

A company is likely to have its own vogue in big words. In one company I ran across the phrase "interpose no objection" in dozens of letters. I thought the writers were favoring this phrase because of their reluctance to agree to certain proposals. "I will interpose no objection" was as if to say "I don't like it, but I won't stand in the way." Nothing of the sort! This was the fashionable though roundabout way of saying "I agree." I later learned that the phrase was once used by an officer of the company in a circular memo. It got around. And it caught on. I've never found the same expression in vogue in any other company, though it is an old favorite of the Federal government.

Chances are there are some big words in vogue in your business which are not on my list. Round them up, especially the pompous ones. See how easily they can be replaced with simple synonyms.

## SIMPLICITY IN SENTENCES

### KEEP 'EM SHORT!

As short idiomatic words and phrases make letters more talkable, short rhythmic sentences make them simpler and more readable.

If letters were written in dialogue, chances are the sentences would all be short. "Good morning. I find there is a mistake in this invoice." "I'm sorry, sir. We'll be glad to correct it." And so on.

But letters are more like monologue. And the longer the speaker is given the floor, the longer and more complicated his sentences may become. If you don't believe me, turn on the recorder the next time someone in your office takes over the conversation. Have your stenographer transcribe his monologue just as he delivered it. When you read the transcript you will find sentence after sentence strung together with conjunctions or interrupted by parenthetical remarks. You may even have a tough job unscrambling the copy. Yet you understood him perfectly as he spoke. Why? Because you had the inflection of his voice to guide you through the twisting and turning sentences.

Dictators sometimes forget that readers are not guided by voice inflection. They try to say too much in one sentence. Then the reader without a voice to guide him, may have to go over the sentence several times to get the meaning.

For easy reading keep the length of most sentences somewhere between fifteen and twenty-five words (about one and a half to two lines of typing). Use a few short short sentences (under fifteen words) and an occasional—very occasional—long one. (When you do use a long sentence make sure it moves straight ahead with no twists and turns to throw the reader off the track.) Sentences of varying length give the letter a pleasing rhythm and if you come up with an average-length sentence of twenty words the reading will be comfortable. You might try shorter sentences, but they are hard to manage in a letter. With only a few sentences in a letter, one long one can cause you to overshoot your mark and a series of short ones will be choppy unless you are skilled in transition.

The problem is, how can you control sentence length in a letter? Those short and rhythmic sentences might come easily in rewriting, but what about dictation?

There is only one thing you can do. Think of a letter as a "*deliberate* conversation," as it was described by Gracian, the Spanish literary stylist. *Don't try to say too much in one sentence.* If you take this advice, the formula will work itself.

Within reason, use one sentence for one thought. It isn't reasonable to separate closely related thoughts that can be expressed in a few words, as "Bannister is better qualified, but Shumaker will win." It is reasonable—and fairly easy—to separate those long qualifying clauses that interrupt the principal thought. Here's how:

When a qualifying thought pops into your head right in the middle of a smooth-running sentence, deliberate. You know instinctively when this happens. Suddenly you feel insecure. You realize that what you are saying won't be accurate unless it is qualified. Suppose, for example, you begin a sentence, "When a disability annuitant recovers, his annuity is continued for a period not exceeding a year—" You want to conclude, "to give him an opportunity to find a job." Then suddenly you remember this statement isn't accurate. What happens? Instead of deliberating, the inclination is to plunge into the qualifying clause then and there. The sentence turns out:

> When a disability annuitant recovers, his annuity is continued for a period not exceeding one year, provided he is not re-employed by the government during this period, in order to give him an opportunity to find a position.

Don't be impatient about getting in those long qualifying clauses. Put some of them in separate sentences like this:

> When a disability annuitant recovers, his annuity is continued temporarily (not more than a year) to give him an opportunity to find a job. If he is re-employed by the government within the year, his annuity stops.

More deliberate conversation is also suggested for complex sentences beginning with as, inasmuch as, because, since or if. If you are thinking of beginning a sentence with these words, don't do it unless you can state the condition in a few words. Compare these sentences:

> Because of the shortage in raw materials / we were forced to shut down the Newark plant.
> Inasmuch as we have received no recent communication of any kind from our borrower / and as the delinquency on the loan still stands from June 5 in the amount of $130 and subsequent payments / with a present unpaid balance of $853, / we are wondering if you have been successful in repossessing our collateral.

The first sentence is easy reading because it is short. Only seven words (because of the shortage of raw materials) suspend the big idea (we were forced to shut down our Newark plant). The second example is tedious and tiring. Here the big idea (have you been successful in repossessing our collateral) is suspended by a statement of three conditions. The reader must hang on to forty-one words before reaching the point. As a better way of handling the thoughts, I would suggest three sentences written by the golden rule. Perhaps:

> The unpaid balance on this loan is $853, with past-due payments of $130 a month dating back to June 5. Still, we have heard nothing from the borrower. So will you please let us know whether you have been successful in repossessing our collateral?

"Since" introduces some of the longest and most tiring sentences in business literature:

> Since distribution of the estate cannot take place until the early part of next year in any event, and the further fact that you will be twenty-one years old on June 3, we could, when the time to do so arrives, petition the court for distribution of the estate and hold the funds in the savings account until you become of age on June 3.

This seems to say:

> In any event, distribution of the estate cannot be made until the early part of next year. We could then petition the court for distribution and hold the funds in the savings account until you become of age on June 3.

For lengthy "if" sentences the Federal government has no peer. Here, though, we find business competing with Uncle Sam:

> *If, as has been indicated by previous information received in this office, the balance of interest and principal which was paid on the primary lien amounted to $6405.49 and the balance of the second mortgage is $1556.09, and as these items add up to slightly under $8000 as compared to the $10,600 recent appraisal made of the property, I believe I can say with full assurance that we can guarantee your principal that they will suffer no loss in connection with the first mortgage.*

This sentence, like other examples given here, is unduly long because of excess verbiage. But even if the excess words were removed, the conditional statements would outweigh the conclusion. The better practice is to state the condition in one sentence and draw the conclusion in another.

condition  
conclusion
> *I understand that the unpaid balance is $6405.49 on the first mortgage and $1556.09 on the second mortgage, a total of less than $8000. The property was recently appraised at $10,600. So I feel confident that your principal will suffer no loss on the first mortgage.*

Finally, I would caution you to pause at the *ands*, *whiches* and *whos*, those frequent junctures between compound sentences. In speech we commonly string sentences together with *ands*. Do the same thing in writing, and the sentence is immature:

> *We wish to bring to your attention that through, round-trip, coach party fares may be purchased at C—— to P——, via our railroad to A——, thence the X Railroad, and return same, for a party of 10 to 49, inclusive, at $8.40 plus tax, per capita, and our ticket agent at C—— will furnish you with round-trip, coach party tickets upon request, and we should be pleased to have your patronage, if possible, in connection with this journey to P——.*

Actually that is not one sentence. It is three. Each big *and* is the beginning of a new sentence. Take out some of the useless words, and the result might be:

> *Through service is available from C—— to P—— over our rail-road to A—— and the X Railroad from there to P——. You may buy your tickets from our agent at C——. The price of the round-trip coach fare for parties of 10 to 49 is $9.24 for each person, tax included.*
>
> *We shall be pleased to serve you . . . and we wish you a pleasant journey!*

After dictating a full-length sentence you may be tempted to tack on another one introduced by *which*.

> *If this installment is received we agree to defer any action until September 15, which should give you enough time to wind up negotiations with Mr. Green for sale of the property.*

Or by *who*.

> *In the event that you desire this done, will you please have 500 of your envelopes sent to Mr. S. M. Peterson, Mailing Division, 8 Center Street, who will see that they are addressed and returned to you.*

Two sentences are neater.

> *If this installment is received we agree to defer any action until September 15. This should give you enough time to wind up negotiations with Mr. Green for sale of the property.*
>
> *If you wish this done, please send 500 envelopes to Mr. M. S. Peterson, Mailing Division, 8 Center Street, Perkinson, Illinois. He will see that they are addressed and returned to you.*

CRAZY WORD MIXTURES

Carelessly arranged words result more often in comical sentences than in misunderstood ones.

> We filed the correspondence in this office between you and Mr. Smith.
> The enclosed booklet explains what you should do when you injure yourself to collect insurance.
> The letter was sent to you due to a clerical oversight intended for another client of a similar name.

What happened to the writers of those sentences happens to everybody sometimes. Of course, it is more likely to happen in free dictation than in letters drafted in longhand or pecked out on the typewriter. Again, the best cure is more of that "deliberate conversation" while dictating. Try to keep your modifiers alongside the words they modify like this:

> The letter intended for a client of another name was sent to you through a clerical oversight.

You'll need some help from your stenographer on this one. Changed meaning from poor arrangement is often difficult to detect in speech. Even after the words go on paper, the trouble may not be readily detected. The following sentence from an office instruction was passed unnoticed by scores of readers.

> The word "concurrence" and the names of necessary officials who must concur should be typed about one inch from the bottom of the page.

The person who first detected the misplaced necessary quipped, "That just about eliminates the need for concurrences."

## SIMPLICITY IN PARAGRAPHS

### SMOOTH CONNECTIONS BETWEEN SENTENCES

No matter how simple and accurate the sentences are, the reader may have rough going—he may even get thrown off—if the connections between them are bad.

There are really only three ways to tie sentences together: *parallel construction, echoes* and *guideposts*.

You have seen countless examples of parallel construction in office instructions like these:

> *Next time you get a hurry-up call for a telegram, don't bother to take the copy you are writing from the typewriter. Sandwich the rush job between the papers already in the machine.*
>
> *1. Turn back the papers in the machine until about two inches of the top margin are showing.*
>
> *2. Insert the first sheet (original) of the rush job behind the papers in the machine.*
>
> *3. Insert a tissue sheet against the coated side of each carbon.*
>
> *4. Turn the platen until the rush job is in place for typing.*

By parallel construction such as this the reader is prepared in one statement for whatever follows. The following sentences are then kept marching in the same direction. Keep that in mind, especially in report and instruction writing where the format is often used. Don't say "turn back the papers" in one sentence and then switch to "the first sheet of the rush job is inserted" in the next sentence. To switch from imperative sentences (do this, do that, or do the other) to declarative sentences (this is done, that is done, the other is done) is confusing to the reader.

Parallel construction also works well in narative reports. Here the scheme is not so obvious, but it can be seen in this report letter from our ambassador to London in 1857:

preparation
*The worst apprehensions are fast seizing upon the merchants. The Bank of England raised her interest on discounts to 10 per cent yesterday.*

similar sentence
structure
*Several heavy failures have been announced . . . Not a ray of sunshine breaks upon the gloom from any quarter as yet. Men look as if they were beneath an impending avalanche and scarcely dare to breathe.*

An echo is a word or phrase repeated from a preceding sentence, or a word—usually a pronoun—that stands for a word or phrase in a preceding sentence, or a wording that suggests a relationship to a preceding sentence. The familiar sound of these echoes carries the reader from sentence to sentence, as in this example:

*As a way of saying thank you for a pleasant relationship we would like to make available to you our Interbranch Courtesy Card.*

"card" repeated
"it" stands for
card
*This card is an exclusive feature of our state-wide banking service. It is designed to give you a quick, easy and convenient means of identi-fication when cashing checks at any of our*

"this" stands for
the last thought
*branches. This is only one of the many special services which we are pleased to provide our customers . . .*

You use echo words like these unconsciously, and normally there is no reason why you should give the matter a second thought. Oc-casionally, though, you will find a misleading echo, as here:

*On August 13 we received $35.50 from Mrs. Clemonts. There is still $80.60 past due on her account. We feel sure that your investigation at the Chicago address resulted in this payment. Will you please continue to follow up on the account.*

Detect the trouble? "This payment" is actually an echo of "$35.50," but the reader would expect it to echo "$80.60." For smoothness and easy understanding the echo should follow the thought that is echoed:

> On August 13 we received $35.50 from Mrs. Clemonts. We feel sure this payment was a result of your investigation in Chicago. There is still . . .

In the next letter, the reader is thrown off completely because of a bad connection between the first two sentences:

> We recently received your report for the week ending May 3, along with your check in the amount of $116.48.
> Enclosed you will find check #7734, dated May 1, 1959, in payment of the above. We are returning this check because of the fact that no signature is affixed. Please affix your signature on this check and return at the earliest possible time so we can make proper application to your account.

Actually, there was only one check. But, with the connection missing, you'd never guess it. Here's the idea:

> Your $116.48 check, forwarded with your report for the week ending May 3, is returned for your signature.

Guideposts, as the name suggests, are word signs—usually adverbs and conjunctions—that let the reader know in what direction he is going. The common guideposts are those that point to exceptions, cause or effect (conclusions), time or place, and additions. This is how they warn the reader:

EXCEPTIONS. Guideposts signifying that an exception will be made to what has just been said or implied: *The question was easy. Yet [still, even so, however, but, nevertheless] none of us knew the answer.*

CAUSE OR EFFECT. Guideposts putting the reader on notice that the new thought states the cause or effect of what has just been said: *Our engineers do not think the machine can be converted to our use.* So [*for that reason, thus, hence, therefore, accordingly*] *we have given up the idea of buying it.*

TIME OR PLACE. Guideposts letting the reader know where he is, in order of what has gone before: *Our first step was to get the property appraised.* Next [*later, then, afterwards, thereafter, subsequently, secondly*] *the question of ownership was settled.*

ADDITIONS. Guideposts letting the reader know that more will be said on the same subject: *As Shakespeare said, "The letter is too long by half a mile."* And [*besides, too, also, what's more, furthermore, additionally, moreover*] *look at the big words!*

These are only a few examples of the many words in the English language that act as guideposts. Despite the wide choice, business writers favor clumsy signs like *accordingly, therefore, however, consequently, subsequently, furthermore* and *moreover*. Can't we make better use of the neater signs like *so, but, now, then* and *too?*

In a thousand letters checked especially for connectives I found only seven sentences beginning with *and* or *but*. Grammarians used to teach that it was improper to begin sentences with these connectives. Nonsense! Even the best writers have always broken that rule. Like any other sentence connective, *and* and *but* become conspicuous when overworked. But if the professional writers can use them judiciously, why can't we?

Both echoes and guideposts are more helpful to the reader when they are introduced near the beginning of a new thought. Notice how Walter Hines Page does it in this charming letter to Sir Edward Grey:

DEAR SIR EDWARD,—*There is an American gentleman in London, the like of whom I do not know. Mr. Edward House is his name. He is the "silent partner" of President Wilson—that is to say, he is the most trusted political adviser and the nearest friend of the President. He is a private citizen, a man without personal political ambition—a modest, quiet, even shy fellow. He helps* make cabinets, to shape policies, to select judges and ambassadors and suchlike merely for the pleasure of seeing that these tasks are well done.

He is suffering from over-indulgence in advising, and he has come here to rest. I cannot get him from outside his hotel for he cares to see few people. But he is very eager to meet you.

I wonder if you would do me the honour to take luncheon at the Coburg Hotel with me, to meet him either on July 1, or 3, or 5—if you happen to be free? I shall have only you and Mr. House.

Very sincerely yours,
WALTER H. PAGE

Now compare the neat connectives in the above example with the clumsy ones in this letter:

> Receipt is acknowledged of your letter dated June 23 regarding the unpaid balance in your account in the amount of $4.16.
>
> You are correct in your understanding that there was a $9.05 credit balance on your account on March 12. Subsequently, however, your account was charged with $13.21, your order number 723 and our invoice A-6957, covering four dozen plastic containers. Consequently, the aforementioned unpaid balance remains outstanding on your account. Therefore, your further payment of $4.16 is requested and will be appreciated.

How would you rewrite the above letter? This is how one student in a letter-writing class did it:

> You are right. There was a $9.05 credit balance on your account on March 12. But the account was later charged with $13.21 (your order 723 and our invoice A-6957) for four dozen plastic containers. So, you can see, that leaves a balance of $4.16.
>
> I would appreciate your check to clear up this small balance.

SIZING THE PARAGRAPH

Long paragraphs suggest complexity. The very sight of them is forbidding.

There is no call for lengthy paragraphs in any letter. All sentences in the paragraph should be related to one idea, but this doesn't mean sentences related to an idea must be confined to a single paragraph. For a pleasing appearance and for ease of reading, try to vary the length of your paragraphs with none running over ten lines. This isn't difficult in letters, because thoughts turn from one to another more rapidly than in some other forms of writing. You can break off and start a new paragraph with any sentence that isn't too closely related to the ones that have gone before.

An effective trick of the professional writers of sales letters is the setting off of single sentences in separate paragraphs. Here is the conventional paragraphing:

> Our business is growing by leaps and bounds. There are now 500 more workers in our plants than there were a year ago— a total of 1,600 plant workers! Our office staff has increased from 240 to 316. Gross sales for the year shot up by more than 8 million dollars. Meanwhile the new plant in southern California is nearing completion, and bulldozers are breaking ground for another one in Alabama.
>
> But that isn't all. In the year ahead we expect to enlarge our Eastern plant, and move into an office building of our own. New markets promise to open for us in . . .

Here is the same copy with two key sentences dramatically set apart in separate paragraphs:

> Our business is growing by leaps and bounds.

There are now 500 more workers in our plants than there were a year ago—a total of 1,600 plant workers! Our office staff has increased from 240 to 316. Gross sales for the year shot up more than 8 million dollars. Meanwhile our new plant is nearing completion in southern California, and bulldozers are breaking ground for another one in Alabama.

But that isn't all!

In the year ahead we expect to enlarge our Eastern plant and move into an office building of our own. New markets promise to open for us in . . .

For interest and emphasis, put some of your big-idea sentences into separate paragraphs.

## SUMMARY

Simplicity, the second of our 4-S virtues, is not just a matter of avoiding the needless word. It also involves the choice and arrangement of words so the reader will know at once what is said, without being especially conscious of how it is said. If you want to make life pleasant for your reader:

1. Know your subject so well that you can discuss it confidently and naturally. Learn the art of clearing up knotty problems by examples. If need be, define technical and scientific terms for your lay readers.

2. Prefer little everyday words to big showy ones. (*Error* instead of *inadvertency; check* instead of *remittance; agree* instead of *interpose no objection.*)

3. Use more idioms. (*I found out* instead of *I ascertained; payments have fallen behind* instead of *payments are delinquent.*)

4. Use short sentences averaging about twenty words. Get some rhythm into the letter by varying the length of sentences.

5. Be careful that modifying words don't get out of place in the sentence.

6. Tie sentences together so the reader can follow you from one to the other without getting lost.

7. Keep paragraphs short, with none running over ten lines.

# STRENGTH

CHAPTER 4 | Your Astonishing
Word Power

*How forcible are right words!—Job 6:25*

IN 1917 the Federal government was building the Alaskan Railroad from Seward to Fairbanks, a project entrusted to the direction of Franklin K. Lane who was then Secretary of the Interior. With things going well on the railroad in September of that year Lane reported to his boss, Woodrow Wilson, with this letter:

> MY DEAR MR. PRESIDENT,—*It will interest you to know that the Commission I sent up this year to Alaska to look into the Alaskan Railroad matters has just returned. The engineer on this Commission was Mr. Wendt, formerly Chief Engineer of the Pittsburgh and Lake Erie Railroad and now in charge of the appraisal of eastern roads under the Interstate Commerce Commission.*
>
> *He tells me that our Alaskan road could not have been built for less money if handled by a private concern; and that he has never seen any railroad camps where the men were provided with as good food and where there was such care taken of their health. They have had no smallpox and but one case of typhoid fever. No liquor is allowed on the line of the road. The road in his judgment has followed the best possible location. Our hospitals are well run. The compensation plan adopted for injuries is satisfactory to the men.*

> *I have directed that all possible speed be made in connecting the Matanuska coal fields with Seward. This involves the heaviest construction that we will have to undertake . . . But by the middle of next year, no strikes intervening and transportation for supplies being available, this part of the work should be done.*

A course in practical English might be built around this letter. Mr. Lane had something worth saying, and he said it directly in few and simple words. That's not all. He chose words that had the power to make his reader see exactly what he meant. His letter has *strength*.

Let's face it: As business writers we are barely tapping our great source of word power. We are not even halfway trying to make good use of this power. And our letters show it.

This is, of course, the kind of sweeping indictment to which I must allow exceptions. If you are an exception, you probably write excellent letters. If not, you can do something about it. You have the word power, all right. Follow the example set by Mr. Lane, and you will be amazed how you can use this power in getting others to work and think with you.

## PICTURE WORDS

The weak writer says:

> *This is to inform you that the Commission which was sent up to Alaska to look into the Alaskan Railroad matters has just returned. A favorable report has been received from Mr. Wendt, the engineer of this Commission, whose background and experience qualify him to make an appraisal of conditions on the road. In his opinion the amount expended on the project compares favorably with similar undertakings. On the basis of his report, the welfare of the workers might be considered above average with respect to health facilities and compensation plans.*

*It is gratifying to note that there have been no recurrences of communicable diseases.*

*I have proposed that connection with the Matanuska coal fields and Seward be made as expeditiously as possible. While this involves considerable difficulties, it may be possible to bring this project to a conclusion sometime within the next year provided no difficulties intervene.*

Compare this example with Mr. Lane's letter. The difference is that between vague, shadowy words and clear, picture words. The weak writer gives you a general idea of conditions on the road, but Lane, who knew the power of words, gives you an exact picture, etching it out with specific concrete words. The weak writer deals in abstract nouns like *experience* and *opinion* and in nonspecific words like *disease* and *labor difficulties*. Lane chose specific concrete words like "Chief Engineer of the Pittsburgh and Lake Erie Railroad," "smallpox" and "strikes." Instead of fogging his reader's perception with a sentence such as "the amount expended compares favorably with similar undertakings," he cut through the fog with "our road could not have been built for less money if handled by a private concern." He was not satisfied with "above-average health facilities and compensation plans." He makes you see what was going on with words like "good food," "well-run hospitals," and "compensation for injuries."

From this comparison we draw our first rule for strength, the third of the 4-S virtues: *Avoid vague abstract words. Use picture words standing for things your reader can see or touch.*

Abstractions like *consideration, location, standpoint, case, instance, nature, degree, character, condition* and *interests*, are literally taking over our business prose. These vague words come to hand readily, deceiving writers with their gloss. I can imagine that the next example of glossy abstractions was dashed off in a matter of seconds:

*Pending full operational completion of the reorganization plan, and as a continuing adjunct to the proper monitoring of produc-*

> *tion, of costs, and of workloads in connection with activities throughout the functional area in the field, need is expressed for a means of rapid assimilation and expression of work progress, manpower utilization, and workload inventories in field offices. Such means must be readily maintained, must cover the full work spectrum, and to be of maximum utility must visualize the elements on which basic operational and managerial controls at this [home office] level may be properly focused.*

That turgid paragraph was written by a management consultant, a member of a profession dedicated to efficiency in office practices. He might have profited from Sir Ernest Gowers' advice, "To be clear is to be efficient; to be obscure is to be inefficient."

Concrete language must sometimes be worked for. It may have been inaccurate to say that the last example was dashed off in a matter of seconds, but it is surely accurate to say that it would take longer to write the same thing in plain English. The attitude that the extra measure of time it takes to be specific is not a worth-while investment is damaging to both the company and the writer. Letters that move others to work and think with us are more valuable than the extra time it takes to write them; and the person most likely to succeed is the one who spares no effort in getting his ideas across. "In literature as in life," said Quiller-Couch, "he makes himself felt who not only calls a spade a spade but has the pluck to double spades and redouble."

Granted there are times when it is difficult to be concrete, granted there are even times when it is dangerous to be specific, I think that the business of writing in abstractions and generalities is, oftener than not, a matter of carelessness. As a general rule, the letter lends itself to specific treatment. The dictator need not go out of his way in search of "pictures." Chances are they are there in the file before him. "Every effort will be made to handle your claim expeditiously" might, from the facts at hand, be expressed as "You may expect to hear from us by September 1 [or other date]." The abstraction "Mr. Green's persistent instability in the manner of repaying his loan" is bound to be backed up by records showing precisely what this means. (For example, "Mr. Green paid only one installment on time. His other payments have been from two to nine weeks late.") And I am sure you will agree that a generality such as this

> The address, Box 493, Apartment 31 is not a distinguishable address for Chicago. Would you please endeavor to get more meaning into this address?

could just as easily be expressed specifically, as

> The Chicago address is incomplete, showing only Box 493, Apartment 31. Will you please try to get the street name and the number of the apartment house?

If you want to strengthen your letters, if you want to get others to work and think with you, begin now to draw on the power of specific concrete words.


## THE VIGOR OF VERBS

Another way to strengthen your letters and at the same time shorten your sentences is to use fewer passive verbs and more active ones. Reread Lane's letter to Woodrow Wilson on the Alaskan Railroad project. You will find two active verbs for every passive one.

The very word *passive* suggests that too many verbs of this form weaken letters while the word *active* suggests that verbs of this form make them stronger. The following sentence is written in both forms. Is there any question in your mind as to which is the stronger?

| Active | Passive |
|---|---|
| Fourscore and seven years ago our fathers brought forth on this continent a new nation . . . | Fourscore and seven years ago a new nation was brought forth on this continent by our fathers . . . |

That, you may say, is unthinkable! Who would spoil the natural order of Lincoln's immortal lines?

You and I may never write immortal sentences, but we can do a thorough job of spoiling the natural order of prosaic everyday sentences like these:

| Active | Passive |
|---|---|
| Mr. Jones was at the meeting. | The meeting was attended by Mr. Jones. |
| Have you *thought* about our proposal? | Has any *thought been given* to our proposal? |
| Please *send* us $76 for the unpaid balance. | Your sending us a check in the amount of $76 for the unpaid balance *is requested*. |
| In the X case, the Supreme Court *upheld* the lower court's decision that the defendant was negligent. | In the X case, the decision of the lower court that the defendant was negligent *was upheld* by the Supreme Court. |
| Mr. Collins *has requested* us to review your securities. | We *have been requested* by Mr. Collins to review your securities. |
| The X Terminal Company *claims* that the package was damaged before it reached them. | *It is claimed* by the X Terminal Company that the package was damaged before it reached them. |

Don't get the idea that passive verbs are to be avoided like poor grammar. Passive verbs are useful:

When the doer of the action is less important than the recipient—

*The defendant has three children. The oldest child is called John.* [Here, the recipient of the action, *the oldest child*, is more important than the doer who may be *they* or *he* or *the child's parents.*]

When needed emphasis is gained by putting the name of the act or the doer at the end of the sentence—

*Divorce laws are enacted by the States.* [Here, the passive voice helps the writer emphasize that the laws are not Federal.]

When the doer is not known or may not be named—

*Much has been said for and against the tariff.*

Oftener than not we lapse into the passive voice thoughtlessly, sapping strength from our sentences and adding to their length. Be especially alert for sentences that make the doer of the action a "byproduct" or hide the doer behind an impersonal passive. Were it not for the preposition *by*—that little friend of the passive voice—and for impersonal passives, this topic would lose much of its importance. Watch how they work:

*Your letter was read by the Manager with interest.* [See how you make your Manager a byproduct? Yet, he is the doer of the action. Why not say *The Manager read?*]

*It is believed that his profession is that of broker.* [Why hide the doer behind the impersonal passive *it is believed?* Why not say *I believe* or *we believe?*]

## THE POSITIVE APPROACH

### SAY IT AS IF YOU MEAN IT

Don't cast doubts on your statements with phrases like "in my opinion" and "in my judgment." And think twice before weakening your sentences with hedgers like these:

| | | |
|---|---|---|
| apparently | in general | normally |
| as a rule | in many instances | ordinarily |
| as a usual case | in most cases | seemingly |
| commonly | it seems | seems to indicate |
| generally | it appears | usually |

By hedging, the writer gives himself a loophole to escape from statements that seem doubtful or not fully inclusive. Of course, this is often a legitimate practice. For example, positive assertions in letters giving investment advice—indeed, positive assertions in any writing offering advice—can be dangerous or misleading.

The weakness of hedging is in statements where it serves no real purpose, leaving the impression that the writer isn't sure of what he is saying.

> *It would appear that we did not receive the money order for $25 mentioned in your letter of September 8.*

Perhaps the writer of the above sentence had some doubt as to whether the money order arrived with the letter. Even so, he might have approached his reader more positively.

> *I can find no trace of the money order mentioned in your letter of September 8. Did you forget to enclose it?*

Needless hedging also raises questions in the reader's mind that may lead to needless correspondence:

When is a report normal?

The report does or doesn't include this figure. Why hedge?

*Normally,* a work-progress report should show both workloads and man-hours. While your report shows the total number of vouchers audited during the quarter ended June 30, 1957, it does not appear to include the total number of personnel on duty during that period.

*Alleged* is the lawyer's and the news reporter's favorite hedger. As an adjective it is used to protect the word it modifies, with the thought that the word may come to trial in a court of law. Unfortunately, it is often pressed into service by letter writers when there is no call for such protection, suggesting to the reader that his truthfulness is questioned.

I once conducted a letter-writing course for a group that handles accident claims. Everybody in the class had had some legal training and, in the manner of lawyers, they had learned to torture plain English unmercifully. I wish I could say that plain English and I came out of that course the winners, but I doubt that this is so. The only claim we can justly make is that we won at least one round hands down. It happened like this:

An accident, I learned from this group, was to be termed *an alleged accident*—never otherwise—until the day the Claims Department made the firm decision to pay the damages. Until then it was "Reference is made to your alleged accident," "Where were you when the alleged accident occurred," "Who witnessed the alleged accident," and so on; or at least it was that way until we won our round.

How did we win it? Easily. We showed the class a picture of an accident victim in a hospital bed, head bandaged, leg in traction. Between fingers that protruded from splints the unfortunate man was holding a letter. The letter began—you *guessed it*—with that familiar refrain, "Reference is made to your alleged accident . . ."

APPEALING WORDS

Readers react to some words more favorably than to others. The letter writer who thinks first of his reader chooses "affect" words carefully. There's strength in positive words like these:

advantage                    appreciate
agree                        benefit

| | |
|---|---|
| can | success |
| faith | service |
| gain | thanks |
| help | thorough |
| honest | thrift |
| now | truth |
| please | valuable |
| recommend | vital |

Words like these are negative, and successful letter writers use them judiciously:

| | |
|---|---|
| allege | fail |
| argument | fraud |
| bankrupt | ignorant |
| blame | impossible |
| cannot | loss |
| cheap | neglect |
| complaint | never |
| contend | ruin |
| dispute | unfair |
| disagree | unable |
| evict | unsatisfactory |

This is not to say that you should search for those mild words known as euphemisms, referring to an *error* as an *inadvertency*, the *poor* as the *underprivileged*, and *death* as *passing away*. Practicing the appeal of the positive is not a matter of disguising words. That weakens your writing. The idea is to approach your subject positively. Emphasize what is *right*, not what is *wrong*; what is *good*, not what is *bad*; what *can be done*, not what *can't be done*.

Read the two versions of the next letter. One writer takes the positive approach, the other the negative. Which letter do you prefer?

Negative

In regard to your letter of August 30, I cannot figure out what you meant by a $25 error. You failed to be specific as to what the trouble is, but I checked back on the carbon copies of the statements and noticed that on August 18 there was a $25 check charged to your account and another one in the same amount on September 3.

If you will look at your statement for August you will see that there is a credit of $7.00 which takes care of the service charges we charged you.

It is requested that you let me know about the $25 item as soon as possible and direct any further correspondence to the undersigned.

Positive

After getting your letter of August 30, I promptly checked our copies of your August and September statements. I find that a check for $25 was charged to you on August 18 and another for the same amount on September 3. Could it be that you overlooked one of these checks?

Our service-charge error of $7.00 was adjusted by the $7.00 credit on your August statement.

If this does not answer your question, Mrs. Clemonts, please let me know at once just what the error seems to be and when it occurred. I am sure I can find the answer for you and clear up the matter to your complete satisfaction.


## WHAT DOES YOUR READER WANT?

Cleveland editor William Feather tells this story of how a single word worked miracles in a help-wanted ad:

Headed for California, a St. Louis publisher ran a classified ad in his paper reading, "Owner wants car driven to West Coast. Will pay all driver's expenses." The ad ran three day with no response. The publisher then asked himself, "What's wrong with this copy?" He decided to change one word and run it again. Result? The first day he got twenty-six replies, and in three days he got more than sixty.

What magic did he use? "Simple," Mr. Feather tells us. "He changed 'car' to 'Cadillac'."

This story brings out a truth that every good copy writer knows. If you want to induce a reader to respond favorably, attend to his wants. Scores of people mildly interested in a free trip to California may have read both ads, but it took something more appealing than the first one to induce anybody to inquire. The luxury, perhaps the importance, suggested by "Cadillac" did the trick.

Writers of sales letters have every opportunity to appeal to human wants. Making the most of this opportunity, the skilled salesman begins a letter, "Did you know your estate may be subject to a mortgage you did not sign?" The reader's interest is immediately aroused. "What? My estate in danger?" He reads on. The writer has succeeded in capturing his reader's attention by appealing to a fundamental want, the want for security. Another sales letter begins, "Here's a real stamp that's worth—at first glance—just 2¢. Actually it's worth dollars—to you." Again the writer is making a direct pitch for the reader's interest. Who wouldn't want to make dollars out of a two-cent stamp? Sentences like these are carefully calculated to appeal to such fundamental human wants as comfort, security, leisure, food, sex, social esteem, recognition and efficiency.

But the writing of sales letters has long since passed into the hands of ad men, professional letter services, or the company's public relations department. Mass-mailed letters, written and dispatched outside the company's offices, are the modern way of flooding the mails with a sales pitch. You may never be called on to write an actual sales letter. Your everyday letters will more likely deal with adjustments, appointments, collections, credit, orders, purchasing, personnel and informational matters—and, of course, those internal memos asking for or setting forth cold facts.

How does the slogan "Make every letter a sales letter" apply to this correspondence?

In the first place, by the very act of writing clearly and concisely you are satisfying one of your reader's wants. Speaking of the psychology of writing, H. A. Overstreet says, "Verbosity, circumlocution, and lack of clearness are psychological in that they fog the stimulus. Abstractness is psychological in that it places too great a tax upon our essentially concrete minds." Professor Overstreet is here explaining an *idea* instead of a thing, and ideas are hard to explain in concrete words. Yet note the stimulus you get from his words as compared to the fogginess induced by another professor's explanation of so concrete a thing as a business report:

> A comprehensive statement of verified facts and impersonal conclusions based on firsthand analysis of present or past conditions or operations and compiled for the information, with or without recommendation, for future action of executives and controlling groups.

Regardless of what the letter is about—even if it is about cold facts—there is always the opportunity to attend to your reader's wants by stating the facts as clearly and concisely as you can.

In the second place, every letter can be written to satisfy one of the great fundamental human wants—the craving for recognition.

A few years ago I stopped for gasoline at a filling station I had never before been to. The service was prompt and courteous, but there was nothing unusual about it. Except for the fact that I happened to be in the same neighborhood two weeks later and in need of gas, I might never have stopped there again. Something happened on that second call, though, that turned me from a chance customer into a regular one. A free car wash? Gift stamps? No. The attendant simply said, "Good morning, Miss Sheppard." How he knew my name I haven't the slightest idea. It isn't important. The important thing is that he recognized me. Like everybody else I appreciate recognition.

You may think that the salutation (*Dear Mr. Jones, Dear Miss Everett*) is enough to give the reader the stimulus that comes from the sound of his name. Oftentimes in short letters it is. But I suggest that you try "name-calling" in the body of those longer letters, especially when you are making an appeal. "May we count on your help, Mr. Jones?" Mr. Jones or anybody else is sure to like it.

Aside from his own name the most important word to your reader is that personal pronoun that stands for him. You. The power of this little word is simply incalculable. And how often we pass up the opportunity to use it! Those dreary office memos:

> *All employees are requested to observe the "No Smoking" sign which was recently posted in the west corridor of the main floor by the Building Superintendent. Until repairs to the west wing are completed this passageway must be used for delivery of materials to the laboratory, some of which are inflammable. In the interest of personal and property protection it is essential that this caution be taken.*

The worker may care about the company's property, but he cares considerably more about his own safety. Get him into the memo—not by the indirect route of association with the word *employees* but by the direct route of you. Begin something like this: "For your own safety, you are urged . . ."

Editor and ad-man Hal Stebbins, in his book *Copy Capsules* (McGraw-Hill), tells a story about another important word. As he tells it, "A group of undergraduates at Oxford—so the story goes—heard that Rudyard Kipling was to get ten shillings a word for a certain piece of work. Scraping together the necessary ten shillings they wired it to the famous author with the naive request 'Please send us one of your best words.' Back came the precious word: 'Thanks!'"

If you have something to thank your reader for, use that ten-shilling word.

Recognition of the reader flows through letters in countless other ways. By words showing him how he stands to benefit from a new office procedure. By a word of praise. By credit for good intentions, as in collection letters. By that extra paragraph of congratulations on a job well done, a marriage, a promotion, a vacation, a new baby—anything that is important to the reader. Even by the simple graciousness of admitting that the reader is right. Not one of these means of recognition can be dismissed by the businessman as "small talk." There's power in any word that has appeal.

One of Abraham Lincoln's letters begins with a word of praise and thanks, and ends with the simple words "you are right and I was wrong."

Washington, July 13, 1863

To MAJOR GENERAL GRANT

MY DEAR GENERAL,—I do not remember that you and I ever met personally. I write this now as a grateful acknowledgement for the almost inestimable service you have done the country. I wish to say a word further. When you first reached the vicinity of Vicksburg, I thought you should do what you finally did—man the troops across the neck, run the batteries with the transports and thus go below; and I never had any faith, except a general hope that you knew better than I, that the Yazoo Pass expedition and the like could succeed. When you got below and took Port Gibson, Grand Gulf, and vicinity, I thought you should go down the river and join General Banks, and when you turned northward, east of the Big Black, I feared it was a mistake. I now wish to make the personal acknowledgement that you were right and I was wrong.

Yours very truly,
A. LINCOLN

In the next letter a personnel director skillfully avoids telling a plant manager he is wrong. Instead he states the problem, then implies a compliment to his reader by asking him how he would solve it.

> *I can understand perfectly well how you feel, Jim. All our plants are feeling the pinch of the manpower shortage, especially the shortage of qualified engineers and technicians.*
>
> *The Atlanta plant is claiming priority because of the pressure on it to meet the schedule on Defense Department contracts. Chattanooga reminds me by daily phone calls of their rights as the producers of our most profitable products. Denver feels neglected because of its remoteness from this office.*
>
> *In the face of these claims—most of them just—is the plain fact that the schools simply cannot satisfy the demands for technicians and engineers. And the competitive bidding for this talent is boosting wages to a height that threatens to put us as well as our competitors out of business.*
>
> *If you can tell me how to solve this problem so as to satisfy your needs as well as those of our other plants, I should be deeply grateful. . . .*

## NONSTOP SENTENCES

Finally I remind you of a trick in word arrangement, a trick that can turn a halting, loose sentence into a strong one. The grammar books call these driving sentences *periodic*. Not a very meaningful word, is it? So let's describe the periodic sentence as *nonstop*. The reader can't "get off" until he reads it through. If he does, he won't get a complete thought. The trick is to hold the big idea for the last words in the sentence, keeping the reader in suspense to the very end.

> *Each week from January 13 through February 21, while ill and absent from her job, she was receiving from the Metropolitan Life Insurance Company a $28.85 check.*

See how it works? See how the sentence keeps going to the very end? In contrast, the next sentence (known as a *loose* one) has two big junctures at which the reader can abandon it comfortably.

*She received weekly checks for $28.85 / which the Metropolitan Life Insurance paid her from January 13 to February 21, / covering the period she was ill and absent from her job.*

Some professional writers lean heavily on the periodic sentence in beginning their stories. Here are some typical sentences from articles in *Reader's Digest*, calculated to lure the reader.

*When a 42-mile-per-hour wind pushed "Galloping Gertie," the mammoth $6,400,000 suspension bridge, into Washington's Tacoma Narrow in 1949 with a splash heard around the world, the Federal Government set up a committee to investigate.*

*In dealing with the school shortage, I wonder whether we clearly ask ourselves what a school is.*

*During the 1930's, when wage inequities were being eliminated, working conditions modernized, wages raised and hours shortened, I asked my elders in the labor movement a simple question: What do we do when these failings of management have been corrected?*

*In everything worthwhile I have ever attempted, I have found some trouble.*

Sentences like these may not come off while dictating. They are more characteristic of studied prose than of conversation. Loose sentences, typical in conversation, are also typical in letters. But an occasional nonstop sentence is worth the calculating, especially when you want to be emphatic or create a strong effect. Sometimes the calculation is a simple matter of switching the order of clauses. "I have found some trouble in everything worthwhile that I have ever attempted," can be turned around as it was in *Reader's Digest*, to focus attention more sharply—"In everything worthwhile that I have ever attempted, I have found some trouble." Similarly these sentences are strengthened

> I was surprised to learn that we have not received your check for the unpaid balance on your account. The thing that surprises me even more is that you have not even shown us the courtesy of a reply, even though we have written you a number of times.

by inverting the order of the second sentence

> I was surprised to learn that we have not received your check for the unpaid balance on your account. Even more surprising is the fact that, although we have written you repeatedly, you have not even shown us the courtesy of a reply.

and this

> I feel I should tell you that I sincerely believe you should accept the General Motors offer, and I tell you this in the spirit of earnest friendship, for, after all, we were friends long before I became the boss.

creates a bigger effect as:

> As your old friend—and not as your boss—I feel that I should tell you in a spirit of earnest friendship that I sincerely believe you should accept the General Motors offer.

## SUMMARY

Are you making good use of your word power?

The strength that flows from right words in the right arrangement is a priceless quality of business writing. It can make others feel and see. It can impel them to work and think with us. Here are five ways of drawing on this power:

1. Avoid vague words. Use picture words standing for things your reader can see and touch. Be especially on guard against the vagueness surrounding abstractions like *opinion, condition, operations, position* and *situation*.

2. Use more active verbs. (*The manager read the letter* instead of *The letter was read by the manager*.) The very word *passive* suggests that too many verbs of this form weaken letters while the word *active* suggests that verbs of this form strengthen them.

3. Approach your subject positively. Don't cast needless doubts on what you say, with words like *apparently* and *in my opinion*. Emphasize what is *right*, not what is *wrong*; what is *good*, not what is *bad*; what *can be done*, not what *can't be done*. Choose affect words judiciously, preferring positives like *success, can, advantage,* instead of negatives like *fail, cannot, loss*.

4. Attend to your reader's wants, especially his want for recognition. Call him by name. Get him into the letter by frequent use of the pronoun *you*. Tell him when he is right, and let him see how he can be benefited. If he has a word of praise or congratulations coming to him, never spare it. And remember that *thanks* is a ten-shilling word.

5. For emphasis and big effect, use some periodic sentences— nonstop sentences that keep the reader in suspense to the very end, as "In everything worthwhile I have ever attempted, I have found some trouble," instead of "I have found some trouble in everything worthwhile that I have ever attempted."

Do these things and you will be astounded by the power of your own words.

# SINCERITY

CHAPTER 5 | Getting Yourself
on Paper

I WAS WANDERING along an office corridor, a big bundle of letters under my arm, when an attractive young woman fell in step beside me.

"Good morning," she said cheerfully. "Are you looking for our conference room?"

"Yes," I replied, getting a new hitch on my burden of letters. "I am beginning to think this is the wrong floor."

"Oh, no. It's just around the corner. I'm headed there, too. Here, let me help you with those papers." Unloading me, she chatted on, "I believe you are going to conduct our letter-writing course. We're looking forward to it. My name is . . ."

When this poised and outgoing young woman told me her name I was surprised. I found it hard to believe that she was the author of those letters I had been reading that very morning. If you are wondering why I was surprised, then read one of her letters:

> Referring to your letter of April 7, 1957, in regard to your interest in a stenographic position with this company:
> I regret to advise you that at the present time this company has no positions open for stenographers. Therefore, it will be unnecessary for you to call on us for a personal interview. However, your letter and application will be kept on file, and should a suitable vacancy occur you will be contacted.

> Pursuant to your request, the photograph forwarded with the application is returned herewith.

Does that sound like the girl in the corridor? In the letter-writing course that followed, here's how she rewrote that letter to sound more like herself:

> If we had any openings for stenographers I would certainly take you up on your offer to call on us for a personal interview. But with no immediate openings here, I feel sure you will want to concentrate on more likely prospects. Meanwhile, I shall keep your application on file, and if anything comes up you can expect to hear from me.
>
> Thanks for thinking of us . . . and all good wishes for your success.

Countless letters are no more like the men and women who write them than the villainous role is like the real-life character of the actor who plays it. The truth is, people who write these unreal letters are themselves playing a role. Completely out of character, they take the part of a pompous scribe at an office desk. They speak in the third person. Coldly impersonal, their letters seem to come from machines rather than from human beings. While subscribing a letter "sincerely yours," some of them muffle the ring of sincerity with artificialities, even though that is the last thing they wish to do.

"Naturalness," said Aristotle, "is persuasive, and artificiality the reverse; for people take offense at an artificial speaker as if he were practicing a design upon them, in the same way they take offense at mixed wines."

If you want the real you to show through your letters, convincing the reader of your sincerity, be natural.

This doesn't mean that you will be pardoned for showing your feelings when an unreasonable customer cuts you to the quick with a scathing letter, when you are hopping mad about that or the other, or bitter over what seems to be an injustice. To be natural and let yourself go under such circumstances would be poor business, hardly calculated to win and keep friends. Our concern with naturalness does not so much involve the writer's feelings. The principal concern is those faulty writing techniques that make a letter sound inhuman whether the writer is at war or peace with the reader.

Earlier chapters showed some of the causes of unnatural expression—oversized and showy words, the practice of repeating questions before answering them, etc. Let's consider now some of the other offenders that rob our letters of the 4-S virtue *sincerity*.

## MODERN SPEECH VERSUS DEAD LANGUAGE

My first suggestion concerns a minor problem, though lots of people seem to think it a major one.

Big, pretentious words were discussed in Chapter 3, but no mention was made of a special variety of pompous expression that comes in words of all sizes. They are the phrases most people think of as the clichés of business, language made popular by commercial schools that sprang up with the coming of the typewriter some eighty years ago. Many articles and books on letter writing still harp on these so-called clichés as the worst sin of business writing. You will recognize them as *beg to advise, beg to remain, esteemed favor, handing you herewith, contents duly noted, deem it a favor, yours of the 9th inst.,* and so on.

The commercial schools of the 1880s and 1890s didn't coin these phrases. They come from way back. Some of them are mannerisms of the eighteenth century. You'll find the same expressions in the letters of George Washington, whose style they suit to a tee. And you'll find a few still surviving, seventy-five years later, in the letters of Abraham Lincoln. The schools simply spread the mannerism throughout the business world where it stuck as *commercialese*.

Today, such mannerisms are almost as rare as roll-top desks—except in the salutation and the complimentary closing. The problem is not as big as some counselors seem to think it is.

Yet a little of that dead language, including latinisms, is exhumed occasionally by some of the older industries, such as railroads. Here are twenty embalmed words and phrases seen oftener than any others:

| *Dead Language* | *Modern Speech* |
|---|---|
| and oblige | thank you |
| annum | year |
| awaiting your further orders | we shall expect to hear from you |
| diem | day |
| enclosed please find | enclosed is |
| in lieu of | in place of |
| in re | about |
| in due course | [omit, or be specific] |
| kindly advise us | please tell (inform) us |
| of even date | today |
| optimum | best |
| party | person |
| per | by, through |
| pursuant to your request | as you requested |
| said (*loan, check,* etc). | the, this (*loan, check, etc.*) |
| same (as "sign and return same") | it, they, them |
| the undersigned | I, we |
| under separate cover | separately |
| up to the present writing | now, up to now |
| yours of the (*date*) | your (*date*) letter |

The fairly common and formal *reference is made, referring to your letter*—which we have dealt with as padding—might also be listed here.

The distinguishing feature of the list is that the words and phrases are seldom if ever heard in conversation. Do you know anybody who talks like this:

*The shipment has a C. O. D. on same of $20.20. Please advise me as to the disposition made of this C. O. D. and oblige.*

*A copy of the invoice is enclosed per request of our Mr. Holmes.*

Keep the language of your letters as modern as the language of your speech!

## THE HUMAN TOUCH

There is hardly a word used to describe a human being that isn't also used to describe a letter. Cold or warm, pompous or natural, efficient or inefficient, long-winded or to-the-point, weak or strong, sincere or insincere—you can think of dozens more.

These adjectives can't actually describe a letter. They describe qualities of a person. The letter is only an image that impresses the reader as a likeness of the writer. Oftener than not, the unpleasant things people say about letters are said because of faulty writing practices that make the writer seem cold and inhuman.

Compare:

| Inhuman | Human |
|---|---|
| It is with regret that the Trust Department must inform you that the above-mentioned incompetent passed away on August 7. | We are sorry to tell you that our ward M—— J—— L—— died August 7. |
| The Division has received a request for investment advice from the aforementioned. | We have received Mr. Smith's request for investment advice. |
| Please inform this office of the present address of this person. | Please give us Mr. Carter's present address. |

| Inhuman | Human |
|---|---|
| According to information just received in this office the subject borrower is now residing with a party at 3401 Fair Street. | I have just learned that Mr. Jones is now living with his sister at 3401 Fair Street. |

You can easily see why the sentences in the left column are "stone" while those on the right are "flesh." Words like *we, I, Mr. Smith* and *sister* instead of *Trust Department, aforementioned* and *party* make the big difference.

If you want your letters to sound human, write in human terms. Use personal pronouns—*you, your, I, mine, my, we, our, he, him, his, she, her, they, them* and *their.* Use the proper names of people—*Mr. Smith, Helen Gibson, Harold M. South.* Use words that stand for human beings—like *child, son, daughter, mother, father, brother, sister.* Use words like these whenever it is fitting to do so.

*You,* it has been said, is one of the most important words in a letter for its power to affect the reader favorably. In "Upgrading Letter Copy," a monthly feature of *The Reporter of Direct Mail Advertising,* Paul J. Binge shows how to humanize and enliven a letter with more *You* and more picture words. Here is the original version:

> . . . *We produce molded products to your specifications and use compounds of either Natural Rubber, GR-S, Neoprene, Nitriles or Butyl, whatever is best for your requirements. In recent years, we have done considerable work in colors and can make them to your satisfaction. Many customers also require rubber bonded to metal.*
>
> *We will be only too glad to quote on your present requirements or on any new developments that you may request as we believe you will be satisfied with our prices and service. If possible, please send us samples of material desired or blueprints and specifications.*

We would appreciate your advising us if you own the molds for your present requirements or if you desire an additional one. If you desire a new mold, we can produce same quickly and very economically.

Here's how Mr. Binge upgraded the letter:

You might think this small rubber part is a collar button, the kind that grandpa found so handy. The bouncing collar button has disappeared but rubber is still doing thousands of jobs no other material can do so well.

This small bumper goes on the door of an automatic clothes dryer. That demands not only shock resistance but also heat resistance. Ordinary rubber won't do, so this bumper is made of silicon rubber, good for more than 600 degrees, wet or dry.

Rubber has come a long way since collar button days. Today there is not only natural rubber, but also GR-S, Neoprene, Nitriles, Butyl and Silicon. There is scarcely a problem of heat, light, solvent or other chemical resistance that cannot be solved with the proper compound.

And color? Just about anything you want. Hardly anybody cares for hot-water-bottle red these days—not with the wide choice of brilliant, glowing colors available for the asking . . .

Just check your interest on the card and mail today. Our man will be along loaded with samples, suggestions, and ideas. No obligation, of course. We like to talk to anyone about rubber and what it can do. May we talk to you?

### WE ARE IMPORTANT, TOO

There has long been a notion among government letter writers that the use of *I* and *we* is unbecoming to a public servant. This notion of the propriety of being impersonal has spread to big business, robbing letters of their humanness. In skirting around *I* and we the writer lapses into impersonal pronouns that chill the tone of even the friendliest letter.

It is hoped *that you will give us the opportunity to serve you.* (*We hope that you* . . .)
It has been determined *from the Personnel Department that Harry F. Fitzhugh has never been employed by this company.* (*Our Personnel Department tells me that Harry F. Fitzhugh has never worked for us.*)

Unlike you, *I* and *we* can be overworked. In its handbook *Bank Notes on How to Write Better Letters* the Bank of America warns its letter writers, "The *I*'s get too big in the eyes of the reader. Too many of them seem to stare at him from the written page . . . and of course it's impolite to stare!" *We* becomes obtrusive, too, especially when used to begin a series of paragraphs.

It is always preferable to write letters from the *you* rather than the *I* or *we* viewpoint, but there is no cause to shun the first person pronouns.

"I" OR "WE"?

When should you use *I*? And when should you use *we*?
A good general rule is to prefer *we* when explaining a company policy, operation or service; prefer *I* when explaining a matter in which you are acting as agent for your company. British authority Sir Ernest Gowers to the contrary, I see no reason why *I*'s and *we*'s shouldn't be mixed in the same letter as long as you stick to this general rule on usage. For example, "*We* do not have a flight to Buffalo. *I'll* be glad to check Capital Airlines for you."
There are five unobtrusive *I*'s in the next letter and only one passive verb. That's how James Huneker went about getting himself on paper in a routine letter about his business affairs.

*New York, New York*
*August 8, 1906*

To DAVID A. MUNRO

DEAR MR. MUNRO,—Here is the copy, relieved of 8 pages, 2000 words. The entire story was nearly 7000 words; it is now not more than 5000. As I couldn't slaughter that first part outright—it would make the study all tail and no head—I made cuts in both sections; which render the affair more symmetrical. I have refolioed the pages and think there are no breaks in transitions. If you wish to avoid the labor of proofreading I shall be only too glad to read the galleys myself. My address until October after Tuesday next will be in care of Forest Hills Hotel, Franconia, New Hampshire.

I can return proofs within 24 hours after receiving them. Again thanking you for your courtesy in this matter.

*I am sincerely yours,*
JAMES HUNEKER

## "COULD NOT" OR "COULDN'T"?

Notice how Huneker used the contraction *couldn't* instead of *could not*. In one company I checked 800 letters for contractions. How many do you think I found? Eight. Only eight contractions in 800 letters. If you were to check five minutes' conversation between any two of the people who wrote these letters, what do you suppose the count would be? Dozens, literally dozens like *I'll*, *we'll*, *you've*, *can't*, *doesn't*, *haven't*, *wasn't*, *isn't*, *wouldn't*, *it's* and *let's*. Perhaps some letters are dictated with these respectable contractions and then changed by well-meaning stenographers. If that's happening to you, ask your stenographer to pass one occasionally. Your letters will sound more like your conversation.

Of course, contractions should not be overworked. Too many look messy on paper. Consider, too, their effect on rhythm and emphasis. *Couldn't* falls naturally in the Huneker sentence, "As I couldn't slaughter that first part outright . . ." Speak these words aloud. Then speak them again, changing *couldn't* to *could not*. You'll feel the difference. Next try the same experiment on this sentence, using first *I will not* and then *I won't*: "I will not [won't] be a party to any such agreement." Here you may find, as I do, that *will not* is more satisfying for its emphasis.

## ? FOR QUESTION

What about a few questions for a conversational touch?

One credit man, a supervisor, once told me that he didn't approve of questions in letters—that is, direct questions followed by question marks. He himself wrote very good questionless letters; and he, like any of the rest of us, should certainly be entitled to at least one eccentricity in letter writing. If this one doesn't happen to be yours, throw in a direct question now and then. Instead of this

> *If there is a copy of the Monsanto Chemical Annual Report for 1955 available from your files, we would appreciate your forwarding it to this office for review.*

try something like this:

> *Do you have a copy of Monsanto Chemical's 1955 Annual Report? If so, may I borrow it, please?*

Direct questions make letters lively and conversational. Here is a good example contributed by a large investment house:

> *We are trying to teach our young salesmen and correspondents to write civilized English, and we should, if possible, like to show them your article "No English" in the Princeton Alumni Weekly (condensed on November 11 in the Wall Street Journal).*
>
> *Are reprints of the whole article available? If so, may we*

*please order 100 copies? We assume either you or the Princeton Alumni Weekly will let us know the cost.*

*If no reprints are available, would it be possible for us to see one copy of the article? Would reproduction, for our own use, be permitted?*

*We shall be grateful for any help you can give us. We are already grateful for your article.*

Don't fear any technique that will give your letter a personal touch. Winston Churchill adds the human touch to his letters by penning the salutation in his own handwriting. Others deliberately put handwritten notes in the margin or at the foot of the letter for the same purpose. You needn't feel your readers will criticize you for these informalities. They are more likely to applaud you.

## EXCUSE IT, PLEASE!

"Everybody makes mistakes" is one of those truisms of which nobody need be reminded. But some of us need to be reminded of how insincere a letter sounds when mistakes are ignored or glossed over with meaningless words. There are dictators who seem to think that the people who get their letters (or perhaps the bosses who review them) would be disillusioned by plain words acknowledging those simple errors that happen sometimes in even the most efficient office.

Let's suppose John M. Smith is notified of a shortage on his account which was actually a shortage on John N. Smith's account. Discovering the error, the ignorer of mistakes writes John M.:

*Please disregard the notice forwarded to you on August 7. The records of this office indicate your account is in good order.*

A trader in meaningless words says to John M.:

*It is the practice of this Department to periodically review all accounts for the purpose of ascertaining their current status.*

From such a review it was discovered that you were notified on August 7 of an outstanding arrearage on your account of $19.60, whereas the account is, in fact, in good standing.

I would like to explain that the large volume of work with which this office is presently confronted and the fact that many of our experienced employees are at this time on vacation, render it difficult to completely avoid small errors of this nature, particularly those originating because of the similarity in names. This department would like to assure you, however, that every effort is being made to give our accounts the best possible service and to prevent the recurrence of such errors.

Any inconvenience which you may have been caused is sincerely regretted.

As a matter of practical psychology, the writer who admits mistakes in plain words is surer of convincing others of his sincerity. Compare the next letter with the one above. Which writer would make you feel more kindly toward him?

We made a mistake in notifying you on July 7 that your account is overdue $19.60. The notice must have been confusing to you because you have always been prompt with your payments. The fact is, your account is in balance, and we hope you will be using your credit with us again.

Please accept our apology with the assurance that we will be more careful in the future.

As a general rule, don't try to explain how clerical errors occur. Half the time it's guesswork. Especially avoid laying the blame on the other fellow, as "We have a new clerk in our office," and excusing yourself because you are busy, as "Due to the pressure of business." The reader could get the idea that you are unwilling to assume the responsibilities of your job. And he isn't one whit interested in how busy you have been!

## PITCHING THE TONE

The suggestions made throughout this chapter—in some measure every suggestion this book has to make on plain letters—will help in the important matter of getting the right tone. But the whole story of what makes good tone cannot be told here or elsewhere. For each of us must create it in his own way.

If you analyze a letter that invokes a pleasing tone you may conclude that good tone is good manners—thinking first of the reader. But there is something more. You feel a sense of balance in reading such letters. They are friendly yet businesslike—neither harsh nor timid, neither brusque nor gushing, neither obsequious nor arrogant.

Not so with letters that leave you cold, displeased or disturbed. Here it is fairly easy to detect what's wrong. And what you detect is something you can avoid.

### OVERWHELMING ADJECTIVES AND ADVERBS

One trouble you may detect is the overwhelming adjective and adverb.

In Chapter 2 we discussed ways of minimizing adjectives and adverbs to shorten letters. There it was suggested that these parts of speech need disciplining also to avoid overintensifying your expressions.

Say to the caller at your desk, "The manager was *extremely* pleased to get your letter," and the caller himself is pleased. Put the same sentence in a letter, and *extremely* does something to the tone. The reader gets the idea that you are putting it on pretty thick.

Some people bubble with intensives when they talk. The intensives of their speech may stand for enthusiasm, a power in any business career. Strangely enough, the same intensives when undisciplined become unattractive on paper, no matter how attractively the writer uses them in his speech. Judge for yourself:

> It was with extreme pleasure that I received your letter dated April 21 in which you requested arrival dates of various cars in the month of January 1958. It is a great pleasure to give you this information.

Who would be convinced that the writer found *extreme* pleasure in a routine inquiry? Or that he was *greatly* pleased to supply what was probably a dull batch of statistics? Most of us would detect sincerity and better tone in fewer words and no intensives:

> I am pleased to give you the information requested by your letter of April 21.

Don't overdo it. You'll get a better tone by going a little slower on words like these:

| | | | |
|---|---|---|---|
| certainly | greatest | most | surely |
| deepest | highest | overly | undoubtedly |
| extremely | indeed | so | very much |

## SURPRISING EMPHATICS

Unexpected emphatics also have an overwhelming effect:

> In addition to cash to be invested we do see that you have your government bonds as well as life insurance.
> It indeed appears that the credits do exceed the charges on your account.

Especially watch that helping verb *do*. It shows up frequently in letters with an annoying emphasis.

Here is a routine letter from an airline official. I think everybody will agree it is of pleasing tone. It is both friendly and businesslike. One emphatic, *indeed*, is used effectively.

> *It was thoughtful of you to write me about your long-overdue refund. I appreciate your giving me the opportunity to straighten out the matter.*
>
> *Our accounting department set up your refund for credit rather than cash, which explains why you did not receive a check as you should have. We corrected this right away, and our check for $32.60 was mailed to you yesterday.*
>
> *I am sorry for the oversight and hope you will not consider it representative of our usual standards, for indeed it was not.*

## OVERPLAYING

Watch out that you don't overplay those "it is a pleasure to serve you" expressions (good business if you don't overdo it).

> *It is a real pleasure to be of service to you, and we do hope that you will write us whenever you have occasion to do so. We look forward to your continued patronage.*

"Eager-to-serve-you" letters sometimes show up in the style of a schoolgirl thank-you note: a short note that says thanks at the outset and a half-dozen lines later says "thank you again." The business version of this sort of thing is found in these two paragraphs from the same letter:

> *We trust that our reports will prove to be both of interest and of practical value to you. Should additional questions arise please feel free to contact Mr. Carson, who will be most happy to place the full facilities of our firm at your disposal . . .*
>
> *Again, we trust that our suggestions prove to be of practical*

value, and at the expense of being repetitious, we should like to again invite you to contact us for specific suggestions.

Overdoing is also found in the most gracious of words, *please*. By overworking this word, the writer seems to make a beggar of himself:

> Please sell our Ford Courier to the party bidding $900, less towing and storage charges. Please send the net proceeds to me, and please do your utmost to return the personal belongings to Mr. Simpson.

We'll charge that one to plain old carelessness.

SOUR NOTES

When carelessness produces a sour tone you can get into trouble by offending the reader. Here you'll detect some of those soured tones:

> As we have told you repeatedly . . .
>
> We are at a loss to understand why you . . .
>
> We gave you benefit of the doubt and requested full payment for only one fare. When we did not receive payment we went to the trouble of . . .
>
> It should have been clear from reading the application that you should have two persons witness your signature.
>
> We suggest that you acquaint yourself with all the facts in the case before writing us again.
>
> It is unfortunate that you are unable to understand my reports.

The off-pitch tones of these examples vary in intensity. Some of the disturbing tones would be heard by everybody. Some would offend one reader and pass another unnoticed. Don't take a chance. You can keep those sour notes out of your letters if you follow these two suggestions:

1. Avoid statements implying that the reader is wrong, misunderstands or has not made himself clear. For example, don't say "You are apparently under the misapprehension that you are entitled to a refund." Instead, simply explain why refund is not due, avoiding implied criticism or condescension.

2. Don't make highhanded statements. For example, don't say aloofly "This office has no jurisdiction over" whatever the reader is interested in. If you know where he can get help, tell him. If you don't, simply say you are sorry you can't be of help.

FORTHRIGHT YET FRIENDLY

Sincerity and good tone are not incompatible in letters offering criticism or saying No. When faced with the task of criticizing a young American's scientific essay, Englist biologist Thomas Huxley wrote this gentle but disarmingly frank letter:

> I should have been glad if you had taken the ordinary, and I think convenient, course of writing for my permission before you sent the essay which has just reached me, and which I return by this post. I should have then had the opportunity of telling you that I do not undertake to read or take charge of such matters, and we should have both been spared some trouble.
>
> I the more regret this, since being unwilling to return your work without examination, I have looked at it, and feel bound to give you the following piece of advice which I fear may be distasteful as good counsel generally is.
>
> Lock up your essay. For two years—if possible, three—read no popular expositions of science. Devote yourself to a course of sound practical instruction in elementary physics, chemistry and biology. Then reread your essay; do with it as you think best;

and *if possible regard [it] a little more kindly than you are likely to do at present.*

The same year Huxley wrote that letter, Theodore Roosevelt, then U.S. Civil Service Commissioner, wrote the following letter about a young man seeking reinstatement in a government job. In a style altogether different from Huxley's, Teddy was nonetheless forthright and friendly in his manner of saying No.

*I am sorry that there is no method by which I could be of assistance to you. The initiative in making reinstatements always rests with the appointing officer. The Commission merely passes upon requests when made. In this case there seems to be no question that the young man was removed for saying what was not true in his application paper. He had very poor advice, indeed, and he ought not to have acted upon it; nor can I understand the reason he did.*

## LINCOLN'S 4-S LETTERS

Many people think that the tone of Abraham Lincoln's plain letters has never been surpassed. Here he explains the reasons for the Civil War in a letter that has all of the 4-S virtues—shortness, simplicity, strength, and sincerity.

*Executive Mansion, Washington*
*August 22, 1862*

To Hon. Horace Greeley

*. . . I would save the Union. I would save it the shortest way under the Constitution. The sooner the national authority can be restored, the nearer the Union will be "the Union as it was." If there be those who would not save the Union unless they could at the same time save slavery I do not agree with them. If there be those who would not save the Union unless they*

could at the same time destroy slavery, I do not agree with them. My paramount object in this struggle is to save the Union, and is not either to save or to destroy slavery. If I could save the Union without freeing any slave, I would do it; and if I could save the Union by freeing all the slaves, I would do it; and if I could save it by freeing some and leaving others alone, I would also do that. What I do about slavery and the colored race, I do because I believe it helps to save the Union; and what I forbear, I forbear because I do not believe it would help save the Union. I shall do less whenever I shall believe that what I am doing hurts the cause, and I shall do more whenever I shall believe doing more will help the cause. I shall try to correct errors when shown to be errors, and I shall adopt new views so fast as they shall appear to be true views.

I have here stated my purpose according to my view of official duty; and I intend no modification of my oft-expressed personal wish that all men everywhere could be free.

Yours,

A. LINCOLN

## SUMMARY

If you want the real you to show through your letters, convincing your reader of your sincerity, be natural. Here are six ways to get the best side of yourself on paper:

1. Speak the language of today. Don't use dead language, like latinisms (re, per, optimum) and the old-fashioned mannerisms (contents duly noted, kindly advise, enclosed please find).

2. Be human. Use words that stand for human beings like the names of persons and the personal pronouns you, he, she, we, they and so on.

3. Admit mistakes. Don't hide them behind meaningless words. Especially avoid laying the blame on the other fellow or excusing yourself because you are busy.

4. Ask some direct questions, followed by question marks.

5. Use some contractions (*I'll* instead of *I shall*, *wouldn't* instead of *would not*, *let's* instead of *let us*, and so on).

6. Don't overwhelm your reader with too many intensives and emphatics, like *extremely, undoubtedly, highly,* and *indeed.*

7. Express yourself in a businesslike but friendly manner, dignified but not arrogant, forthright but not blunt.

CHAPTER 6

# Planning
# and Dictating
# the Letter

> Much of the redundancy and excess verbiage in let-
> ters would, in my opinion, be eliminated if all
> dictation were forcibly abandoned for a month or
> two. . . . In the usual business practice, a dictator
> faces a machine or a stenographer without even hav-
> ing closely read the letter he is answering.
>
> —WILLIAM FEATHER

PLANNING, it has been said, is the only cure for rambling letters, and the few extra minutes it takes are well invested even on the busiest day.

William Feather was hardly exaggerating when he suggested that free dictation is the root of letter-writing troubles. Supposedly, letters are dictated as final compositions to be signed and mailed after the first typing, but an appalling number of them have to be revised and retyped. One company discovered that six out of every ten of its dictated letters had to be done over. A survey by a government department revealed that 44 per cent of the letters prepared for the administrator had to be rewritten after reaching his office, and this survey doesn't tell us how many of these letters were revised and retyped before they were sent to the administrator.

Anyone who writes letters can easily recognize the hazards and wastefulness of free dictation. Even so, much costly and time-consuming rewriting can be avoided. All it takes is a little planning.

## YOU DON'T NEED A PRESCRIPTION

The idea prevails in some quarters that a business letter calls for a formal plan built around a statement of the subject, the body (or exposition), and the "tag" or signing-off sentence. This idea encourages the deadly prescribed manner of beginning with "This is in reply to your letter" or "This is to inform you," and ending with such hackneyed tags as "It has been a pleasure to be of service" and "Thanking you again."

You don't need a prescription for arranging your ideas. You can plan each letter individually with the parts so meshed that the reader is unconscious of the three elements of winding up, having your say, and signing off. One of the most gracious of gracious letters, from William James to his students, is such a unit:

*Cambridge, Apr. 6, 1896*

*DEAR YOUNG LADIES,—I am deeply touched by your remembrance. It is the first time anyone has ever treated me so kindly, so you may well believe that the impression on the heart of the lonely sufferer will be even more durable than the impression on your minds of all the teachings of Philosophy 2A. I now perceive an immense omission in my psychology—the deepest principle of Human Nature is the craving to be appreciated, and I left it out altogether from the book, because I had never had it gratified till now. I fear you let loose a demon in me, and that all my actions will now be for the sake of such rewards. However, I will try to be faithful to this one unique and beautiful azalea tree, the pride of my life and the delight of my existence. Winter and summer will I tend and water it—even* with my tears. Mrs. James shall never go near it or touch it. If it dies, I will die too; and if I die, it shall be planted on my grave.

Don't take all this too jocosely, but believe in the extreme pleasure you have caused me, and in the affectionate feelings with which I am and shall always be faithfully your friend.

WM. JAMES

The unity of this letter is apparent from the first to the last sentence. James might have achieved unity by gluing his little exposition between an *I wish to thank you for* and *Thanking you again.* But he didn't follow the prescription, and therein lies the difference between a solid composition and one that is glued together.

Another example of the unit with component parts unobtrusive is this modern letter from The Mutual Benefit Life Insurance Company to the wife of a new salesman:

When your husband came to the Mutual Benefit Life he brought you into the Company also. We are glad to welcome you. We hope you will enjoy all the associations that will come to you through his new work.

The Home Office counts on you as an important person in his success. Very frequently we have observed among Mutual Benefit underwriters that understanding sympathy and support at home have made the difference in the progress of new men. You may be sure that we all are much interested in your husband and in you, too, who will share his adjustments to life insurance sales work. Best wishes to both of you.

You like that friendly letter, don't you? Then cut loose from those old prescriptions. Make your own plan for each letter, keeping three things in mind:

1. How much the reader knows
2. What ideas you need to put across
3. Where each idea should fall in place for logic and for best effect on the reader.

## GETTING OFF TO A GOOD START

Think of what you would say if the reader were sitting on the other side of your desk. Do this and you'll never begin another letter with *reference is made, receipt is acknowledged,* etc.

If you have something to thank your reader for, you should decide whether the thank-you will be more effective at the beginning or the end of the letter. "Thank you for your letter" is a good approach—but watch out! This, too, can lead you off on a rehash of the question. "Thank you for your letter of March 15" is usually enough, without saying what the letter was about.

And don't feel that you must give thanks for *every* letter. Wearied to distraction by *reference is made* and *this is in reply to,* the president of one company issued a circular memo suggesting *thank you for your letter* as a better beginning. He was right; but the staff took the suggestion as a command performance and began offering thanks for every letter, even abusive ones.

If you consider it a polite convention to make mention of the incoming letter, do so casually, as "The catalog requested in your April 15 letter was mailed yesterday" or "After getting your letter of April 15, I . . ." Sometimes you can make the incoming letter the subject of your opening sentence, as "Your letter of April 15 touches on a subject of considerable interest to this company."

The following natural and to-the-point examples will suggest a number of ways to raise the curtain on a 4-S letter. Culled from old and modern letters, these good examples should be compared to the stuffy and wordy manner in which less skilled writers might have begun the same letters.

### Natural and to the Point

After getting your letter of April 9 we corrected our records to show your first name as James instead of John.

Here, with my thanks and best wishes, are a countersigned copy of the contract and a check for the first installment of the advance.

Your letter was a friendly act of the most genuine and helpful kind. I shall remember it as an expression of your interest.

It isn't often that I have you on my conscience but you have been there of late a great deal. I was meaning this day—even before your letter came—to get you into another and better place.

You mustn't think because I do not call or write that I am any the less sensible of the many favors you do me.

### Stuffy and Wordy

In accordance with the authority contained in your letter of April 9, 1954, the records of this office have been amended to show your name as James H. Grayson rather than John H. Grayson.

Enclosed herewith you will find a copy of the contract which has been countersigned by this company, together with a check in the amount $1500 in payment of the first installment of the advance.

I would like to express my appreciation of your recent suggestions which I am sure you made with the intentions of being helpful.

I have just received your letter of June 23, and I wish to take this opportunity to apologize for the delay in answering your previous correspondence because of out-of-town business engagements. However, I had intended to write you today.

Please accept my thanks for . . . . I have intended to write you, but the pressure of business has been such of late that I haven't had a minute to catch up on my correspondence.

| Natural and to the Point | Stuffy and Wordy |
|---|---|
| Appearances are against me. Don't believe them. I have written you in intention a dozen letters. | I am reminded of the fact that I was supposed to get in touch with you regarding . . . I should like to explain that . . . |
| The Bible record of your birth may be all you need to prove your age. | This is in reply to your letter of May 2, 1954, expressing concern over the fact that you do not have a birth certificate, and asking if a Bible record of your birth is acceptable proof of age. |
| Senator . . . sent me your letter of June 3, with the thought that we may have a job opening for a proofreader. | Reference is made to your letter of June 3 to the Honorable . . . , which has been referred to this office for attention and reply in connection with your interest in a position as a proofreader. |
| As much as I dislike doing so, I must decline your invitation to speak at the . . . luncheon on March 14. | I have received your letter of February 7 in which you do me the honor of requesting that I address the luncheon meeting of . . . on March 14. It is with the deepest regret that I must decline your invitation. |
| You are absolutely right about G. M.—and yet, I think you are wrong too! He is, as you say, far and away the most valuable man for . . . But the operations for which we are considering him . . . | In response to your suggestion about G. M., I would like to say that I do not think it is a good idea to keep him here when his talents can be put to better use in the field. |

### Natural and to the Point

I know you are human enough to like appreciation, so I am sending you this word—no more than I feel! Your address this morning was a bit of real literature.

Your interest in employment with this company is a compliment for which I thank you.

Thank you for the fine account you have just opened at this Bank. We shall always try to merit your business through the years to come.

### Stuffy and Wordy

I want to take this opportunity of telling you that I heard your address before . . . this morning. Please accept my congratulations. In my opinion your fine speech was in the category of real literature.

We have received your letter of June 8' in which you inquire about the possibilities of employment with this company.

It has come to my attention that you have just opened an account with this Bank, and I want you to know that it is a pleasure to be of service to you.

## REPLY LETTERS

### STRAIGHTAWAY ANSWERS

You have seen how straightaway answers can fortify us against indulgence in tedious detail. Even if we have details of interest to offer the reader, it is advisable to hold them until his questions are answered.

Suppose you were to ask a fellow worker, "What time is it?" Suppose he begins to tell you what make his watch is, how many jewels it has, and why it keeps accurate time. Finally having exhausted the subject, he says, "It is now three o'clock."

To yourself you might say, "Whew! That fellow is long-winded!" On the other hand if he tells you the time and then tells you about his watch, you may find him not such a bore. He may say just as much in each instance, but in the second instance he does not keep you waiting for the answer to your question. He does not tax your patience.

A letter developed on the following pattern taxes the reader's patience just as much as the office bore taxes yours:

> We are replying to your letter of August 17 in which you ask about surrendering the above-numbered policy.
>
> We should like to explain [then follows an explanation of the loan value, how much it is, how to go about getting a loan, and how it is repaid].

Finally the letter ends:

> The cash surrender value of this policy is $970. The appropriate form is enclosed for your use in the event you decide to surrender this insurance.

Those facts about a loan were given in the interest of the reader as well as the company. A better-planned letter might give the same facts, but it would not give them until the reader's immediate question had been answered. That is how Mildred Stone, author of *Better Life Insurance Letters*, tackles the subject:

> You may use the enclosed white form to request the Company to pay the cash value of your policy (number). That value is now $——, including dividend credits. Your policy should be forwarded when you send us the signed request.
>
> Perhaps you are considering surrender because you need cash. Then may we suggest the possibility of a loan. You may borrow now, on the security of your policy, $——. To borrow simply complete the enclosed form and send it to us. You need not send your policy.
>
> If you give up your policy the protection for your beneficiary (name of beneficiary) is lost. If you borrow (he or she) is still

protected for the amount of the policy, $——, less the loan. You may repay the loan at any time, in full or by installments.

Naturally you are in a better position than we to consider all the circumstances. We will serve you promptly if you decide to surrender. On the other hand we want to help you keep your valuable life insurance property if that is best for you. As soon as you send us one of the signed forms (and policy if you are giving up the insurance) we will take the next step.

Even in the letter saying "No," there is usually more merit in directness (not bluntness) than in beating around the bush. Here, again, Miss Stone proves the point:

Your request to reinstate your policy (number) could not be approved by the Company. We are sorry that it was not possible to restore the full benefits of your permanent insurance. However, we are glad to remind you that your temporary extended insurance under the policy protects you for $——. This will continue until (date).

The enclosed check is a refund of the amount you paid with your application for reinstatement. We shall appreciate your cooperation in cashing the check within a month.

If ever we can be helpful to you in connection with this policy or your life insurance program, please feel free to call upon us.

KEY SENTENCES

When you must introduce a matter the reader is not expecting, work out (before dictating) the key sentence that will tie this matter to your reply. If you don't you may find yourself leaning on that old crutch "We should like to explain."

"Perhaps you are considering a surrender because you need cash," is the key sentence with which Miss Stone introduced the subject

of a loan in reply to an inquiry about cash surrender. The word
surrender echoed the principal subject as she introduced a fresh one.

## GOOD NEWS FIRST

If the reader has several questions, don't feel that you must
answer them in the order asked. It is preferable to start on a pleasant
note. So if you must say No in answer to one question and Yes
in answer to another, or agree on one point and disagree on another,
take advantage of the opportunity to give the good news first. See how
a branch manager did it in a letter to one of his salesmen who had
some ideas on how to run the branch and the company:

> You are right about following up on those old sales prospects,
> Jim. There must be several hundred good ones buried in our
> files. I'm asking our file clerk to get busy and dig them up.
> Thanks for reminding me.
>
> There's also a lot to be said in favor of your suggestion on
> cutting down the length of field reports. I know you fellows
> are hard pressed for the time it takes to fill out those detailed
> forms. The problem gets thrown around at nearly every sales
> meeting in New York, but for some reason it has never been
> resolved. You can count on me to try again at the next meeting,
> which comes up in June. What you have to say on the subject
> gives me some good ammunition.
>
> When it comes to higher commissions for what you call
> "above par" sales, I have to remind you that this branch or any
> other branch ahead of quota actually gets more in commissions
> than the branches that are falling behind. So I wouldn't feel
> justified in asking New York to consider your "above par" idea.
>
> Reports from your territory are good. Keep it up . . . and by
> all means let me have any other suggestions that will help us do
> a better job in this branch.

## DIPLOMACY ON PAPER

Reply letters include those written in response to complaints, suggestions and comments. Here you have the opportunity to show your skill in the art of diplomacy.

Your own right attitude toward a complaint is the secret of how well you handle it. Regardless of what you think about the injustice of a criticism, remember that the reader is equally convinced of its justice. Never attempt to answer these letters while your dander is up; or, if you simply must get it out of your system, put your reply aside for a day or two. I can almost guarantee you'll never mail it. Your purpose is to win the reader to your way of thinking or acting, and your best chance of success is a rational reply in quiet tones. Only the most perverse reader would find the next letter argumentative or unconvincing; yet the writer (editor of a small-town newspaper) does justice for himself:

> *Yes, we know there were some errors in last week's paper. We will further agree that there were errors in the issue of the week before, but before you bawl us out too unmercifully about it, we want to call your attention to these facts: In an ordinary newspaper column there are 10,000 letters, and there are seven possible wrong positions for each letter, making 70,000 chances to make errors and several million chances for transposition. There are 48 columns in this paper, so you can readily see the chances for mistakes. Did you know that in the sentence "to be or not to be," by transposition alone, 2,759,022 errors can be made? Now aren't you sorry you got mad about that little mistake last week?*

In planning your reply to a complaint or criticism—indeed, in planning any reply—think first of the reader and secondly of yourself. Begin by admitting an error if there is one. Attempt to explain only if you have a convincing explanation, and then be brief about it.

If there is no convincing explanation, simply express regret and assurance of your good intentions. Sure, the reader may be wrong. He misunderstands—or he is afflicted by plain old cussedness. Just the same, it's profitable business to be the soul of patience. If you find no point of agreement you can save face for the reader by letting him know that you understand his viewpoint.

Oftener than not those who offer suggestions or criticisms are expressing an interest in your business. They give you the customer's views that you may never get otherwise. Notes on the margin of the next letter show how the writer might have laid out his plan before dictating his reply:

| | |
|---|---|
| thanks and expression of understanding | *Thank you for telling us about your recent experience while traveling with us. I readily understand how you feel about charges for excess baggage. It is a problem with which we, too, are concerned, especially when it seems to our passengers that we are less liberal than our competitors.* |
| explanation of tariff requirements | *As "common carriers" we are obliged to operate according to tariff regulations. Once a tariff is established we are subject to penalties if we fail to charge the established rates. Tariffs state that hand luggage, carried in the cabin, must be considered in the total weight of the baggage and the total weight must be compared to the free baggage allowance. To clarify this point, I am enclosing information from our current timetable. You will note a paragraph defining baggage that must be weighed and that which may be carried by hand without inclusion in the total weight.* |
| key sentence | *Although the 40-pound free baggage allowance has existed for many years, some airlines became careless about the handling* |

violations

*of excess weight charges. A few of the lines avoided the assessment of the charges simply to obtain a competitive advantage over other*

establishment
of enforcement
office

*lines. As a result, an enforcement office was set up several years ago. Now a number of investigators are traveling constantly throughout the United States, watching to be certain that all airlines are observing the tariffs. We ourselves, notwithstanding an honest intent to abide by the tariff, have been found in violation at least twice in the past year. One*

example

*of these violations involved the failure of our agent at Midway Airport to charge for one pound of excess baggage. We were fined $500 as a result.*

summing up—
focusing
reader's
attention on
effect

*So you see, Mr. ——, that observance of the tariff is not a matter of the desires or whims of the individual airline. With the intense activities of the enforcement officers, it is only a matter of time before all carriers will be conscious of their obligations and travelers will find uniform practices everywhere. For our part we have always tried— and will continue to try—to operate in a busi-*

and on company
ethics

*nesslike manner. As a party to tariff agreement we feel a moral obligation to do everything in our power to behave like ethical businessmen.*

bidding for
good will

*We appreciate your patronage, and I hope we may be privileged to continue to receive it. It is your respect we want, and we will do everything in our power to deserve it.*

An answer to a letter expressing appreciation of a product or service requires no special planning. A few sentences of gracious

acknowledgment will do the job, as in this note from a hotel to one
of its guests:

> Nothing pleases us more here at Cambridge Towers than a
> note such as yours saying how much you enjoyed your vacation.
> Your presence added to the enjoyment of our other guests,
> and it was a pleasure for our staff to serve you. We hope you
> will come again.

## INITIATED LETTERS

Both in government and in business the volume of initiated
letters exceeds the volume of replies. A reply is motivated by an
incoming letter, phone call or telegram. An initiated letter has the
simple distinction of being motivated by the writer's requirements
rather than the reader's inquiry. It is the writer—not the reader—who
determines the subject of these letters. There is an advantage in
this. Many initiated letters can be planned as forms or patterns,
ready for use when needed. (See Chapter 10.)

We might broadly classify initiated letters as *asking, good will, informing, reporting,* and *instructing.*

### ASKING

An asking letter has a twofold duty: (1) to state what is wanted,
and (2) unless the reason is obvious, to tell why. "To be able to
ask a question clearly," said Ruskin, "is two thirds of the way to
getting answered." Clarity is certainly essential, but courtesy and
persuasion are also on top of the list.

Your decision in planning an *asking* letter is whether the big idea
(*what* is wanted) should be stated at the beginning, with an explanation (*why*) following, or whether the reverse order will be more
effective. In some asking letters, as a request for payment of a

past-due account, there is a psychological advantage in holding the big idea until the end. It is then the last impression on the reader's mind.

|   |   |
|---|---|
| suggestion of problem | *When a good customer like you lets payment on his account fall behind we try to determine what the trouble may be.* |
| why | *Just now while looking over your account I noticed that your June 23 invoice is still unpaid. But I also noticed that we've received several checks from you in payment of later purchases. So the thought occurs to me that you have simply overlooked the June 23 invoice, a copy of which is enclosed.* |
| big idea (what) | *If there is an error in this billing please let us know and we will correct it. Otherwise, I am sure you will wish to keep up your good payment record by promptly mailing us your check for $37.60.* |

There is an element of suspense in letters like these, designed to hold the reader's attention while building up to the big idea. Franklin D. Roosevelt's letter on rubber conservation is an artful example of suggestion and suspense, followed by the big idea.

|   |   |
|---|---|
| suggestion of what's coming | *Following the submission of the Baruch rubber report to me in September, I asked that mileage rationing be extended throughout the nation. Certain printing and transportation problems made it necessary to delay the program until December first.* |
|   | *With every day that passes our need for this rubber conservation grows more acute. It is the Army's need and the Navy's need. They must have rubber. We, as civilians, must conserve our tires.* |

why
(suspense)

*The Baruch Committee said: "We find the existing situation so dangerous that unless corrective measures are taken immediately this country will face both a military and civilian collapse. . . . In rubber we are a have-not nation.*

*Since then the situation has become more acute, not less. Since then our military requirements have become greater, not smaller. Since then many tons of precious rubber have been lost through driving not essential to the war effort. We must keep every pound we can on our wheels to maintain our wartime transportation system.*

what
(big idea)

*We must do everything in our power to see that the program starts December first because victory must not be delayed through failure to support our fighting forces.*

Again, the big idea—what you want—may be effective when set forth straightforwardly in the first sentence. Then, if the letter runs to several paragraphs, a reminder may come at the end:

what
(big idea)

*May we extend to you a cordial invitation to take advantage of our "No Co-Maker" personal loan plan? Under this plan personal loans are made solely on the basis of character and earning power, and on your signature alone.*

why

*These loans are made at the rate of $7 per $100 a year. This cost is 50 per cent less than the rate prescribed by State law for licensed small-loan companies.*

*Why pay more?*

reminder of
big idea

*We hope you will accept our invitation when you need this service, and that you will refer to us any of your friends and business associates whom you believe to be entitled to similar consideration.*

Should you begin your asking letters with *what* or with *why*? Do whichever seems more likely to capture and hold the reader's attention.


## GOOD WILL: LETTERS YOU DON'T HAVE TO WRITE

Some of the most important initiated letters are those you don't have to write. Commonly known as good-will letters, these are the ones that let customers, business associates, and employees know that you're on top of your business, alert to their interests and welfare. The airlines have set a good example of the value of good-will letters in building confidence in their industry. The following examples are exhibited by courtesy of United Air Lines whose customer-relations program has won the warmhearted approval of thousands of travelers.

To a patron: regrets for an unavoidable delay

> *We certainly did not anticipate that Flight —— would have to be delayed. Irregularities of this kind fortunately do not happen often on United, but I realize how inconveniencing they can be to our patrons. Please accept my apology.*
>
> *Our management is working to provide truly dependable service under all conditions. I feel confident that your future flights with us will be free of such aggravating circumstances.*
>
> *Your stewardess, Miss ——, has asked me to thank you for the courtesy you displayed. We hope to redeem ourselves by giving you the finest Mainliner service on future flights.*

To a business associate: congratulations

> *Today's Aviation Daily carries the story concerning your election to the presidency of the Airport Operators Council at the annual meeting last week. My sincere congratulations!*

*I expect the new assignment will involve a lot of additional work, but I don't know of anyone better able to handle it.*

*I'll be looking forward to seeing you soon. Until then, my very best.*

To an employee: a pat on the back

*It is apparent from the attached letter that Mr. ——— is most grateful for your courtesy and efficiency. We are, too!*

*Such service adds real meaning to our slogan "Extra Care," and means much to United in terms of good will and repeat patronage.*

*Thank you . . . and keep up the good work.*

In 1957 United originated 17,000 letters to passengers who had been involved in some trip irregularity and to whom the company felt an explanation or apology was due. Such letters frequently bring responses like this one:

*Your thoughtful letter is an example of how things should be done. Not only am I grateful because you give me, as an individual, a most satisfying reply and thereby make me feel good, but also I am indebted to you for an example to my own associates as to proper handling of a customer complaint or suggestion.*

Letters of good will should be brief, informal, and as personal as you can make them. There is no problem planning the composition of these letters. The problem with most of us is in getting ourselves to write them. We may think it is a good idea, but for some reason we keep putting it off until it is too late or we forget we ever had the idea.

There are occasions for good-will letters in everybody's business, not alone in the affairs of company presidents and vice-presidents, and public-relations staff writers. I know a salesman in a small town whose wife works with him as an ambassador of good will. She watches the local paper for announcements of business promotions, weddings, births and deaths. On any of these occasions the customer gets an appropriate note. This salesman has been financially successful, and he and his wife are among the most respected citizens in their community.

Never underestimate the reader's appreciation of your interest in him.

### INFORMING: THE "HAPPY ENDING"

> We applied $5,062.60 of the $5,167.02 check received today from the California Pacific Title Insurance Company as full payment of principal and interest on your loan—original amount $5,500. The balance of $104.42 has been deposited to your joint commercial account at our 21st and Broadway Branch.
>
> Enclosed are the note marked "Paid" and a duplicate deposit tag.
>
> It has been a pleasure for us to have had a small part in establishing you and your family in your new home.

This letter, exhibited in the Bank of America's handbook *Bank Notes on How to Write Better Letters*, exemplifies a businesslike and friendly manner of informing a customer about a routine business transaction. Many of our modern business letters fall in the "informing" category—notices of actions on claims and applications, announcements of various kinds, and everyday transactions in buying, selling and accounting. Most of these letters are "matter-of-facts," and dictators sometimes feel at loss on how to go about warming them up with a personal touch.

It isn't always easy. When it seems especially strained you might ask yourself whether what you are seeking is actually called for.

You will notice that the personal touch added by the last sentence in Bank of America's letter is effective because it is specific and natural. Anything dealing with the subject—something the reader might expect in conversation—makes a happy ending for these letters or any others. An expression of good wishes for a holiday season or a new business venture—any timely and appropriate amenity—will also serve.

Here are a few examples of "happy endings" I have found substituting for the overworked sentences like "It has been a pleasure to be of service to you" and "If we can be of further assistance, please do not hesitate to call on us."

*With our congratulations on having achieved this goal we extend our best wishes for many successful seasons.*

*It is a privilege to count you among our clients. We look forward to a long and pleasant business relationship.*

*Thank you for your nice order. You can always count on us to do our best to merit your business.*

*I hope we have handled this to your complete satisfaction, Mr. Osborne, and that you'll be calling on us again very soon.*

*When you are in this branch I would appreciate the opportunity to meet you personally. Just step over to my desk and say, "Hello!"*

*We count this as the beginning—and not the end—of our business relationship. The opportunity to serve you will always be welcomed.*

*Thanks and best wishes for a prosperous New Year.*

REPORTING

Terseness is characteristic of the writing of executives who often complain of the long-winded and stuffy style of others. Those formal narrative reports, often turned out as memorandums, are the target of their criticism. The fault that touches off this criticism comes not so much from lack of planning as from poor planning that follows academic prescriptions for report writing. The plan is there, meticulously laid out (according to the "book") as *purpose,* scope, *definition*, and so on. In trying to follow this prescription the writer labors to give words to a definition that isn't needed or to a purpose that speaks for itself. It is something of a paradox that businessmen should write so formally to their fellow workers, while hailing them as "Joe" or "Hank" or "Betty."

Walter Hines Page was a master hand at writing reports. The effectiveness of his reporting lies in its directness, vigor and color. You won't find a trace of formality or stuffiness in any of his report letters, not even those directed to the President of the United States. Although he used the format of the conventional letter, his technique would be just as effective for narrative reporting by memorandum.

6 *Grosvenor Square, London*
*October 24, 1913*

big idea

DEAR MR. PRESIDENT,—*In this wretched Mexican business, about which I have read columns and columns and columns of comment these two days and turned every conceivable proposition back and forth in my mind —in this whole wretched waste of comment, I have not seen even an allusion to any moral principle involved nor a word of concern about*

antithesis

*the Mexican people. It is all about who is the stronger, Huerta or some other bandit, and about the necessity of order for the sake of financial interests. Nobody recalls our action in giving up Cuba to the Cubans or our pledge to the people of the Philippine Islands. But there is reference to the influence of Standard Oil in the American policy. This illustrates the complete divorce of European politics from*

conclusion

*fundamental morals, and it shocks even a man who before knew of this divorce.*

*In my last talk with Sir Edward Grey I*

amplification
by incident

drove this home by emphasizing strongly the impossibility of your paying primary heed to any American business interest in Mexico— even the immorality of your doing so; there are many things that come before order. I used American business interests because I couldn't speak openly of British business interests and his Government. I am sure he saw the obvious inference. But not even from him came a word about the moral foundation of government or about the welfare of the Mexican people. These are not in the European governing vocabulary. . . .

color:
direct report-
ing by quotes

I ran across the Prime Minister at the royal wedding reception the other day.

"What do you infer from the latest news from Mexico?" he asked.

"Several things."

"Tell me the most important inference you draw."

"Well, the danger of prematurely making up one's mind about a Mexican adventurer."

"Ah!" and he moved on.

Very heartily yours,
WALTER H. PAGE

Page's letter suggests how you can make your reports more stimulating:

Hitting the big idea in the first sentence
Drawing a conclusion as soon as possible
Antithesis (the other side of the story)
Examples
Color by direct quotes
An end that "bangs"

Here are eight suggestions on planning those long reports:

1. Get the purpose (if there is need to state it) as well as the subject into the subject line or opening sentence.

2. Summarize recommendations and findings at the *beginning instead of the end.* If your reader is a busy executive he may learn all he needs to know without reading another line.

3. Use headings to break up the subject matter. Get some punch into those headings. For example, if you are writing about the handling of blueprints and you want to explain what the study covered, avoid a dull heading like "Scope." Try something like "From Drawing Board to Production Line."

4. Don't feel that you must include a standard part just because the "book" says so. Omit any standard part that serves no purpose.

5. Avoid sweeping generalities. Use specific examples or findings to make your points.

6. Keep related ideas together. If storage of blueprints is one of the major points, have your full say on this subject once you introduce it. Don't take up the matter of cabinet storage in one part of the report and then launch into a discussion of drafting techniques before disposing of the subject of shelf filing. Your subject headings will help you stay on the right track.

7. Keep marching straight ahead, moving from one idea to another in the order your reader will expect after reading the summary at the beginning of the report.

8. Don't get the idea that a report must be written in the third person to be objective. That doctrine has had more deadly effect on the style of report writing than anything that was ever dreamed up in the ivory tower. It is difficult to make a report convincing without a spokesman.

## INSTRUCTING

Anybody who has a part, however small, in directing office affairs or supervising others will have occasion to write an instruction. Larger companies usually issue their standard operating procedures as revisable manuals, but letters and memorandums are used for temporary or nonstandard instructions covering everything from an order to attend a sales meeting to directions on how to invest a million-dollar fund. The total effect of these letter-style instructions on company operations is enormous; and, as with reports, it is the longer and more detailed instruction that should be more carefully planned. In this planning you might call on any of Kipling's six honest serving men:

> I keep six honest serving men
> (They taught me all I know);
> Their names are What and Why and When
> And How and Where and Who.

If you want to be sure a job gets done right, let your reader know as much as he need be told about what it is, who is to do it, why, when, where, and how.

But this axiom is not to be followed to the point of being ridiculous. What sometimes shows up in the form of a definition nobody needs. The person getting an instruction on the preparation of a blueprint or a payroll or an invoice knows perfectly well what is meant by these terms.

This is a good way to tackle the plan for an instructional memo: Write down the six words—who, where, what, why, when, and how—and consider them one at the time, trying to put yourself in the place of the readers. Dismiss any serving man your readers won't be needing, and set the rest of them to work in the order most helpful. Three thoughts:

1. Leave small matters to the reader's judgment. He need not be told how to cross every t and dot every i.

2. Avoid labeling the parts as "What," "How," "Why," etc. These labels have been overworked, and are not likely to evoke any special interest. The *whats* and *hows* should speak for themselves. Get some originality into those headings.

3. Invite your reader's suggestions, giving him a proprietary interest in whatever is to be accomplished.

The instructional memo on the next page was contributed by Kay Pearson who, with Everett Alldredge of the General Services Administration in Washington, is waging the government's war against gobbledygook and for shorter, simpler letters. Miss Pearson's memo is a good example of informal instruction writing. It also contains, for supervisors, some helpful hints drawn from her experience in directing plain-letter courses for nearly 100,000 government writers.

*Office Memorandum*   •   UNITED STATES GOVERNMENT

TO      : Supervisors of Letterwriters      DATE: January 23, 1959
FROM    : Kay Pearson, General Services Administration
SUBJECT : Training letterwriters

Are you a top sergeant commanding your subordinates to write good letters? Or are you a teacher tactfully and patiently teaching your fellow workers to improve their letters?

Many times it is easier to rewrite a person's letter than to guide him in rewriting his own. If you take the easy way, you deprive that person of needed training. Besides, you will go on forever rewriting the letters of others.

Why not develop your writers and turn out better letters at less cost? To these ends you can:

1. Set clear standards for letterwriting
2. Help each writer to meet the standards
3. Let each writer know how he is doing

The standards you set must apply to quality of writing and to accuracy of content. For quality of writing, ask your workers to review "Plain Letters" and to apply the 4-S formula to every letter they write. For accuracy of content, keep your group up to date on changes in laws, policies, and procedures.

When a writer fails to meet a standard you have set, tell him exactly what his shortcoming is and suggest a remedy. Never scrawl a blunt "Please rewrite" across the face of a letter and send it back without a word of help. If you must revise a letter before talking it over with the writer, send him a copy of your revision and, if needed, an explanation of the changes.

Let each person know his rating as a letterwriter. From month to month check his progress with him. Compare his letters of today with those he wrote several weeks ago. Show him where he has improved and where he yet needs to improve. When a person prepares an unusually good letter, praise him warmly and post a copy of his letter in the center of the main bulletin board.

THOSE HANDY MEMOS

> *"The honor of the moment,"* the King went on, *"I shall never forget."*
>
> *"You will, though,"* the Queen said, *"if you don't make a memorandum of it."*—LEWIS CARROLL, Through the Looking Glass

Government and big business are taking the Queen's advice seriously nowadays. The memo has virtually replaced the conventional-style letter for internal company messages. It is used not only for messages within a building but also for those between company offices in different cities. So popular has the memo become that some of us are in the habit of using it to take up trivial matters with people in offices across the hall, even across the room. Prudent managers are concerned about this reliance on writing when a phone call would do the job as well and more economically. After waging a campaign against nonessential memos one company cut down its typing costs by roughly $20,000 a year.

Still, writing is essential in conducting an endless variety of internal affairs, and the memo is ideal for the purpose. Beginning with a brief statement of the subject, like

*Subject: Production report for week ended November 7, 1958*

you can let the reader know at once what to expect. If you are initiating the memo you can pitch right into your subject without further preliminaries. If you receive a memo that must be answered, the same straight-to-the-point technique can be applied.

*Subject: Production report for week ended November 7, 1958.*
      (See your memo 11/10/58)
We*re there 7 or 9 people absent? Line 7, column 2, shows 7, but the recap shows 9.*

Back comes the answer:

*Subject: Production report for week ended November 7, 1958.*
*(See your memo 11/15/58)*
*Sorry, my error! The correct number of absentees is 7.*

Don't think of the memo as a letterhead to be used just because it is prescribed by your company for internal communications. Think of it as a format suitable for terse style, and plan what you have to say accordingly. Sometimes you can reply on the bottom of an informal memo and send it back to the company man who wrote it, saving time, paper and filing space.

## "WRITING OUT LOUD"

Planning dictation may call for nothing more than a few minutes of "thinking it through." Again, you may want to jot down some notes; or, if you are writing on a new and tough subject, have your stenographer make a rough, double-spaced draft.

Dictating is "writing out loud." The descriptive phrase originated, so far as I know, in the Navy Department as the title of a pamphlet giving helpful hints on how to dictate.

When you pick up the mike or say to your secretary, "Take a letter, please," you enter into a partnership. From that moment until the letter is ready for mailing, your secretary shares your responsibility for it. You can make life pleasant for her and she can help you do a better job if you will:

1. Let her know you welcome her suggestions.

2. Encourage her to correct ineptitudes in grammar and sentence structure. You might even suggest that she watch out for some of the troublesome words and phrases rounded up in this book. When any of these words invade your dictation—as they will everybody's at times—let her feel free to delete them or make suitable replacements.

3. Give her all the information she needs to set up the letter as you want it. If she is your secretary she will need only special instructions for exceptions; but if she is a member of a stenographic department serving a number of dictators she may need complete instructions. Give these in the order in which she goes about setting up the letter.

   a. Begin by saying how many copies you need. Her first task is to assemble the carbon pack. If a special letterhead is to be used, say so. Delaying these instructions until the end of the dictation makes her job harder. The delay may mean retyping.

   b. Next, give any special instructions such as airmail, registered mail or special delivery.

   c. After dictating the letter, tell her who is to receive the copies.

4. Pace your speech—neither hurried nor slow. Don't mumble or speak in monotones. Be especially careful about those "uhs" with which most of us sprinkle our speech. These may turn out as "ands" in long compound sentences.

5. Spell out unusual words, especially proper names. For most punctuation you can rely on the guidance of your voice and her judgment, but unusual punctuation and paragraphing should be specified.

6. Be clear about corrections. If possible, make them as they come up. If you use a dictating machine the manufacturer will be pleased to give you some helpful pointers on the best way to record corrections on his equipment.

7. Be natural. Address a stenographer through a dictating machine just as you would if she were your secretary sitting opposite you.

## SUMMARY

Planned dictation is the only cure for rambling. You don't need a prescription for the manner of planning a letter. Be original, planning each letter individually and keeping three things in mind: (1)

how much the reader knows, (2) what ideas you need to put across, (3) where each idea should fall in place for logic and best effect.

This chapter contains eight suggestions on how to go about planning:

1. Give answers straightaway; then explain if necessary.

2. Start on a pleasant or a positive note. If you must say No in answer to one question and Yes in answer to another, or agree on one point and disagree on another, take advantage of the opportunity to break the good news first.

3. Don't attempt to reply to a complaint letter when your dander is up. Put the letter aside until you can think it over a little.

4. In making a request of the reader, consider the twofold duty of an asking letter: (a) to state *what* is wanted; and (b) unless the reason is obvious, to tell *why*. Begin with either, depending on the better way of capturing the reader's attention. Where persuasion is needed, it is sometimes more effective to suggest what is wanted at the outset; then tell why, concluding with a definite request.

5. Take good-will letters into your plans. Apologies to a customer for a product or service not up to par, congratulations, notes of condolence, a pat on the back for an employee—these are letters you don't have to write, but they are the ones that show you are on top of your business.

6. Forget everything you ever learned about laying out reports and office instructions under such dull headings as "definition," "purpose," "scope," etc. You can enliven reports by hitting the big idea in the first paragraph, antithesis, examples, color, and an end that bangs. For an office instruction, call on any of Kipling's serving men—What, Why, When, How, Where and Who—but don't press any of them into a service that is uncalled for.

7. Before dictating an internal memorandum, consider whether a phone call will do the job as well, quicker, and more economically.

8. Make your stenographer a full partner in the letter-writing job. Let her know you welcome her suggestions. Encourage her to correct ineptitudes in grammar and sentence structure.

Part Two

# THE PRACTICAL
# APPROACH TO
# GRAMMAR AND
# PUNCTUATION

CHAPTER 7

# Forty Points
# on English Usage

As COMMONLY understood, grammar suggests a body of arbitrary rules and conventions for handling words. The purist decides what is good or bad grammar—or, more properly, what is grammatical and what is ungrammatical—by applying these rules strictly. But, as business letter writers, we are not concerned with the niceties of the purist. Our concern is the extent to which we should be governed by conventions in order to keep within the bounds of what most educated people consider acceptable grammar.

There is both safety and danger in the rules of grammar. Ignore them altogether and we are in trouble. Follow them too closely and our letters may sound cold and unnatural.

Happily there is a middle course between the vulgate level of English usage (unsuitable for written communication) and formal English (suitable for literary, scientific, technical, and academic writing). This middle course, which most letter writers follow quite unconsciously, is neither pedantic nor substandard. It is the practical approach to the grammar of business letters.

As defined by Porter G. Perrin, this middle course, or *informal English*, is the "speaking and writing of educated people in their private and business affairs." Informal English is the level of usage suitable for business letters, advertising, news stories and features, magazine articles, books on subjects of general interest, and most fiction. The written informal English of this level allows certain freedoms from grammar-book rules that are not allowed in formal prose. Just the same, informal English is *good*, for the simple reason that it is natural, understandable, and acceptable to most educated people. Office workers are well equipped to handle informal English, and business letters are admirably suited to informal usage.

My suggestion is this: Don't be too concerned about strict grammar-book rules. Have confidence in your ability to handle informal English—and not just in your ability to handle it, but also in your ability to handle it without going too far toward vulgate usage.

A number of points on usage are offered here to help you decide how well you are handling informal English. These are points which have come up frequently in my letter-writing courses. If you are within bounds on these points, the chances are you have no problems with grammar.

AGREEMENT IN NUMBER. Everybody reading this book knows that a subject and its verb should agree in number. Yet there is always the temptation, especially in dictating, to make the verb agree with a nearby noun which is not its subject.

> *The several serious mistakes in billing which have occurred since the system has been operating in the Chicago Branch seems [seem] to offset the advantage of the new machine.*

The verb "seem" was so far removed from the subject "mistakes," the dictator missed the proper agreement. This kind of mishap is bound to occur sometimes, even with the most careful writers, but frequent offenses leave the impression of slovenliness. Unless you are careful you may get into the same trouble with pronouns, as this dictator did:

> *Each employee who has had two or more years service with the company is eligible to participate by contributing two per cent of their earnings [his earnings].*

Our worst troublemakers are verbs that precede compound subjects.

*Enclosed is the note marked "paid" and duplicate deposit tag.*
*There is one typist in my office and three in the Denver office.*

You can see that *are* is required for proper agreement in both of the above sentences. Watch this.

See "as well as, together with"; "collective nouns"; "connectives in pairs"; "everyone, everybody, nobody"; "none."

AMONG, BETWEEN. The Merriam-Webster Dictionary is as explicit on the use of these prepositions as anything you'll find. If the proper usage is helpful in making meaning clear, it should be observed.

*Among* implies that more than two persons or things are involved; *between*, in a literal sense, applies to only two objects or persons.

*The company distributed the profits among the workers.*
[more than two workers]
*The supervisor divided the work between his helpers.* [two helpers only]

But *between* is applied to more than two objects to suggest individual relationships, as:

*I hope that between answering the phone, dictating letters, attending conferences and interviewing applicants, you will find time to lunch with me.* [between doing any two of these things]

"Between you and I" is often heard in conversation, but the correct form "between you and me" should be used in letters.

AS, THAN. *As* should not be followed by the objective in a sentence like this:

*He can handle the General Motors account as well as me.*

"As I can" is understood, so the second *as* (a conjunction) should be followed by the nominative *I*. Similarly, *than* is incorrectly used as a preposition in this sentence:

> *I admit that he is better qualified than me.*

Say *than I*, remembering that "than I am" is implied.

AS WELL AS, TOGETHER WITH. When these prepositions join a singular subject to a related noun, the verb is singular.

> *The check, as well as the bills, was* [not were] *left on the desk.*
> *The remittance advice (together) with a copy of the purchase order is filed* [not are filed] *in the purchase-order folder.*

*Together* is unwanted in the last sentence.

BETWEEN. See *Among, between.*

BOTH . . . AND. See *Connectives in pairs.*

CAN, MAY. *May* suggests permission or possibility; *can*, ability.

> *May I call on you at 10 A.M. next Wednesday?* [permission requested]
> *You may be on the right track.* [possibility]
> *She can type a letter faster than I can dictate it.* [ability]

When the meaning is clear with either *can* or *may*, as it usually is, there is no reason to be fussy about a distinction. Still, it is considered polite to use *may* with *I* and *we* when requesting permission:

> *May* [not can] *I show you our latest model?*

COLLECTIVE NOUNS. *Company, committee, majority,* and *number* are typical of collective nouns recurring in letters. A collective noun is treated as singular or plural, depending on the meaning. If you are writing of the group as a whole, consider the noun to be singular. If writing about individuals of the group, consider it plural.

The committee meets on Tuesday to elect its chairman. [group as a whole]

The committee were divided in their opinions. [individuals in the group]

The whole-or-several rule isn't much help when applied to nouns like *majority* and *number*. Theodore M. Bernstein, in *Watch Your Language*, suggests that it is preferable to treat *majority* as plural when it means *most of.* He also passes along this suggestion from Professor R. W. Pence of DePauw University: "Preceded by *the*, *number* is singular; preceded by *a*, *number* is plural." These suggestions work well here:

The majority of errors were due to carelessness.
The number of errors is small.
A number of errors were found in the transcript.

Singular treatment is preferred for the name of a company:

The Corinth Company is putting on a sales drive to move its winter merchandise.

CONNECTIVES IN PAIRS. Corresponding connectives are:
Both . . . and

| Misplaced: | Both in the opinion of Mr. James and Mr. Clark the merchandise is overpriced. |
| In place: | In the opinion of both Mr. James and Mr. Clark the merchandise is overpriced. |

Either . . . or

| Misplaced: | We can either make arrangements to meet you in Chicago or Cleveland. |

In place: *We can make arrangements to meet you in either Chicago or Cleveland.*

*Neither . . . nor*

Misplaced: *I neither have a price list nor a catalog.*
In place: *I have neither a price list nor a catalog.*

*Not only . . . but also*

Misplaced: *I found not only errors in his statements but also discovered that some items were omitted.*
In place: *I not only found errors in his statements but also discovered that some items were omitted.*

As illustrated by these examples the members of a pair of connectives are followed by the same part of speech—noun for noun, verb for verb, adjective for adjective, and so on. When one of a pair of connectives is followed by a singular noun and the other by a plural noun, let the verb agree with the nearer noun:

*Neither the supervisor nor members of his staff want [not wants] to work overtime.*

DIFFER, DIFFERENT FROM. To express the idea of disagreeing you may use either *with* or *from* with *differ*.

*I differ with you in my views.*
*This lot differs from the last in color.*

But in expressing the idea of being different the preferred idiom is *different from*, not *different than*.

*The styles this spring are different in every respect from [not than] those of last spring.*

DIRECT, DIRECTLY; SLOW, SLOWLY. If you want to be proper, use *direct* when you mean *straight*, and *directly* when you mean *immediately*, as:

> *Please reply direct [straight] to Mr. Jones.*
> *I will come to your office directly [immediately].*

Business writers seldom use *directly* in the sense of *immediately*, preferring the more natural expressions *at once* or *promptly*. *Directly*, however, is often used in the sense of *straight*.

Like *direct* and *directly*, *slow* and *slowly* both serve as adverbs. Distinction serves no purpose here, but *slow* seems less formal.

> *We are moving slow [or slowly] on the project.*

DANGLING PARTICIPLES. See *Replying to your letter.*

DATA. See *Latin plurals.*

DUE TO. Merriam-Webster on the subject: "Prepositional *due to*, meaning *because of* and introducing an adverbial modifier, though objected to by some, is in common and reputable use." *Due to* is frequently used as a preposition in business letters, as in this example:

> *Due to weather conditions at LaGuardia, American canceled its flight.*

If you object to the prepositional usage, substitute *because of* to modify a complete thought (*The flight was delayed because of bad weather*) and reserve *due to* to modify a noun (*The delay was due to bad weather*).

EACH, EVERY. For word economy as well as logic omit *each* and *every* in sentences like these:

> *It's a long time between each payday [between paydays].*
> *There is a healthy rivalry between every member of the staff [between members of the staff].*

You can't get "between" an *each* or an *every*. But illogical though it is, I think most readers would agree that *every* as used in the last example is a more natural means of gaining emphasis than the formally correct way of saying "between each member of the staff and the rest."

EITHER . . . OR. See *Connectives in pairs.*

EVERY. See *Each, every.*

EVERYONE, EVERYBODY, NOBODY. Like *each* and *every*, these pronouns are singular, calling for verbs and pronouns that agree in number.

> Everyone *is looking forward to his vacation.*
>
> Everybody *knows that the reorganization plan is to his interest.*
>
> Nobody *at the meeting would admit he was present when Mrs. Appleby refused to wait on the customer.*

Although the singular *he* used with pronouns like these traditionally suggests both sexes, some writers are unhappy in leaving the women out of the picture. If you feel that way or if you wish to emphasize that a number of persons are involved, it is better to express the idea in another way.

FARTHER, FURTHER. Of *farther* and *further* Perrin says, "In colloquial and informal English the distinction is not kept and there is a definite tendency for *further* to be used in all senses."

Here informal English gives you a choice. If you want to be strictly correct use *farther* to indicate distance, *further* to indicate quantity or degree: *Go farther away; hear nothing further.*

FEWER, LESS. In formal usage, *fewer* refers to number; *less* refers to degree, quantity or extent: *Write fewer pages and use less ink.* The distinction is not as apparent in the next example, and the choice may fall on either without offense to the average reader:

> We are getting along with six *less* [formal English *fewer*] typewriters.

FOCUS. See *Latin plurals.*

FOLLOWING. If you use *following* as a preposition in the sense of *after,* you have lots of company among informal writers. Only the purist is likely to condemn you for the usage. Still, *after* is sharper. So why not be correct?

> We expect business to be slow following [after] the year-end sales.

FORMER, LATTER. For ease of reading, avoid *former* and *latter.* Repeat words rather than ask your reader to look back for the right antecedent.

> Jim Conrad and Mike Jones disagreed violently throughout the conference.
> The former [Conrad] argued that . . . while the latter [Jones] insisted. . . .

FORMULA. See *Latin plurals.*

FURTHER. See *Farther, further.*

IDIOMATIC PREPOSITIONS. Because prepositions overlap in meaning, it is sometimes difficult to decide on the best ones to combine with other words. Here are a few combinations usually preferred:

accompanied by
accord with
acquiesce in
adhere to
adverse to
agree with a person
agree to a thing
agreeable to
compliance with
concur in an opinion
concur with a person

disappointed in
discrepancy in a thing
discrepancy between two things
dispense with
dissent from
identical with
incompatible with
parallel with
perpendicular to
retroactive to

IF . . . WERE. See *Subjunctive*.

ITS, IT'S. The possessive of *it* is written without an apostrophe, as:

*I have no idea of its value.*

*It's* is a contraction of *it is*:

*It's time to take stock.*

Although *it's me*, *it's him*, and *it's them* are common in speech, in unquoted writing this usage is generally considered a vulgate. Use the nominative:

*It's I who must make the sales quota.*
*It is he who insists on a higher quota, not I.*

KIND, SORT. *Kind of a* and *sort of a* are seen often in letters: *kind of a letdown*, *sort of a tool*. The grammarians say this is incorrect; that *kind* and *sort* are used in referring to a class of objects instead of an individual object, as:

*the kind of letter everybody likes to read*
*a sort of crutch until we can do better*

The question of correct or incorrect grammar doesn't seem important here, but *kind of a* and *sort of a* are such awkward phrasings we should try to avoid them.

Because *kind* and *sort* are both singular nouns the grammarians also frown on plural usage of these words, as *these kind of things* and *those sort of things*. But the plural is so common, it is unlikely to be held against you.

LATIN PLURALS. The commonly used Latin words *memorandum*, *formula* and *focus* may be written in the plural as *memorandums*, *formulas* and *focuses*. The Latin plurals *formulae* and *foci* are seldom seen, but *memoranda* is fairly common. The important thing is, be consistent.

*Data*, though plural, may be used with a singular verb. The singular form *datum* is seldom seen.

LATTER. See *Former, latter*.

LAY, LIE. These little verbs confuse many of us because the past tense of *lie* (meaning *recline*) is the same as the present tense of *lay* (meaning *to place*).

> He *lies* on the floor. [present tense]
> He *lay* on the floor. [past tense]

*Lay* in the sense of placing never takes the form *lie*. It is also distinguished by taking a direct object.

> *Lay* the papers on the desk. [present tense]
> He *laid* the papers on the desk. [past tense]

The past tense of *lie* (recline) never takes the form *laid*.

> *While* he *lay* [or was lying] there on the floor, the nurse called the ambulance. [Don't say he laid on the floor.]

LEND, LOAN. Both *lend* and *loan* are good as verbs.

> *Will* you loan [or lend] me $20?
> The bank loaned [or lent] him $20.

LIKE. The use of *like* to introduce a clause of comparison ("Winstons taste good—like a cigarette should.") is still opposed by some, though I suspect that nine out of ten readers never question the usage. According to the grammarians *like* is not a subordinating conjunction and for this reason should not introduce a clause of comparison.

*Why don't we use cycle billing as [not like] so many companies are doing nowadays?*

*It looks as if [not like] Jones will have the largest volume of sales for this fiscal year.*

Notice that the clause with its characteristic verb, *companies are doing* and *Jones will have,* warns you to avoid *like.* When used as an adverb followed by a complement in the objective case, *like* is correct:

*He spoke like a man with authority.*

There's another catch, though. When the predicate is omitted but understood, *like* is again ruled out as in this example from Merriam-Webster:

*He took to figures as [not like] a duck to water. [Duck takes to water is understood.]*

MAY. See *Can, may.*

MEMORANDA, MEMORANDUMS. See *Latin plurals.*

METAPHORS MIXED. Figures of speech play a small role in business letters. Even the favorite metaphors of government and business (*backlog, bottleneck, off the ground, blue chip*) are surprisingly infrequent. We might wish that better use could be made of figurative speech for liveliness and getting ideas across in few words.

But if you plan to cultivate the metaphor, take care you don't overdo it. Too many become tiresome. Besides, there is always danger of mixtures and incongruities. Critical readers delight in analyzing metaphors, deriding us for incongruities

*When I get off the ground with this records project I hope to drop by your office.*

*On May 1 our Credit Manager wrote Mr. Henry hoping to knit together any bad feelings that may have occurred.*

or mixtures

> *I will be glad to lend my small weak voice to your strong right arm to see if we can do something about this problem.*

The last example, from a letter by a member of Congress, shows how the politician, always fond of figurative speech, is sometimes trapped by it.

MODIFIERS MISPLACED. Modifiers cause trouble when they get out of place in the sentence, changing the meaning. In the next sentence *only* can take five positions with a definite change of meaning in four of these positions.

> Only *James Brown wanted to work on Saturdays in July.* [This means nobody but James.]
>
> *James Brown* only *wanted to work on Saturday in July.* [Here the meaning becomes fuzzy. This may be interpreted variously— *James* only *wanted (but didn't do anything about it)*, or *"James had no wish for anything but Saturday work in July."*]
>
> *James Brown wanted* only *to work on Saturdays in July.* [This means that James wanted nothing else.]
>
> *James Brown wanted to work* only *on Saturday in July.* [This means that James wanted Saturday work in July, but did not want to work on the other days of that month.]
>
> *James Brown wanted to work on Saturdays* only *in July.* [This means James had no wish for Saturday work in the other 11 months of the year.]

That's what happens when one little word gets out of control. Now you need not be precise about getting adverbs like *only* in the right place as long as the meaning is clear. If you say "he only carried a brief case" when you mean "he carried only a brief case," there is little likelihood that your meaning will be misunderstood. Even an obvious misplacement such as "your letter only came yesterday" will usually go unnoticed.

More trouble comes from group-word modifiers—phrases and clauses. These should fall in place to read easily and understandably as in the following sentences:

> In filling out your application, *you overlooked question number 12.*
> We sent the papers to the address *you gave us* in your letter of September 2, *but they were returned unclaimed.*

Short sentences will help solve problems of group-word modifiers. In addition:

1. Keep an unmistakable kinship between the modifier and the modified. If a prepositional phrase makes the kinship doubtful as here

> *Historians may be cheated of many valuable papers* by hiding them in file cabinets.

cut out the preposition

> *Historians may be cheated of many valuable papers* hidden in file cabinets.

If the trouble is the simple matter of the position of the modifier

> *In developing first our diagnosis and then our recommendations we certainly will include any ideas of people on the job that are good.*

attach the modifier to the proper part of the sentence

> *In developing first our diagnosis and then our recommendations we certainly will include any good ideas of people on the job.*

2. As a general rule don't separate a principal verb from its auxiliary by a cluster of words. Instead of

> The marginal accounts were during the week covered by this report 40 per cent past due.

shorten the distance

> The marginal accounts were 40 per cent past due during the week covered by this report.

3. As a general rule don't separate the key verb and its object by a cluster of words. Instead of

> Applications from handicapped persons in the nearby cities were also accepted.

close ranks

> Applications were also accepted from handicapped persons in the nearby cities.

MYSELF. Grammarians say this pronoun and others of its class (himself, herself, themselves) are used incorrectly in sentences like these:

> Frank and myself were working the 3 o'clock shift when the fire started [Frank and I were . . .].
> The boss selected Frank and myself to represent the company at the meeting [selected Frank and me . . .].

Myself and companion words are correctly used when their antecedents are expressed.

> I blame myself for what happened.
> He reported the accident himself.

If you get out of bounds on this one, don't let it trouble you. That great letter writer, Abe Lincoln, was not a strict grammarian. He frequently used *myself* when *me* would be according to the rule, as in his save-the-Union letter to Greeley, "I have just read yours of the 19th, addressed to myself through the New York Tribune," and his letter to Governor Joel Parker of New Jersey, "Yours of the fifteenth has been received, and considered by the Secretary of War and myself."

NEGATIVES DOUBLED. Two negative words in the same statement must be ruled out as crude.

| Not This | This |
|---|---|
| We haven't but two colors in style 873. | We have but [or *only*] two colors in style 873. |
| I couldn't hardly believe my eyes. | I could hardly believe my eyes. |

NOBODY. See *Everyone, everybody, nobody.*

NONE. Despite the suggestion of singleness, *none* may be plural or singular, as

> *Of all the men in this office none is more loyal or has more years of service than Hitchcock.*

or

> *Of all the men in this office none are more loyal or have more years of service than Hitchcock.*

but not

> *Of all the men in this office none is more loyal or have more years of service than Hitchcock.*

If *no one* is used instead of *none* the reader expects singular agreement.

*We studied several systems, no one of which is any better than ours.*

NOUN AND PRONOUN COMBINATIONS. When a pronoun is combined with a noun, as *we business writers*, the pronoun takes the same case form as the noun. In the next sentence *business writers* as the subject of *are helped* is nominative; hence the nominative *we* is used.

*We business writers are helped by this rule.*

In the next sentence *business writers* becomes the object of the verb, making *us* correct.

*This rule helps us business writers.*

Similarly, *us* follows the preposition:

*The rule has been helpful to us business writers.*

POSSESSIVES AND THE VERBAL NOUN. When verbs ending in *-ing* are used as nouns, modifying nouns and pronouns usually take the same form that would be used if the verb were a noun. You would not say "I look forward to him letter"; and so you may not wish to say "I look forward to him writing," although you will find enough examples of the objective pronoun in this usage to make a case for yourself. Other examples:

*I hope you will not be inconvenienced by Mr. Green [Mr. Green's] going out of town.*
*He doesn't approve of them [their] smoking in corridors.*

Perrin points out that a plural noun is more likely to take the common form than the possessive, and here the common form certainly seems more pleasing. Ninety-nine persons out of a hundred will like the sound of "He doesn't approve of women smoking in corridors" better than "He doesn't approve of women's smoking in corridors."

If you have trouble following this rule, don't get the notion your grammar is bad.

PREPOSITIONS AT THE END OF SENTENCES. A preposition that falls naturally at the end of a sentence need not be shunned, but an awkward or unwanted one should be. When the preposition has an adverbial value it is always defensible:

> While he was addressing the conference the lights went out.
> He read the report because he had to.

In context the next sentence as it is written was emphatic, and there was no reason to rearrange it to avoid the preposition at the end.

> A 10 per cent increase in sales is what we are working for.

In the next example the preposition should be left off because it is unwanted and crude.

> Before you leave Chicago please let me know where you will be going to.

PRIOR TO. The correctness or incorrectness of prior to as a preposition is unimportant, but I often wonder why we business writers are so fond of this stuffy phrase. Time and again I have noted sentences like this:

> Prior to the announcement of the sale we must make every effort to insure that our warehouses are prepared to meet the demands of the distributors.

Use before.

PROVIDING, PROVIDED THAT. Say "Providing low-rental housing

is a problem," but say "We agree to build a plant in Chicago provided that low-rental housing is made available." *Provided that* serves its best purpose as a stipulation. For a simple condition *if* is preferable to *provided:*

> *I will make a down payment of $3000 if [not provided] you agree to sell.*

REPLYING TO YOUR LETTER. This phrase, more than any other, gets us into the difficulty known as a dangling participle.

> *Replying to your letter of June 9, the order was shipped on June 8.*

Although there is no trouble understanding this sentence, it is illogical. How can an order reply to a letter? Here's a dangler that is even sillier:

> *Replying to your letter of August 10, Miss Green left our company and is now in South America.*

To set these sentences right you must say something like this:

> *Replying to your letter, I wish to say . . .*

That's needlessly formal. Avoid this participial construction and similar ones such as "referring to your last question" and "now turning to the matter of."

SET. See *Sit, set.*

SHALL, WILL. Both of these verbs are now used with *I* and *we* for simple future tense.

> *I shall [or will] write you again.*
> *We shall [or will] look forward to meeting you.*

SHOULD. See *Subjunctive*.

SIT, SET. Don't use *set* in the meaning of "she sat at the typewriter," and don't use *sat* in the meaning of "he set the typewriter on the desk." Remember that people and things *sit* (past *sat*), and in this sense the verb doesn't take the form *set*. *Set* (past *set*) in the meaning of *placing* never takes the form *sit* or *sat*. *Set* is also distinguished by taking a direct object.

> He stood while she sat.
> I sat [or was sitting] in the last row of the second balcony.
> Set the figures in columns three inches apart.

SLOW, SLOWLY. See *Direct, directly*.

SORT. See *Kind, sort*.

SPELLING. Incorrectly spelled words may leave the impression that similar sloppy habits exist in your manner of conducting business affairs. Mishaps will occur sometimes, but with a good dictionary at hand there is no excuse for repeated offenses. If you are not sure of the correct spelling, don't take a chance. Look up the word. Ask your stenographer to do the same.

SPLIT INFINITIVE. An adverb between *to* and the verb (*to finally arrive*) is a split infinitive, frowned upon by purists. Yet the sequence if often natural. When it is, "split" with confidence that your reader won't mind. The following orderly sentence would not be improved by changing the position of *fully:*

> It would take a whole book to fully explain this subject.

If the construction seems awkward, as I find it to be in the next sentence, you might avoid it; but I see no reason why a letter should be rewritten if you get trapped:

> He managed to convincingly speak for the minority.

This is plainly a case where you can rely more on your ear and less on the rule.

SUBJUNCTIVE. The commonest use of the subjunctive is in the statement of a condition that may not be fulfilled or does not exist.

*If I were you I'd go by plane to Los Angeles.*

Whether or not you are a stickler for the subjunctive depends on how you are "tuned in." *Were* in the sentence "if I were you" is considered a must by most writers, but *was* is not likely to offend a sensitive ear as used in this conditional sentence:

*This would be a better letter if it was a shorter one.*

Similarly, both *should* and *would* are used in informal English for the future conditional, although formal English would have us use *should*.

*We would [or should] be grateful for any suggestions you could give us.*

*We would [or should] be better off if we could shut down our plant for the next six months.*

Note the difference in connotation of the last sentence when *would* is used instead of *should*. To most readers *should* implies a doubt that is not suggested by *would*.

THAN. See *As.*

THAT, WHICH. *That* refers to both persons and things. *Which* refers to things only. There is another and finer distinction I recommend to you, not for the nicety of grammar but as an aid to more exact meaning. Use *that* to introduce a clause that limits your meaning —one you can't omit without changing the sense of the sentence. Use *which* to introduce a clause that simply explains—one you can leave out without materially changing the sense of the sentence:

*The truck that was wrecked is in the garage.*
*The truck, which was wrecked, is in the garage.*
*The wrecked truck is in the garage.*

The first sentence suggests that another truck is somehow involved. Thus, *that* serves to limit the meaning to one of two or more trucks. Out of context, the second and third sentences convey no substantial difference in meaning: *which was wrecked*, like *wrecked truck*, simply describes the condition of the truck without implying that other trucks are in any way involved.

Some modern writers are allergic to *which*, finding it a disturbing word of more ill effect than good. Others find it useful in emphasizing a secondary thought. "The truck, which was brand-new, was demolished" seems to give more emphasis to newness than does "the brand-new truck." Of course, if you want to avoid *which* there are always other ways of gaining emphasis, as: "The truck, a brand-new one, was demolished."

THERE IS. See *Agreement in number.*

VERBS USED AS NOUNS. See *Possessives and the verbal noun.*

WHO, WHOM. When Arthur Godfrey came out with that emphatic *whom* in questioning his talent scouts ("*Whom did you bring us?*") you may have felt that he was making a big show of correctness. Most speakers would say "Who did you bring us?" I find that most letter writers also use the nominative in sentences like Godfrey's while using the objective in sentences like this:

> I employed Bernice Carroll, whom the Personnel Director decided was the best qualified for the job.

What happens is that nine out of ten persons go by what sounds right to them, not by what the grammar book says. If you are one of those who plays this one by ear I don't think it will help to remind you of the rule. With the sentences on paper you can see that *whom*, as the object of *bring*, is correct as Godfrey uses it, and that *who*, as the subject of *was the best qualified*, is correct in the sentence about Bernice. Say "This is Bernice Carroll, whom the Personnel Director selected for the job," and *whom* is correctly the object of *selected.*

This is another case of "don't bother to rewrite the letter" if you slip up. But it's worth a little more care while you are dictating.

WILL. See *Shall, will.*

WOULD. See *Subjunctive.*

## SUMMARY

If you are concerned about strict grammar-book rules, don't be. Unwarranted fear of grammar and the striving for formal usages account for much of the coldness and unnaturalness of letters. Informal English is admirably suited to letters, and office workers are qualified to handle it. Your grammar may not always please the purist, but it is good as long as it is understandable, natural, and acceptable to most educated people.

The forty points on English usage here discussed will help you decide whether your informal English is up to the standards most of us in business try to maintain. If you are "within bounds" on these usages, chances are you're safe.

# Where Does the Comma Go?

COMMAS and periods are the only punctuation marks used in nine letters out of ten. (Of course I must make an exception for the colon following a salutation.) Convention gives us little choice in the use of periods, but when it comes to commas we often have a choice. If a writer is heavy-handed with his commas, his punctuation style is known as "close." He might use nine commas in this short and simple memo:

> Your report for May, 1958, with comments on the proposed Newark Warehouse, has come to my attention. I see your point of view, and am glad that you have given this matter some thought. How do you, and how does McGill, think we should go about reappraising our plan? Of course, you are right in saying that we have pretty sketchy information about other suitable locations. When you are in Syracuse next week, I'll ask McGill to get together whatever information we have. Then, the three of us can talk it over, coming to some decision as to what should be done.

When commas are used only for sense and ease of reading, the punctuation style is known as "open." Following this style the same memo might be written with only one comma.

Your report for May 1958 with comments on the proposed Newark Warehouse has come to my attention. I see your point of view and am glad that you have given this matter some thought. How do you and how does McGill think we should go about reappraising the plan? Of course you are right in saying that we have pretty sketchy information about other suitable locations. When you are in Syracuse next week I'll ask McGill to get together whatever information we have. Then the three of us can talk it over, coming to some decision as to what we should do.

Short sentences remedy comma troubles in that they create fewer slight pauses (commas) and more full stops (periods). Remedy, I say—not cure. Those who are fond of commas, like the writer of the first example, can find legitimate but nonessential use for them in short sentences as well as long ones. We must also remember that a series of short sentences with their full stops may be less restful than a longer sentence with a few slight pauses.

Styles in punctuation are as varied as the men who set them. Contract with a publisher for a book and he stipulates the right to change punctuation to conform to the style of his house. Similarly my views on punctuation may conflict with yours, and both of us may have supporters for our cause. My principal purpose is to remind you that excessive commas deface the page like so many spilled-over periods and keep attracting the reader's attention when he could move on. Think of your reader's requirements. Don't lavish commas on him, but give him those that he needs for guidance and "breath." Your common sense will help you more than my suggestions, but here are a few points for what they are worth.

## UNWANTED COMMAS

The commas in parentheses in the following sentences are not needed, although most of them are defensible.

1. Apparently(,) he wants to do business with us.

2. Thus(,) the time has come when we can no longer afford to overlook the competitive factor.

3. After the meeting(,) Vincent called to say that he is on our side, a lucky break for us.

4. In a literal sense(,) the public domain is gone.

5. He(,) therefore(,) returned the merchandise with the request that the charges be removed.

6. His viewpoint is(,) obviously(,) that the prime contractor(,) rather than his company(,) is responsible to us, and(,) you must admit(,) that he may be technically correct.

7. The only thing to do(,) under the circumstances in the case(,) is to give him credit for the books.

8. Our experience in writing sales letters was so limited(,) that we decided to employ a consultant.

9. I have your letter telling me your sad experience with Washington red tape(,) and how you finally extricated yourself.

10. When the machine is installed(,) and is actually producing, three employees can be transferred to the Order Department.

11. Employees who are likely to object(,) should not be questioned.

12. We are showing a handsome(,) green coat in Forstmann wool.

13. We read both of your reports carefully(,) and we agree with you on the points made in each of them.

14. When you are in Syracuse next week(,) I'll ask McGill to get together whatever information we have.

15. Since May(,) 1958(,) Lockman has been guiding the affairs of this office.

16. *Address:* Mr. J. S. Smithson(,)
            1620 River Road(,)
            Brandywine, Maryland
   *Close:* Sincerely yours,
            A. J. Donaldson(,)
            Chief, Order Department(,)
            The Carson Company

Sentences 1 through 4 are smooth and clear without commas after the introductory word or phrase. Although there is nothing wrong with these commas, they are not required for ease of reading.

The commas setting off *therefore* and *obviously* in sentences 5 and 6 provide an unwanted emphasis, as do those setting off the phrase in sentence 7. Those setting off *rather than this company* and *you must admit* in sentence 6 are needless interruptions. Sentence 8's comma is indefensible. The words following this comma are so closely knitted to the sentence that a comma is like a knot in the thread of thought.

The comma separating the two objective clauses in sentence 9 is unexpected, as is the one separating the two verbs in sentence 10's dependent clause.

The subject of sentence 11 is *employees who are likely to object*, not *employees* alone. The writer recognized this is preferring to omit the comma after *employees*. There was then no reason to interrupt the reader with a comma after *object*.

In sentence 12 it is the green coat that is handsome, not just a coat; so *handsome* and *green* are not adjectives of equal rank calling for separation by comma.

The co-ordinate clauses in sentence 13 are so closely related that a writer favoring open punctuation would omit the comma. He would also omit the comma following a short dependent clause at the beginning of a sentence, as in example 14.

Commas setting off the year (sentence 15) are optional, but are not favored by modern stylists. Had the day of the month been included (May 7, 1958) these commas would be purposeful.

Open punctuation (example 16) is the modern style for addresses and closes.


## A DOZEN PRACTICAL USES OF THE COMMA

A comma is useful:
1. To prevent momentary confusion.

> *To begin with, the objections he raises were never made known to me.*
> *When I awoke, my watch said 4* A.M.
> *Besides, a draftsman can handle the job as well as an engineer.*

Compare these examples with the first four examples under "Unwanted Commas." You see the difference, of course. Here we have opening phrases that can't be fused into the sentence without momentarily confusing the reader.

2. To separate a series of equal-ranking words, phrases and clauses.

> *Officers, supervisors(,) and clerks are expected to volunteer.*
> *We found useless records in offices, in Central Files(,) and in warehouses.*
> *Lane said that the men on the Alaskan Railroad project were well fed, that their hospitals were good(,) and that they were satisfied with their compensation plan.*
> *You need a short, simple, strong sentence.*

Note that the last comma (preceding the *and*) in the first three sentences may be omitted, but many typists feel that these commas lend balance. The last example illustrates how adjectives of equal rank are set off by commas. Compare this example with example 12 in "Unwanted Commas."

3. To clarify.

*Officers, supervisors, and clerks, living in the city, are expected to volunteer.*

Here the commas setting off *living in the city* serve to show that this modifier applies to all three groups: officers, supervisors and clerks. Change the punctuation in the following manner and *living in the city* applies only to clerks:

*Officers, supervisors, and clerks living in the city, are expected to volunteer.*

4. To set off nonrestrictive modifiers.

*Pettingill, who has no interest in the job, is likely to be appointed.*
*Hardy, a seasoned merchandiser, is Lockman's choice for the job.*
*Our credit losses for the past year were less than one tenth of one per cent, the best record we ever had.*

Compare the first of these sentences with sentence 11 in "Unwanted Commas." Note that the commas are omitted in sentence 11 because the restrictive clause is an essential part of the subject, as it is in this sentence:

*The man who is least concerned about the job is the most likely to get it.*

5. To provide a "breath."
*Following a long or losely connected dependent clause:*

*Considering the fact that this account has been past-due for more than three months without a word from you about your intentions to pay it, you must agree that we have been very patient.*

*Whatever he thinks about the matter, I am resolved to transfer my membership to a club where my clients will feel more at home.*

Compare with example 14 in "Unwanted Commas."
Between long or loosely connected co-ordinate clauses:

*A time study shows that for cash disbursements it takes 35 minutes to get everybody's signature, and who wants to stand in line that long?*

Compare with example 13 in "Unwanted Commas."
Before a dependent clause, especially if it is loosely related to the main clause:

*The men on the job must be getting along all right, because I have heard nothing from them.*

6. To emphasize.

*The recommendations of the Committee are, obviously, the handiwork of Guy Smithson.*

Here commas emphasize the obvious fact that Smithson was responsible for the recommendations. There is even a hint that the writer is a little critical. Remove the commas and this shading of meaning is no longer there.

7. To show that something is omitted.

*Pettingill is the first choice; Hardy, the second.*

8. To follow a clause that is out of its natural order.

*That Hardy is a good man for the job, I grant you.*

9. To interrupt with parenthetical matter and with adverbs such as *however, therefore,* and *moreover.*

> *The time is right, in the opinion of my investment counselor, to buy some good oil shares.*
>
> *The Board's conclusion, therefore, was that we should not attempt to enter the foreign markets.*

*However* seems to trouble some typists. I frequently find it incorrectly punctuated as in this example:

> *We had expected a more substantial payment, however, we appreciate the good faith you have shown by sending us this $25 check.*

When *however* connects two complete thoughts, separate the thoughts with a period or semicolon.

> *We had expected a more substantial payment; however, we appreciate the good faith you have shown by sending us this $25 check.*

Or

> *We had expected a more substantial payment. However, we appreciate the good faith you have shown by sending us this $25 check.*

*However* is set off by commas only when it interrupts one thought.

> *We had, however, expected a more substantial payment.*

The same rules of punctuation apply to the other adverbs of this class like *therefore* and *moreover.*

For commas unwanted with these adverbs see sentences 5 and 6, "Unwanted Commas."

10. To show opposition and contrast.

*This is a cause for which we should work together, not apart.*
*I made it clear that this job required the services of an experienced technician, but neither our personnel office nor the employment agency has referred anybody with more than six months' experience.*

11. To introduce a quotation in a sentence.

*When I pressed him for payment he said, "I won't pay you a cent until the contractor makes good his agreement to modernize the kitchen."*

12. To separate a year from the day of the month, a city from a state or county, and a title from a name:

*It happened January 4, 1958, in Miami, Dade County, Florida.*
*E. J. Lockman, president, made a full statement of the company's position.*

## SOME OTHER MARKS

COLON (:). The colon (aside from its use in the salutation) is used in letters principally to introduce a series of statements, a long example or a long quotation. The matter following the colon is then set in a separate paragraph. We might use this mark oftener to introduce within the paragraph short emphatic statements and questions that are not quoted, as:

*This is the final decision: Go ahead and buy the Yates property.*

*I figure it this way: no risk, no gain.*
*The question is: What per cent of this sum is overhead?*

As a usual practice a capital letter follows the colon when it introduces a complete sentence; a small letter, if the sentence is incomplete.

DASH (—). The complaint that the dash is overworked cannot rightly be lodged against letters. Sir Ernest Gowers notes that the dash lends itself to rhetorical uses that may be out of place in humdrum prose. My suggestion is this: If letters are humdrum, let us do what we can to enliven them by mechanical devices of writing. The dash may add a note of surprise. Use the dash sparingly, but don't hesitate to use it for a little variety.

1. To take the place of a comma or parenthesis.

*After all the papers on the case are assembled—correspondence, remittance advice, and purchase orders—put them on the supervisor's desk.*

*The plant itself—an old and dilapidated affair—is not worth $25,000, but I think we can meet the price if the owner agrees to sell the adjoining property.*

Dashes, you see, are not reserved for emotional writing. In the above sentences they serve a practical purpose in taking over the job of commas that would clutter these sentences when added to others that cannot be dispensed with. Parentheses might have been used, but the effect would have been less emphatic.

2. To sum up.

*Correspondence, purchase orders, and remittance advice—all these papers are missing from the folder.*

3. To break off.

*There is nothing—though Elliott thinks there is—to prevent our acquiring the Hendricks property.*

These sudden breaks are likely to come up in dictation. They are conversational and should not be avoided.

The dash is also the typewriter symbol in hyphened words. Although the hyphen isn't popular nowadays, you can't always dispense with it and make your meaning clear. A phrase such as "a small tool manufacturer" needs a hyphen to show whether you mean *small tool* or *small manufacturer*. If you mean *small tool* write "small-tool manufacturer." If you mean *small manufacturer* write "small tool-manufacturer." Similarly a "half-fried chicken" is one thing, and a "half fried chicken" quite another. If you like your chicken rare you might settle for the *half-fried*.

ELLIPSIS ( . . .). An occasional ellipsis adds interest and variety, especially to sales letters.

> *It is new . . . it is different. You child will cherish this toy.*

In suggesting that the ellipsis be used in this way, I must caution you that it soon loses its effectiveness when overworked. I have seen few sales letters that could take more than a few of these marks without leaving the impression that the writer was striving for drama.

PARENTHESES ( () ). Parentheses are useful for citations.

> *The form (example 4) is for office use only.*
> *The rule is clearly stated in the note to Forth v. Stanton (1 Saund.210, note b).*

and for long explanatory statements.

> *Of course, you know, we're on rations now—yet we suffer no inconvenience on that score. But these queer people (they are the most amusing and confusing and contradictory of all God's creatures, these English, whose possibilities are infinite and whose actualities, in many ways, are pitiful)—these queer people are fiercely pursuing food-economy by discussing in the*

*newspapers whether a hen consumes more food than she pro-
duces, and whether what dogs eat contain enough human food
to justify the shooting of every one in the Kingdom.*

The above passage from one of Walter Hines Page's World War I
letters to President Wilson is a typical example of interruptions
one might expect in conversation. The combined use of parentheses
and dashes makes it easy for the reader to follow this seventy-word
sentence.

Parentheses attached to a sentence are followed, not preceded, by
the mark that would be used if the parenthetical matter were not
inserted. Detached from the sentence, the parentheses enclose any
other mark required.

*We have 30,000 empty drums (tabluation attached), all of
which could have been returned for credit six months ago.*

*Technical language should not be used in letters to customers
(Rule 6).*

*Technical language should not be used in letters to customers.
(See Rule 6, Chapter XXII.)*

QUOTATION MARKS (" "). Does the comma go inside or outside
the quotation mark? Don't be puzzled. Always place the comma
inside—well, nearly always. Legal writers sometimes have reasons
for wanting it outside. Periods, too, go inside the quotation marks.

*We simply pulled a "boner," Mr. Adams.*

*When I asked him about the past-due balance he said, "I've
written you people repeatedly that I did not order or receive
any merchandise from your company in July." Then I showed
him a copy of the order. "By George!" he exclaimed. "Do you
know I completely forgot about that order?"*

When an exclamation or question mark ends a quotation, it goes
inside the quote mark as in the last example When these marks

belong to the complete sentence—not just the matter quoted—
they usually go outside:

> What do you suppose he meant by that gobbledygook "denial
> is premised on the obvious proposition"?
> Now that's what I call a "big deal"!

SEMICOLON (;). Page used the semicolon freely.

> Every nation in Europe knew that Germany was preparing
> for war. If they had really got together for business and had
> said to Germany, "The moment you fire a shot, we'll all fight
> against you; we have so many billions of men, so many men-of-
> war, so many billions of money; and we'll increase all these if
> you do not change your system and your building-up of armies"
> —then there would have been no war.

Again:

> I suspect that in spite of all the fuss we have made we shall
> at last come to acknowledge the British blockade; for it is pretty
> nearly parallel to the United States blockade of the South during
> the Civil War. The only difference is—they can't make the
> blockade of the Baltic States against the traffic of the Scandi-
> navian neutral states effective. That's a good technical objection;
> but since practically all the traffic between these States
> and Germany is our products, much of the real force of it is
> lost.

But Page's letters were written more than forty years ago. Semi-
colons are not as popular today as they were then. The infrequency
with which they are used in letters causes me to wonder whether
this mark is taught any more in general courses in English. It can
be very useful in shortening sentences while keeping them closely
related, as in the first sentence of the last example; and it is handy

for separating a series of co-ordinate clauses as in the first example. You will also find it useful in sentences like these:

*Pettingill is the first choice; Hardy, the second.*
*Winston is a technician; Harrison, an engineer.*

## SUMMARY

The biggest problem in punctuation is the comma. In excess, commas deface the page and keep attracting the reader's attention when he could move on. To punctuate with a purpose, think of your reader's requirements. Don't lavish commas on him at every opportunity, but give him those he needs for guidance and a "breath." Your common sense is more helpful than rules in deciding where the comma should go.

In addition to suggestions on more purposeful use of commas, this chapter contains a number of tips on making better use of other marks, especially those that replace the comma.

Part Three | PRODUCTION

AIDS

CHAPTER 9

# The Appeal of Good-looking Letters

*I am trying to get the hang of this new fangled writing machine, but am not making a shining success of it. . . . The machine has several virtues. I believe it will print faster than I can write. One may lean back in his chair and work it. It piles an awful stack of words on one page. It dont muss things or scatter ink blots around. Of course it saves paper.*

—MARK TWAIN

MARK TWAIN is said to be the first author to have bought a typewriter, purchasing one for $125 about a year after the machine was first put on the market. Delighted with his newfangled writing machine, he wrote his brother on December 9, 1874, describing its virtues and displaying his ineptitude at operating it. A few sentences from his letter are quoted above.

The modern typewriter is a miracle machine compared to Twain's clumsy contraption. With a little attention to layout, even a relatively unskilled typist can turn out attractive letters on today's streamlined models.

The pleasing appearance of the letter is principally a matter of balance between white space and type. White space may be expensive, but the generous amount framing the letter and separating its parts adds class to the "package" and makes reading easier. Crowded margins and solid pages of type are forbidding. Similarly, disproportionate margins create a lopsided appearance that is disturbing. I think most businessmen will agree that it is more important to entice our readers than to pinch pennies on paper costs.

## MATERIAL

Good-quality stationery is the essential material. Professions that do not advertise would be expected to have a more formal letterhead than those that do. That bit of color now preferred by some companies can be used effectively by any business or profession, but elaborate printing along the side margins creates the appearance of an ad rather than a letter. A simply designed letterhead is in good taste in any company.

The larger companies have at least three types of letterheads distinguished as "executive" for use of officials (usually a good quality watermark bond), "standard" for routine letters, and "memorandum" for internal communications. There may be a number of special-usage letterheads within these three general types.

Standard business stationery is 8½ by 11 inches, but the Federal government insists on size 8 x 10½ for its letters, supposedly to save paper. It doesn't work out that way, though. Too many government letters spill over a line or two onto a second page.

If you want to save paper, stock some letterheads 8½ by 7⅓ inches, keeping the standard width and reducing the length by a third. Easily 40 per cent of today's business letters can be attractively laid out on paper that size. The standard size can then be reserved for longer letters, with the same standard envelopes used for both sizes.

## LAYOUT

There are a number of minor deviations in the manner of framing a letter to give it a picturelike look, but the essentials are much the same. You may have your own manual of style practices that takes into account these essentials. If not, the suggestions offered may be helpful. These suggestions apply only to standard stationery 8½ by 11 inches, but it is a simple matter to make adjustments for odd sizes.

DATE. Three positions are preferred for the date, all beginning two to four lines down from the last line of the letterhead: (1) alined with the right margin; (2) beginning at the center of the page or slightly to the right of the center; (3) blocked at the left margin. The first is the hardest to handle because it involves right-to-left positioning which will vary with the months. The second style, beginning approximately at the center of the page, is easier and has the added advantage of alinement with a blocked close. On the other hand, right-margin dates balance right-margin file references. The third style, calling for the date blocked at the left margin, goes well with blocked paragraphs.

FILE REFERENCES. Most companies still prefer the right-hand position for file, invoice, claim, order and other identifying numbers; but these numbers are just as conspicuous and many feel that the letter looks neater, when they are blocked at the left. In any event, file references should be set apart from the rest of the heading, halfway between the date and the next entry and separated by double spaces. The word *reference* written in full or abbreviated is unnecessary.

Order 1011-A
Invoice C-94716

Your letter 10/19/58
Claim 8937
Your file NY 1432

PERSONAL AND CONFIDENTIAL. Usually underlined and written with initial caps, the words *Personal and Confidential* or *Personal* or *Confidential* are preferably blocked at left margin three spaces above the address.

ADDRESS. The address may be typed at the beginning or at the foot of the letter, flush with the left margin. The usual style is at the beginning, but some writers like to place it at the end of a formal letter; others prefer the address at the end for business letters to personal acquaintances. Three lines of typing look better than two; so if there is no street address put the name of the state on a separate line.

Mr. Calvin S. Pritchett          Mr. Calvin S. Pritchett
Little Falls                     1020 River Road
Massachusetts                    Baltimore 10, Maryland

Titles may be placed on the same line with the addressee's name or on the line with the name of the organization, depending on length.

Miss Regina Mae Pettingill       Mr. B. R. Grove, Vice-President
Secretary, Women's Art League    Monarch Electroplating Corpora-
4480 East Lake Avenue            tion
Dallas 14, Texas                 1444 East High Road
                                 Richmond 22, Virginia

Abbreviations are unattractive. Unless the typist is crowded for space she should spell out all words in the address including titles, states, and *corporation*. *District of Columbia* is the exception; *D. C.* is preferred. For modern styles of punctuating dates, address and closes, see Chapter 8.

SUBJECT. If a subject line is used it may be centered or written at the left margin two spaces above the salutation. The word *subject* is not needed, but when it is omitted the entry is underscored. If there is more than one line in the subject, underscore the last line only.

SALUTATION. *Dear Mr.* (*surname*) is friendlier than *Dear Sir;* and *Gentlemen* and *Ladies* are preferable to *Dear Sirs* and *Mesdames.* The secretarial schools that set our styles preach that *My dear Mr.* (*surname*) is more formal than *Dear Mr.* (*surname*). You may not think this is logical, especially since some of the style-setters also insist that *My dear Mr.* (*surname*) should not be used in a letter signed by a company; for surely those impersonal company-signed letters are more formal than letters in which an individual speaks for the company. Except for letters to dignitaries, don't feel that you must be governed by conventions in the form of address and salutation. In formal letters to dignitaries it is courteous to conform to these conventions. See "Forms of Address," Appendix.

The salutation may end with a comma or a colon. Your choice!

If a letter is directed to the attention of someone, note this, two spaces above or below the address. Above the address it is usually blocked at the left margin. Following the address it is blocked or centered.

| | |
|---|---|
| Attention Mr. Ben R. Grove | Monarch Electroplating Corpora-<br>tion |
| Monarch Electroplating Corpora-<br>tion<br>1444 East High Road<br>Richmond 22, Virginia | 1444 East High Road<br>Richmond 22, Virginia |
| | Attention: Mr. B. R. Grove |
| Gentlemen: | Gentlemen: |

The salutation is made to the company, not the individual, when an attention line is used.

MARGINS. With an approximate idea of the number of words in the letter, it is easy to frame it on the page. This scale will guide a typist in setting up letters on a page 8½ by 11 inches with paper centered at 50 for elite type and at 42 for pica:

| | | Side Margins | | | |
| | | Elite | | Pica | |
| Length | Address begins about | Left | Right | Left | Right |
| Under 100 words | 22 lines from top of page | 24 | 78 | 20 | 65 |
| 100–200 words | 20 lines from top of page | 18 | 84 | 15 | 70 |
| 200 words and up | 18 lines from top of page | 12 | 90 | 10 | 75 |

For more precise margins a typist can make her own chart, keeping in mind that standard office typewriters produce six single lines to the inch, down the page, whether the type is elite or pica. Across the page elite type has twelve spaces to the inch, whereas pica has only ten. The allowance for the right margin is determined by subtracting the number of spaces in the left margin from 102 for elite and from 85 for pica. Even on the longest letters the left margin should be at least one inch and the space left at the bottom of the letter should equal that of the left margin.

If the body of the letter is four lines or less, double spacing is preferable. Other letters look better single spaced with double spacing between paragraphs.

PARAGRAPHING. Blocked paragraphs (no indentation on the first line) hit the peak of their popularity several years ago. Today more and more companies seem to be preferring an indentation ranging anywhere from five to ten spaces. They have learned that the idea of saving time by blocking paragraphs is a myth. Set tabs for indentation and the half-dozen strokes saved by blocking is so insignificant that the "efficiency expert" who peddles such piddling economies must be pressed for ideas. I am not attempting to influence you in your choice. The letter can be attractive whether the paragraphs are indented or blocked. All I am saying is this: Don't be influenced in your choice by the idea that you'll save a few postage stamps.

Occasionally, outlining is used in letters. If the headings are numbered, this format may be followed:

*For many divisions:*
 I. Roman numeral
   A. Capital letter
     1. Regular number
       a. Small letter
         a-1. Small letter and figure
         a-2. . . .
       b. . . .
       c. . . .
     2. . . .
   B. . . .
 II. . . .

*For only two divisions:*
 1. Regular number
   a. Small letter
   b. . . .
 2. . . .

TWO-PAGE LETTERS. Here are a few hints on setting up letters that run more than one page:

Leave enough white space at the bottom of the page for a pleasing balance. Avoid beginning a paragraph at the bottom of the page unless you have room for at least two lines. Similarly, try to carry over at least two lines of the paragraph to the next page. It won't always work out this way, but when it does the letter is more attractive.

Avoid dividing a word between two pages. This goes for hyphened words, too.

Begin the first line of typing on second and suceeding pages about six lines from the top. Keep the side margins the same as those on the first page. Whether the second page of a two-page letter is numbered is a matter of choice, but it is always advisable to number the second and succeeding pages of longer letters. Some companies like to show the addressee's name and the date of the letter on the second and succeeding pages. A good balance comes from centering the page number between the addressee's name and the date.

Mr. Carl R. Smithson                — 2 —                June 28, 1958

Leave three spaces between this identifying information and the body.

COMPLIMENTARY CLOSE. If you are a stickler for conventions you may think that *yours truly* and *very truly yours* are proper closes for business letters to readers unknown to the writer. If not, you may wonder why *sincerely* and *sincerely yours* should be reserved for what the style books call "a friendly relationship between reader and writer." In truth, there is little distinction between these mannerisms of closing a letter. It is a simple matter of choice.

*Cordially* and *cordially yours*, long reserved by the style books as a treat for personal acquaintances, have been gaining popularity in the last few years, and are often used in letters to clients with whom the writer is not personally acquainted. When it comes to writing personal acquaintances, the complimentary close can take any form that is in good taste. Those fragmentary last sentences, staunchly opposed by the style books, are to be found in some of the best letters, as

> *With the warmest regard, in necessary haste,*
>
> > *Cordially yours,*

and

> *I look forward to seeing you in Chicago. Until then . . .*
>
> > *Yours as ever,*

and

> *Hoping you are well,*
>
> > *As ever,*

As ever, as always, yours, yours as ever, and your friend are suitable complimentary closes for letters to those who are both friends and business associates. Respectfully yours, very respectfully, and respectfully are characteristic of formal letters to dignitaries.

CLOSE (NAME AND TITLE). The penny-pinching efficiency expert can make more of a case for himself with his suggestion on blocking the close. Centering a name over a title is tedious business hardly worth the trouble. In style this form is out of keeping with blocked paragraphs. The common-sense approach is to center the name over the title or to center the title under the name only when there is a spacing problem.

Sincerely yours,                                    Very truly yours,

William J. Donovan                                  J. J. Green
Vice-President                          Vice-President and Controller

Here is another fussy practice taught by the style books: If the first-person plural (we) is used in the letter, then you are supposed to type the company name at the close above the signer's name; but if the first-person singular is used, the name of the signer comes first. The style books don't say the company name is a must as part of the close, but some companies seem to think that is the idea. With the company name on the letterhead, only those who think like file-clerks or neon-sign ad men can justify repeating the name at the end of every letter. One tells you that it is needed to identify the carbon copy; the other says it is a good idea to display the company name at every opportunity. The only good usage I can think of is in this setup:

Yours truly,

MONARCH LITHOGRAPHING COMPANY

By

IDENTIFYING INITIALS. Initials identifying the typist or both the dictator and the typist are placed at the left margin one space below the last line of the close. If the letter is signed by the person who dictates it, only the typist's initials are needed.

mec [or] JRL:mc [or] JRL/mc [or] JRL:MC [or] JRL/MC [or] J. R. Lane: mc

Formal letters and those prepared for company executives usually omit this identifying matter from the original. Again this is a convention. There is no really good reason why it should not be omitted from the original of all letters except that it takes a little longer to adjust the typing. Rarely does any reader refer to these initials in later correspondence.

SPECIAL MAILING INSTRUCTIONS. Why make these instructions conspicuous on the letter by typing them in all caps in a heading that may be crowded with other data? Airmail, special delivery or registered mail is neater when typed at the left margin, a space or two below the last entry.

| MLC:is | M. E. Jones/is | isc |
|---|---|---|
| Encl 2 | | Enclosure |
| | Registered mail | |
| Airmail | | Special delivery |

ENCLOSURES. Flush with the initials and on the next line, the word enclosure may be written in full or abbreviated. If there is more than one enclosure the number is shown.

| KRS/ct | M. T. Jones: en | esr |
|---|---|---|
| Enclosure | Encl | Encl 4 |

INFORMATION COPIES. If others than the addressee are to receive copies, a notation is made at the left margin one or two spaces below the last entry. The name of the first person to receive a copy is preceded by copy or cc.

Copy Mr. S. M. Kelly        cc Mr. S. M. Kelly
                               Mr. Ralph Hendricks

THE SIMPLIFIED LETTER. A number of years ago the National Office Management Association attempted to sponsor the simplified letter—a letter omitting the salutation and complimentary close and beginning all lines of typing at the left margin. By motion studies NOMA proved that the saving in typing time was over 10.7 per cent on a 96-word letter. But most of this saving comes from the use of the window envelope, not from left-margin alinement and omission of the salutation and close.

The simplified letter is informal and neat. Perhaps the informality accounts for the fact that business has been slow to adopt the style and government has rejected it altogether. Most business writers tell me that they feel the letter is incomplete without the salutation and complimentary close. It is true that a "touch" must be added to the opening paragraph to make it suitable to the style. But this touch is nothing more than you have been taught in this book as a friendly and informal way of beginning letters. In addition, the addressee's name is usually thrown into the opening sentence, as: "You are right, Mr. Jones. We did ship your order collect when you requested that we charge it. Why this should happen to a good customer like you, it is difficult to understand."

In time we may come to see the salutation and complimentary close as mannerisms belonging, like "I beg to remain" and "esteemed favor," to another age. In the meantime any zealot for the cause might direct his ardor to more important matters. If I receive a simplified letter I usually reply in kind as a compliment to my reader's taste; and that the simplified letter is in good taste, there is no question. Don't hesitate to use it if you like it. Here is the setup:

February 25, 1959

Miss Miriam T. Foote
Chief, Stenographic Section
Atlas Letter Service
350 Fifth Avenue
New York 1, New York

Simplified Letters

You are right, Miss Foote. Our company has been writing simplified letters for several years. This letter is an example.

The format is extremely simple. All typing begins at the left margin. Salutation and complimentary close are omitted. When a window envelope is used—as it is for most of our letters—we are careful to place the address where it will fall in the window with a simple three-way fold of the page.

At first some of our staff objected to this form. No effort was made to require its use. Now practically everybody likes it, though I must admit that some write letters better suited to the style than others.

Usually the appearance is good. The exception is the letter with a number of short left-margin entries: attention line, subject, personal and confidential, special mailing instructions, and so on. When these pile up along the left margin the letter is truly a lopsided affair.

Thank you for your interest. If you have any other questions I shall be pleased to answer them.

Janice Cummings
Chief, Stenographic Department

ec
Enclosure

ENVELOPES. A blocked address beginning a little to the right of the center of the envelope is preferred nowadays whether the letter is set up in formal or informal style. The Post Office Department likes the name of the state on a separate line, and if you are not crowded for space you might as well go along with this. The best order for lines is: (1) individual's name; (2) company name; (3) room, apartment or box number; (4) street address; (5) city and zone; (6) state. If a letter is directed to a foreign country, the name of the country should be set on a separate line in all caps. A street address is preferable to a building name. If you have the street address, there is no reason to show the building unless you know the room number in which case the entry is made as "314 Grand Union Building."

Street numbers below 10 may be written in figures or words, but those above ten are preferably written only as figures. Except for envelopes addressed in quantities for mass mailings, when it is important to save time, street, avenue, road, building, etc., should be spelled out for better appearance. North, Northeast, East, Southeast, etc., are abbreviated as N or E., NE or N.E., and so on.

Special mailing instructions, such as airmail, special delivery and registered mail, are more conspicuous when typed above and to the right of the address. Other instructions as hold for arrival, attention and personal may be typed at the lower left corner.

## PROS AND CONS OF STANDARD STYLE

One thing should be clear: It is unwise to attempt to prescribe a standard style practice for every letter. Although the larger companies can profit from a manual of general guidance, no such manual should be in the form of an army regulation. Nothing is more disconcerting to a typist than an inflexible rule which she knows should be broken at times for a better layout. Too often manuals are developed by a member of a management team who counts efficiency in terms of standardization and savings in typewriter strokes, or by a secretary enslaved by conventions. I have seen manuals with paragraphs numbered like a Dewey Decimal file, written in the third person, and prescribing a layout like a law. Following the rules of such a manual, stenographers in one company were placing subjects, claim numbers and file references at the left margin under the salutation. Who could make a letter sound friendly after throwing in all this matter between the salutation and the message? But this, I was told, was in the interest of standardization and efficiency. Is business letter writing to become a mechanical monster for the sake of standardization?

The most helpful style guide is written informally, designed to inspire the typist to apply her own skills and imagination. The *musts* are few. A blocked paragraph or an indented paragraph can be a *must* without affecting the appearance of any letter. But when it comes to a prescribed placement for dates, attention lines, personal and confidential notations, subject, and so on—watch out! Unless you can devise a placement suitable for every combination of these entries, you'll find them bunching up where they are least attractive. Instead of prescribing a placement, provide a preferred placement subject to adjustment; and in making your suggestions think more of appearance and less of saving a few typewriter strokes. The value of standards is in their excellence, so that your readers come to distinguish your style as a trademark of your business just as they come to distinguish the style of a first-class publication.

## ABBREVIATIONS

In typewriting as in printing, unabbreviated words are more attractive than those that are abbreviated. So it is preferable to spell out words in letters directed outside the company, except those like *Mr., Mrs., Dr., Sr., Jr.,* and so on, and footnotes like *encl* and *cc.* Names of the states and months are spelled out in the heading as well as in the body of the letter. (District of Columbia is an exception.)

Informal internal communications may be abbreviated freely.

## CAPITALIZATION AND UNDERSCORING

Like abbreviations and overpunctuations, excessive capitalization and underscoring spoil the appearance of the typed page. Of course, initial capitals are used for proper names, principal words in titles, and the first word of the sentence; otherwise, it becomes a matter of judgment as to whether capitals are called for. Underscoring in the body of the letter should be avoided.

A few hints on capitalizing:

BUSINESS TITLES. Even when referring to a specific person, titles usually are not capitalized in printed matter. There is no reason why we cannot follow the same practice in typing, but this is a matter of choice. You may write "J. Fenwick Sommers, vice-president and general manager" or "J. Fenwick Sommers, Vice-President and General Manager" in the body of the letter, though initial caps are preferable for titles in heading and close. Be consistent.

FAMILIAR NAMES. Do not capitalize the words *father, mother, sister, uncle,* and so on, when preceded by a personal pronoun. You may capitalize these words when the the personal pronoun is not used.

*I wrote Mother last week.*
*Have your aunt sign the enclosed paper.*

GEOGRAPHIC NAMES. Such words as *northern, eastern, street, county, river* and *ocean* need be capitalized only when part of a proper name designating a territorial division.

| *This* | *Not This* |
|---|---|
| southern Virginia | Southern Virginia |
| the southern counties | the southern Counties |
| Lower California | lower California (unless you are distinguishing the general location rather than the territory) |

|              This              |            Not This            |
| ------------------------------ | ------------------------------ |
| Dallas County                  | Dallas county                  |
| the Orient                     | The Orient                     |
| Mississippi River              | Mississippi river              |
| southeastern Oklahoma          | Southeastern Oklahoma          |
| Mulberry Street                | Mulberry street                |
| Western Hemisphere             | western Hemisphere             |
| Pacific Ocean                  | Pacific ocean                  |

HEADINGS. Prepositions and conjunctions of less than three letters need not be capitalized in headings:

|            This             |            Not This            |
| --------------------------- | ------------------------------ |
| The Style of Modern Letters | The Style Of Modern Letters    |
| Time and Place of Meetings  | Time And Place Of Meetings     |

All-cap headings should be avoided in short compositions like letters.

JUNIOR AND SENIOR. When these words are abbreviated, capitalize them.

James R. Nicholson, Sr.
James R. Nicholson, Jr.

SEASONS. Do not capitalize the words *summer, fall, winter* and *spring*.

SENTENCES FOLLOWING COLONS. As a general rule, use an initial cap with a complete sentence following a colon; lower case with a fragmentary sentence.

*My suggestion is: Sell our property east of the highway and buy the 30 acres adjoining the plant property.*

*The results are indifferent: some fair, others just passable.*

THE. Capitalize *the* only when it is part of the title.

| *This* | *Not This* |
|---|---|
| the United Air Lines | The United Air Lines |
| The Evening Star | the Evening Star |

In the first example *the* is not part of the title; in the last example, it is. If the title is used as a modifier, *the* goes down, as "the Evening Star editorial."

When a common noun substitutes for a title it need not be capitalized.

| the bank | your committee |
|---|---|
| our company | their firm |
| this corporation | the company |

## DIVISION OF WORDS

Even dictionaries differ on word division—sometimes; but the division suggested by any good dictionary is acceptable. A typist need not consult a dictionary very often if she remembers these ten suggestions:

1. Divide words according to pronunciation: *han-dled* instead of *hand-led, prob-ably* instead of *pro-bably,* and so on.

2. Usually divide between double consonants: *pos-sible, neces-sary, begin-ning* and *bid-der.* Exception: If the basic word to which an ending has been added ends in a doubled letter, the division follows the basic word, as *pass-ing* and *full-er.*

3. Don't divide contractions such as *shouldn't, wouldn't* and *couldn't.*

4. Don't divide one-syllable words such as *straight, width, course, planned* and *shipped.*

5. Avoid dividing words at the end of two consecutive lines. In fact, avoid dividing. The fewer divisions, the better.

6. As a general rule don't divide a two-syllable word, and never divide on a single letter. For example, don't separate the short syllables in these words:

| | | |
|---|---|---|
| e-dition | camer-a | sever-al |
| i-dentify | fa-miliar | peri-od |

7. Don't divide words of five letters or less: *carry, idea,* and *begin.*

8. Divide hyphened words at the hyphen.

9. Never divide figures and abbreviations. Divide dates between the day and the year instead of the month and the day.

10. As a general rule, avoid separating initials from a name and dividing a proper name. When there are several initials or a long name, follow the style of printing and divide.

## NUMBERS

Numbers come up often in business letters. Except at the beginning of a sentence they are usually written as figures rather than words, regardless of the size or sequence. If you prefer this style as a convenience in quick reference, that is all you need to know on this subject. If you prefer a more formal style, then you might follow these suggestions:

WHEN TO WRITE NUMBERS AS FIGURES. Write as figures:

1. Isolated numbers of 10 or more.

*Representatives from 15 regions attended the conference.*

2. Several numbers in related context, regardless of size.

*Only 8 of the 1500 letters received in the last 6 months were complaints.*

3. Quantities and measurements—ages, time, dates, decimals, mathematical expressions, percentage, etc.—regardless of the size of the number.

| | | |
|---|---|---|
| 1 foot | 15 days | 10:03 A.M. |
| 2 acres | January 1 | 57th year |
| 9 gallons | 17.8 per cent | 11 miles |

When the name of the month precedes the date, it is preferably written.

> *The conference is scheduled for June 17.* [Not *June seventeenth or June 17th*]

When the number precedes the month, it is written, as "the 3rd of January." Dates should not be abbreviated in the body of the letter (7/19/58), except perhaps in informal internal communications.

4. Reference numbers in text, regardless of the size.

> *page 3, Section 10.58, Chapter IX.*

5. Sums of money, regardless of the size.

> *We need more Christmas merchandise retailing under $5.*
> *We shall expect your check for $13.89 by return mail.*
> *The small credit balance of 62 cents [or 62¢] was refunded.*

Decimal points and ciphers are not called for in writing even sums ($60 instead of $60.00), except in tabulations for uniform appearance. Large round sums may be expressed by a figure and a word, as in *30 million.*

WHEN TO WRITE NUMBERS AS WORDS. Write as words:
1. The isolated numbers 1 through 9.

> *Get nine crates    The numbers 7, 14 and 29*

2. Any number at the beginning of a sentence except in footnotes.

> Seven days after the sale began we were sold out.
> Forty-three years ago a lone man with $10 cash founded this company.

3. Numbers representing centuries, as *twentieth* century.
4. Round or indefinite numbers.

> *midthirties*          *fortyfold*          *hundreds of persons*

5. Enumerations of 100 or less preceding a compound modifier.

> *three 4-inch pipes*          *twenty-one 32-inch wheels*
> *149 4-inch boards*          *seven $5 bills*

In printed matter, you will find variations in the style of writing numbers. It all depends on the publisher's preference. The practices suggested here for letters may also be varied and still be in good style. Consistency and clarity are what count.

## SPACING AFTER PUNCTUATION MARKS

Proper spacing after punctuation marks is a detail that gives the "package" a professional look.

| After | Leave |
|---|---|
| colon | 2 spaces |
| comma | 1 space |
| dash | 1 space each side (in hyphened words, no space) |
| exclamation point | 2 spaces |

| After | Leave |
|---|---|
| parentheses | 1 space (if followed by another mark of punctuation, no space) |
| period | 2 spaces (1 space if period is used for abbreviation) |
| question mark | 2 spaces |

Spacing after quotation marks is governed by other marks alongside. No space is left between the quote marks and the matter enclosed.

## SUMMARY

The pleasing appearance of a letter is principally a matter of balance between white space and typing. Crowded margins and solid pages of type are forbidding, as are disproportionate margins. The general guides on style discussed in this chapter are designed to help you develop your own in such matters as layout, capitalization, abbreviations, salutations and complimentary close.

Standards in style should not be treated as inflexible rules. The most helpful style guide is written informally, designed to inspire the typist to applying her own skill and imagination. The value of standards is in their excellence, so that your readers come to distinguish your style as a trademark of your business just as they come to distinguish the style of a first-class publication.

CHAPTER 10 | Capturing Subject Matter

*I have not had time to write you a short letter;
therefore I have written you a long one.*
—PLINY

*I have made this letter rather long only because
I have not had time to make it shorter.*
—PASCAL

*If I had more time, I should have written you a
shorter letter.*
—MADAME DE STAEL

THE PURPOSE of this chapter is to suggest how you can manage your correspondence so there will be more time for shorter and better letters.

Let's start with the simple theory that functions and responsibilities are clearly defined in any good businesss organization. With this theory in practice we go to the office each morning knowing in advance what our work will be like. We also know in advance what our office letters will be about. A finance officer does not recruit workers. A personnel officer does not purchase supplies. Orders go to the order department, and credit applications are handled by the credit department.

Without leaving your desk or making a single telephone call you should be able to tell which office writes letters about job opportunities or purchase orders or adjustments or credit. In terms of your own letters this means that you may be responsible for only a slice of a pie chart representing the total subject matter with which your business is concerned; the larger your company, the smaller may be your slice; and the smaller the slice the more limited is the scope of your subject matter.

Suppose we go on from there. You can see that everybody except the Jack-of-all-trades writes business letters on a limited number of subjects. All of us know generally what our letters are about. Why not capture more of the subject matter? Why not use more form letters? That's a good way to get that extra time you may need for shorter and better letters.


## WHAT DO YOU GAIN?

Some business men are skeptical of so-called canned letters. They believe that letters must be individually dictated to please their customers. That is sometimes true, but only when the ready-made letter is hastily and poorly written or when its use is inappropriate.

We've all heard about those "wooden" and misused form letters. My own favorite story goes back to the days of the New Deal and the National Recovery Administration with its colorful administrator, General Hugh Johnson. Like most government departments, the NRA had a number of form letters. One of these letters was a typical brush-off, designed to take care of requests that could not be granted. It was set up for the General's signature and when mailed was signed in his behalf by a member of his staff. The day came—or so goes the story—when an admirer of the General's wrote to request his autograph. Back to the autograph seeker went NRA's brush-off letter signed with the General's name: "I regret that due to the pressure of business it is impossible to comply with your request."

That's the sort of mishap that can occur with form letters. But remember this: Mishaps also occur with dictated letters. It isn't sensible to ban the ready-made letter as a precaution against accidents. It is sensible, though, to ban a form letter as a reply to personal letters, such as the one requesting an autograph. If you do that, serious mishaps are unlikely.

Actually those ready-made letters should be the best in any type of business. They give us the opportunity to edit as zealously as the professional writers. Knowing that the letter will be used over and over again, we can afford to spend the time that is needed to polish it. We cannot lean on that old excuse, "If I had more time I would write a shorter letter."

Of course you know that you can save money with form letters, but do you have a good idea of what a dictated letter costs in comparison to a form? Perhaps you have never been convinced by those sweeping generalities that would have you believe the average cost of dictated letters is $1.75 or $2 or $2.50 or whatever figure somebody happens to come up with. I haven't either. Average-cost figures applied to business generally are meaningless. Many factors influence cost, but the principal factors are the complexity and length of subject matter and the salaries of the dictators. Letters written in a corporation engaged in scientific research are far more costly than those written in a mail-order house. The thing that counts is the cost of *your own* or your *company's* letters; and the only way to determine that cost and whether it is too high is by a time study. I have made many such studies, finding average costs of dictated letters ranging from a few pennies under $1 to a fantastic high of $9.60.

But never mind about the average cost of dictated letters. Our concern now is with the comparative cost of dictation and form letters. A table from the General Services Administration handbook *Guide Letters* (U. S. Government Printing Office) gives a rough idea of the cost difference between dictation and the two classes of form letters: (1) those that are printed; and (2) those that are individually typed from a predrafted pattern.

| | TIME AND COST FACTORS IN CREATING A TYPICAL ONE-HALF PAGE, 175-WORD LETTER | | | |
|---|---|---|---|---|
| | Minutes Required | | | |
| Action | Steno Dictation | Machine Dictation | Guide Letters | Printed Letters |
| Planning What to Say | 10 | 10 | 0 | 0 |
| Dictation | 10 | 5 | 0 | 0 |
| Looking up a Letter | 0 | 0 | 2 | 1 |
| Transcribing– Typing | 7 | 8 | 6 | 1.5 |
| Reviewing–Signing | 2 | 2 | 1 | .5 |
| Total Minutes | 29 | 25 | 9 | 3 |
| Cost in Terms of Salary | $.70 to $2.45 | $.60 to $2.25 | $.20 to $.30 | $.08 to $.15 |

This table, says the handbook, is based on studies of correspondence operations in a number of government offices. Note that it shows not an average cost but a typical cost of a typical 175-word letter. The time shown for planning dictation may seem unrealistic, but bear in mind that no time was allowed for rewriting, which always adds considerably to the amount of time expended on dictated letters.

## HOW TO DEVELOP FORM LETTERS

There are seven essential steps in developing efficient form letters. By following these steps you can develop your own "bank" of predrafted letters and paragraphs; or, if you happen to be a supervisor or office manager, you can develop the bank on which others in your office will draw.

Step 1. *Collecting.* Have an extra copy made of each dictated letter. Collect these copies long enough to get a fair sampling. In a large department a two-week sampling is usually enough. In small departments (or if you are collecting only your own letters), three to eight weeks may be required to get a representative coverage.

Step 2. *Sorting.* Make a list of the key subjects of the correspondence. A key subject is comparable to a primary subject in a filing system. For example, if your correspondence is on credit and collection, you may think of your key subjects as *requests for payment, pay or attorney, holding orders, extending time, unearned discount, credit inquiries,* and *credit investigation.* Sort the collection of letters according to these key subjects.

Step 3. *Classifying.* Take one key subject at a time and classify the sorted letters according to the specific situations with which they deal. For example you might subdivide the key subject *request for payment* as *first, second* and *third requests.* Then you might again subdivide each of these as *highly rated customers, marginal accounts,* and so on. Be sure to note how often each subject comes up. This information will help you decide whether it is practical to print the letter or to have it manually or automatically typed. Don't bother with subjects that do not recur.

Step 4. *Organizing.* Organize the subject classifications so that any subject can be located in a matter of seconds, keeping subdivisions under the corresponding key subject. Give each classification a number.

Step 5. *Drafting.* Carefully analyze the letters on each subject. Then put your best efforts to writing a top-quality letter or paragraph on every repetitive subject, observing the 4-S principles of letter writing. Number each letter or paragraph to correspond with the number you have given the subject.

Step 6. *Testing.* Find out how well your predrafted letters work by trying them out in actual use.

Step 7. *Packaging.* Put the collection of predrafted letters in a manual or a card file visibly indexed by key subjects and numbers. You can then look up a letter by subject, and you can let a typist know what you want simply by giving her the number of the letter you choose.

## PRINTED LETTERS

Two tests should be applied in deciding whether to print a letter. One is for appropriateness; the other for economy. A printed letter used inappropriately may damage customer relationship. And obviously there is no advantage in printing a letter that can be typed from a pattern at the same or at little additional cost.

A printed letter is appropriate if:

It is about a routine business or informational matter.

It is not, in fact, a personal letter; or it does not deal with a subject that would be considered personal.

It does not carry news that will be unwelcome by the reader.

Printing is usually economical when:

There are 5 to 10 lines in the letter and the monthly usage is 20 or more.

There are 10 to 15 lines in the letter and the monthly usage is 15 or more.

There are 20 or more lines in the letter and the monthly usage is 10 or more.

In modern correspondence, notices are frequently being used in place of conventional letters. A notice used in volume can be designed with that eye-appeal which professional copy writers and layout men strive for. Figure 1 is an example of such a notice.

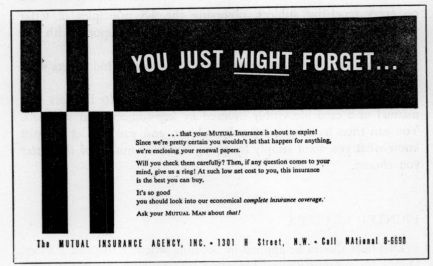

Figure 1. Printed Notice Replacing Letter

Printed on quality paper in subdued shades of gray and green, it speaks well for the good taste of its company.

Again, repetitive business letters can be converted to box-type forms when a number of entries must be made by typewriter or longhand. Figure 2 exemplifies this technique.

Figure 2. Box-type Form Replacing Letter

If the subject matter doesn't lend itself to notices or box-type forms, we must fall back on the letter style either with or without salutations and complimentary close. Letters to be printed should be designed so they can be easily prepared for mailing and will still be attractive when typewriting is added.

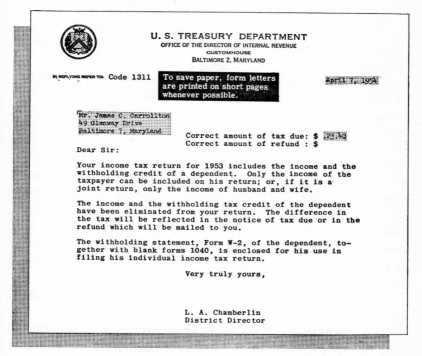

**U. S. TREASURY DEPARTMENT**
OFFICE OF THE DIRECTOR OF INTERNAL REVENUE
CUSTOMHOUSE
BALTIMORE 2, MARYLAND

IN REPLYING REFER TO: Code 1311    To save paper, form letters are printed on short pages whenever possible.    April 7, 1954

Mr. James C. Carrollton
49 Glenway Drive
Baltimore 7, Maryland

Correct amount of tax due: $ 23.40
Correct amount of refund : $

Dear Sir:

Your income tax return for 1953 includes the income and the withholding credit of a dependent. Only the income of the taxpayer can be included on his return; or, if it is a joint return, only the income of husband and wife.

The income and the withholding tax credit of the dependent have been eliminated from your return. The difference in the tax will be reflected in the notice of tax due or in the refund which will be mailed to you.

The withholding statement, Form W-2, of the dependent, together with blank forms 1040, is enclosed for his use in filing his individual income tax return.

Very truly yours,

L. A. Chamberlin
District Director

Figure 3. Letter with Typewritten Entries at Heading

There are only three basic designs for printed letters:

PLAIN. A plain letter is one to which nothing is added by typewriter except perhaps the date, address and salutation. Sales letters, letters to stockholders, and letters making announcements are usually set up in this fashion. Sometimes the salutation is omitted. Sometimes it is printed as *Dear Friend* or *Dear Customer*.

FILL-IN. Printed letters requiring the addition of typewriting other than date, address and salutation, should be designed so the added matter will not be scattered throughout the letter. Often the typewritten data can be placed at the head or the foot. See Figure 3, page 217. When typewritten matter must go into the body of the letter, blank spaces should be left at the end of a paragraph or line whenever possible. This makes it easier to take care of entries of varying lengths. Seldom will the first draft of a letter come out in this fashion, but language is so flexible that changes can be made to get the alinement desired.

CHECK LIST. For a number of optional statements, a suitable form is developed by printing a box at the beginning of each statement. When the letter is prepared for mailing, the applicable statement or statements are checked. Check-list memos are good for internal communications, but check-list letters to customers should be used cautiously. Avoid the hodgepodge that comes from listing many and unrelated items. Although the insurance companies normally take pride in their form letters, they are sometimes guilty of cooking up check-list letters that look like a reference work, with numerous entries written on both sides of the page. This may save a few dollars, but a full page or more of items strikes a reader as absurd when only one item expressing a simple idea in a single sentence is checked for his information.

No matter what style you choose (plain, fill-in or check-list), these tips are helpful:

ADDRESS. If the form letter is to be mailed in a window envelope, show the place the address should begin by printing a single bracket ([) or a dot (.) on the heading.

SALUTATION. If you want to use a salutation, print it in full as *Dear Sir* or *Dear Customer* or *Dear Friend*; otherwise leave the salutation space blank. Don't print *Dear* with the idea of having the typist tack on the name. That's tedious. It's easier for her to type in the full salutation as *Dear Mr. Harris*. When no part of the salutation is printed, be sure to leave enough space for it between the address space and the printed message.

CLOSE. Mass-mailed form letters that serve their purpose in one mailing are usually reproduced with the facsimile signature. But an imprinted signature on a form letter that is stocked may become obsolete before the supply is used up. Take this possibility into consideration before printing.

REPRODUCTION. For a letterlike appearance the offset process is preferable for reproduction. Letterpress is suitable for letters reproduced in large quantities and for notices requiring display type. Mimeographed letters can be neat, but the appearance is never in the class with offset.

COPIES. File copies of form letters are usually unnecessary. When the letters are mass-mailed, the mailing list showing the date of mailing is sufficient for the record. For scattered mailings of forms about routine business transactions, notations of form letter numbers and the dates of mailing can be made on the basic files. Copies of routine form letters clutter records and consume valuable filing space.

## GUIDE LETTERS

Guide or pattern is the name by which most of us know those form letters that are individually typed, automatically or manually. The guide letter has many advantages over the printed form. It can be adjusted for a personal touch to make it indistinguishable from an individually dictated letter.

Experience in countless companies has proved that offices writing quantities of letters can develop a bank of forms—printed or patterns or both—on which letter writers can draw for 60 to 90 per cent of their requirements. A bank of form letters is particularly useful when the subject matter concerns adjustments, personnel, credit and collections, orders and purchasing. With the subject matter captured and classified as suggested earlier in this chapter, the dictator can quickly locate a letter suitable for his purpose. Suppose, for example, a credit man is seeking a letter of apology for a past-due notice mailed in error. Scanning the subjects in his bank of letters he finds a guide that the typist can personalize. All he needs to do is give her the number of the letter—no fuss and bother about dictation. In a few minutes she makes ready an apology that might read something like this:

> You are right, Mr. Abbott. That letter we recently wrote you asking for payment was absolutely uncalled for. How we happened to send you a past-due notice when your account is current, it is difficult to understand. We simply pulled a "boner."
>
> I regret this error and sincerely hope you won't hold it against us.

Simple? Yes. But the short simple letter that talks may be the most difficult one to write. Those who have little time and patience can make up for these shortcomings with a bank of models. Then the time saved can be profitably spent on planning those letters that must be dictated.

## SUMMARY

One would expect a company's form letters to exemplify the best techniques of letter writing. In predrafting letters you have the opportunity to edit as zealously as a professional writer. Knowing the letter will be used over and over again, you can spend more time polishing it than you can when you must dictate letters individually.

There are two classes of form letters: (1) those that are printed, and (2) those that are individually typed from patterns. This chapter contains a number of suggestions on how to capture subject matter and develop an efficient bank of forms on which those who write a quantity of letters can draw for most of their requirements.

Part Four | EXAMPLES

CHAPTER 11 | Reading Your
Way to Plainer
Letters

*One good example is more valuable than twenty
precepts written in books.*
—ROBERT ASCHAM

As WE come to the last chapter of this book I am aware that I must
at times have painted a gloomy picture of the modern letter. Much
has been said about what is wrong and perhaps too little about
what is right. This cannot be helped if the book is to serve its
purpose, but I should be sorry to give comfort to those who think
of letter writing as a lost art. To compare our letters with those
of the past is unfair, for only the best of the past has been preserved.
There is no reason to believe that the garden-variety letters of
yesterday were any better than our own. And there is every reason
to believe that the average office worker of today is better prepared
to handle written English than ever before.

The lost-art school thinks only in terms of personal letters in
which men expressed their innermost thoughts and in which
literate men took great pride. Letter writing today is principally
a practical art. The increased extent to which the letter is now used
for practical purposes will be seen from the Hoover Commission
Task Force Report on Paperwork Management (1955). Anybody

who has the notion that other means of communication are replacing the letter may be surprised to learn from this report that the federal office worker of today is writing ten times as many letters as his counterpart of forty years ago. Letter style changes. Even language changes. But how can any art be lost as long as men have need to practice it?

Quality letters are to be found not only in histories and biographies and archives, but also in the current files of business and government. Those exhibited here are not necessarily the *best* letters, although all of them are outstanding examples of good plain letters. These particular letters were selected because they illustrate many of the points made in this book and many of the subjects on which we commonly write. A few of them are historical, but most of them are contributed by contemporary business and government. Contributors of good examples exhibited in this book include *American Telephone and Telegraph Company, Bank of America, Hamilton Watch Company, International Latex Corporation, Ladies' Home Journal, Merrill Lynch, Pierce, Fenner & Smith, New York Stock Exchange, Life Magazine (Time, Inc.), United Air Lines, The Mutual Benefit Life Insurance Company of New Jersey, The Mutual Insurance Agency of Washington, D. C., The Wolf Magazine of Letters (The Wolf Envelope Company), Cleveland, Williamson-Dickie Manufacturing of Fort Worth, Woodward & Lothrop of Washington, D. C., Wyandotte Chemicals Corporation, General Services Administration, Internal Revenue Service,* and *Veterans Administration.*

## THE ART OF SAYING NO

### No Job

Abraham Lincoln's letter to Schuyler Colfax explaining the reason for rejecting him as a cabinet member is a notable example of forthrightness and tact.

Your letter of the 6th has just been handed me by Mr. Baker of Minnesota. When I said to you the other day that I wished to write you a letter I had reference, of course, to my not having offered you a cabinet appointment. I meant to say, and now do say, you were most honorably and amply recommended, and a tender of the appointment was not withheld, in any part, because of anything happening since 1858. Indeed, I should have decided as I did easier than I did had that matter never existed. I had partly made up my mind in favor of Mr. Smith— not conclusively, of course—before your name was mentioned in that connection. When you were brought forward I said, "Colfax is a young man, is already in position, is running a brilliant career, and is sure of a bright future in any event; with Smith, it is now or never." I considered either abundantly competent, and decided on the ground I have stated. I will now have to beg that you will not do me the injustice to suppose for a moment that I remember anything against you in malice.

Sixty-three years before Lincoln wrote this letter to Colfax, Thomas Jefferson was in Paris struggling with problems of our young nation. There, in reply to a stranger seeking a job, he demonstrated the art of saying No:

The circumstances escaped me of my having the honor of being made known to you by Mr. Walker of Charlottesville. However, I should not have been the less ready, had it been in my power, to have aided you in procuring employment in some bureau here. But stranger that I am, unconnected and un-acquainted, my solicitations in your behalf would be as ineffec-tual as improper. I should have been happy to have been able to render you this service, as I am sincerely concerned at the circumstance which has placed you in need of it.

As to the paper money in your hands, the States have not yet been able to make final arrangements for its redemption. But, as soon as they shall get their finances into some order, they will surely pay for it what it was worth in silver at the time you received it, with interest. The interest on loan-office certificates is, I think, paid annually in all States; and, in some of them, they have begun to make payments on the principal. These matters are managed for foreigners by the consul of their nation in America, where they have not a private friend to attend for them. . . .

Some of the same attributes of a good "No" letter are found in the following examples from contemporary business:

Your letter expressing an interest in a job with us is a compliment which we appreciate. There is no doubt that your experience qualifies you for a responsible position in sales; and if we had an opening in the Sales Department we would certainly want to consider you for the position. But with no immediate openings in view I am sure you will want to concentrate on more likely prospects.

Thank you for thinking of us and best wishes for your success.

## NO MORE CREDIT

It was a pleasure to hear from you, even though we cannot respond favorably to your request for additional credit.

Please do not feel that we are being arbitrary. In your case, as in all cases, we must take into consideration the financial information furnished us as well as the size of the balance owing and the age of the transactions this balance represents.

I realize that the picture may change—and I sincerely hope it will improve as we are eager to co-operate with you. Just as soon as you can give us more up-to-date and complete financial information which would justify an increase in the credit limit we shall be happy to make a change.

AN IDEA REJECTED

For ideas from our consumers on how we can better serve them with our products we are always grateful. So, first of all, let me say "thank you" for the interest which prompted your friendly letter.

There's a lot to be said in favor of your idea on packaging a S—— Aid Kit. You have expressed the "pros" well and convincingly. In this age of attractively packaged merchandise many homemakers, like you, must wonder why our company has passed up those eye-appealing packaged units.

Our side of the story is this: We want to produce and market top-quality products at the greatest possible savings in the retail cost to our consumers. We would, of course, have no choice but to pass the packaging cost on to you—the buying public. Most of our S—— items are small, which would mean a proportionately higher cost for individual packaging, and we have avoided collective packaging so you can always choose and purchase only those items you need.

As a token of our appreciation of your interest in our products we are sending you today—parcel post—a number of those small home aids so useful to you and to thousands of other homemakers. Remember, any one of these items can be purchased separately as you need it—and for only a few cents!

NO SALE!

Your excellent demonstration of the A—— machine was enjoyed by all of us who attended the showing last week; and I have thought seriously about your proposal on installing the machines in this office.

There is no doubt that you have a good machine and an efficient system for turning out letters accurately and economically. But, frankly, I am not convinced that our volume of correspondence—or what you call the "convenience" factor —warrants our purchase of the machines at this time. As our business grows we may be needing your help, in which event I'll not forget you.

Thank you for your courtesy.

JOB TURNED DOWN

No sampling of letters is complete without at least one by Henry Adams. Adams' voluminous published correspondence is personal, high-lighted by intimate accounts of his travels and of prominent people of his time. But here is an early business letter declining Whitelaw Reid's offer of a job on the New York Tribune. The trip to Europe, given as the reason for declining the offer, was to be Adams' honeymoon.

For my own satisfaction and amusement nothing would please me better than to join your fraternity and obtain an education for the press under your head, under the Tribune. Perhaps one of these days I may be glad to accept an invitation to do so. Just now, however, I can do no press work, because I am on the point of starting to Europe on a year's vacation. If you feel like calling me when I return, I may succumb to the invitation though I am tied here [Harvard] by the leg.

A VIGOROUS NO

H. G. Wells once wrote, "While the poor little affairs of obscure, industrious men of letters are made the subject of intensive research, the far more romantic, thrilling and illuminating documents about the seekers and makers of great fortunes are neither gathered nor cherished." Those who interest themselves in the literature of business will find infinite truth in that observation.

The last half of the nineteenth century and the early years of the twentieth were the golden age in the romance of business, with great fortunes in the making. Business letter writing became a fine art at the hands of men like Henry Lee Higginson, Clarence King, and C. B. Perkins who counted among their correspondents Henry Adams, William James, John Hay, John La Farge, the Howells, and Raphael Pumpelly.

As C. E. Perkins' broker, Henry Lee Higginson once offered to make good a loss which he felt may have been due to his carelessness. In response to this magnanimous offer, railroadman Perkins replied with a vigorous No.

I have your letter of August 23rd, and while it is very good of you to suggest paying my losses on Wisconsin Central, I think, on reflection, that you will agree with me that it is an utterly impracticable scheme, and one which I cannot consent to for a moment.

In the first place, supposing you did buy the bonds for me without an order to do so (which I am not sure about), I nevertheless knew about it within a very short time, and could have sold out then and there had I chosen to do so; but, as I preferred to take the chance of profit, I also necessarily took with it the chance of loss. Had I sold at once I could, no doubt, have gotten out even or better.

In the second place, since that time, and perhaps before, you have put me into things or let me into things out of which I have made money. So if you are to pay losses on these Wisconsin Centrals, we must go through the books for about forty years and have an accounting; and I must pay you back, no doubt, considerably more than you are now proposing to pay back to me.

In the third place, considering our relations for the last forty years, I shall agree to nothing of the kind, and will see you damned first!

## ANSWERS THAT "TELL" AND "SELL"

### THE HUMAN TOUCH

In the next letter, responding to an inquiry about life insurance, note how deftly the human touch is applied by personal pronouns.

Thank you for your inquiry concerning twenty-year endowment insurance for your grandson. The rate for $1,000 is $—— at his present age of 14. You will be glad to know that in giving him such a policy you would be starting him with the regular adult form of contract. It has cash values, annual dividends, and also the settlement option privileges which might be so important to him when he is older.

You will need the help of an agent and medical examiner in making the application. We are asking one of the Company's Boston representatives to get in touch with you about the next step. If your grandson does not live near you, the Boston office can nevertheless serve you in handling the purchase.

We look forward to helping you give your grandson a gift for which he will always thank you.

### A GOOD BEGINNING

Few of us will ever be called on to write letters about the history-making affairs of government and business, but all of us can profit by studying the style of men who have the power to make us see the big issues through their written words. In the next letter, vintage 1915, note how neatly Walter Hines Page referred to Edward M. House's letter which he was answering.

The sinking of the Arabic is the answer to the President and to your letter to me. And there'll be more such answers. You said to me one day after you had got back from your last visit to Berlin: "They are impossible." I think you told the truth, and surely you know your German and you know your Berlin —or you did know them when your were here.

The question is not what we have done for the Allies, not what any other neutral country has done or has failed to do— such comparisons, I think, are far from the point. The question is when the right moment arrives for us to save our self-respect, our honour, and the esteem and fear (or the contempt) in which the world will hold us.

Berlin has the Napoleonic disease. If you follow Napoleon's career—his excuses, his evasions, his inventions, the wild French enthusiasm and how he kept it up—you will find an exact parallel. That becomes plainer every day. Europe may not be wholly at peace in five years—maybe ten.

REPLYING IN THE PUBLIC INTEREST

With the following modern letter Keith Funston, president of the New York Stock Exchange, gives a clear answer on how the nation's market place is coping with a problem involving the public interest:

It was good of you to send along the forceful editorial on stock swindlers. This is a matter that concerns us deeply, and your own interest in it is of great encouragement.

Much of our educational effort in the Exchange Community in recent years has been directed at exposing and wiping out phony stock promoters. These operators are comparatively few, but we agree completely that they hurt not only their victims, but the economy as a whole and the responsible members of the securities industry.

Our own approach to the problem has been to warn the

public, through all media available to us, that quick overnight profits are rare, but that glib promoters are not; that sound investment stocks can be found and are good to have, but they don't make millionaires of the average investor. Accordingly, we have developed a series of yardsticks to guide the average investor and these are stressed in all of our advertising and educational material.

For example, we stress that there are risks as well as rewards in share ownership, and that one should tailor the risk to what he can afford. Equally, we urge people to stay away from tips, rumors, and vacant promises. We emphasize the need to understand investment objectives, get the facts and deal only with a reputable broker. One example of the kind of constructive work we can undertake is found in the booklet issued earlier this year, "How to Protect Yourself from Stock Swindles," which was prepared by the Better Business Bureau of New York, the New York Stock Exchange and other groups in the securities industry. If you have not seen it, I believe you will be interested in the enclosed copy.

In the long run, of course, education is necessarily a slow process. We have found that through rules and regulations we can protect people against a good many things—but not against their own cupidity.

For this reason we are always grateful when powerful editorial voices focus additional attention on this and other aspects of our investment life. Your constructive approach is welcomed. We are constantly exploring new ways to get our story before the public.

ON CLOSING AN ACCOUNT: A GRACIOUS REPLY TO BAD NEWS

I was sorry to learn from your letter of June 24 that you are closing your account with us. It is sincerely hoped that this interruption of our business relationship will be temporary only and that we may have you with us again soon. It has been a pleasure to serve you.

This severance of our business relationship should in no way affect our personal association; so please feel free to call upon me if I can be of service to you in any way. Stop in for a visit whenever you are in this area.

Kindest regards!

ADJUSTMENTS WITH A SMILE

Recently Mr. A—— in our San Francisco warehouse passed along your letter about invoice S 9032 for $174.30. We regret that a duplicate shipment was made and have extended the dating on the invoice to February 1, as you requested.

Our best wishes for the holiday season and the New Year!

Of course you may return the blue blouse. How we happened to send you a blue one when your order plainly specified white, it is difficult to understand. Thanks for giving us the opportunity to make the exchange.

As soon as we receive the blue blouse we will issue you a credit. Meanwhile you would probably like to have the white garment, so we are mailing it today and charging it to your account.

I don't blame you in the least for questioning our action in charging your account for $30.20 in unearned discount. We did so only because the payment was not received until October 7, more than a week after the discount period had expired. Now that you tell us that your check was mailed on September 29, we certainly do not want you to lose a discount because of a delay for which you are not responsible.

Credit to offset the $30.20 charge will appear on your next statement. Thank you for helping us set the matter straight.

## LETTERS THAT GET ANSWERED

### "DO ME A FAVOR"

Dale Carnegie (*How to Win Friends and Influence People*) tells how sales promotion manager Ken Dyke got a 500 to 800 per cent increase in responses to his letters by applying the "do-me-a-favor" psychology. By the manner of asking a simple favor we can make our readers feel a sense of importance, as in this letter:

> I wonder if you'll help me out of a little difficulty?
>
> About a year ago I persuaded our company that one of the things architects most needed was a catalogue which would give them the whole story of all J-M building materials and their part in repairing and remodeling homes.
>
> The attached catalogue resulted—the first of its kind.
>
> But now our stock is getting low, and when I mentioned it to our president he said (as presidents will) that he would have no objection to another editon provided I furnished satisfactory evidence that the catalogue had done the job for which it was designed.
>
> Naturally, I must come to you for help, and I am therefore taking the liberty of asking you and forty-nine other architects in various parts of the country to be the jury.
>
> To make it quite easy for you, I have written a few simple questions on the back of this letter. And I'll certainly regard it as a personal favor if you'll check the answers, add any comments that you may wish to make, and then slip this letter into the enclosed stamped envelope.
>
> Needless to say, this won't obligate you in any way, and I now leave it to you to say whether the catalogue shall be discontinued or reprinted with improvements based on your experience and advice.
>
> In any event, rest assured that I shall appreciate your co-operation very much. Thank you!

THE COMPLIMENT

Moved by a simple compliment, Abraham Lincoln replied:

> Everyone likes a compliment. Thank you for yours on my little notification speech and on the recent inaugural address. I expect the latter to wear as well as—perhaps better than—anything I have produced; but I believe it is not immediately popular. Men are not flattered by being shown that there has been a difference of purpose between the Almighty and them. To deny it, however, in this case, is to deny that there is a God governing the world. It is truth which I thought needed to be told, and, as whatever humiliation there is in it falls most directly on myself, I thought others might afford for me to tell it.

The effectiveness of a compliment will be seen in this modern letter requesting information which was promptly furnished:

> So many good reports have reached me about your company pension plan that I am eager to learn more about it. Any information you are willing to give me about your plan will certainly be appreciated.
>
> Your company has earned a fine reputation for employee-employer relationships—one of which you may well be proud.

## VOICE OF THE PEOPLE

Taxpayers and customers often write letters offering comments, suggestions and opinions on the manner of running government and business. Of these letters Thomas Jefferson had this to say in a letter to a Committee of the Merchants of New Haven:

> I have received the remonstrance you were pleased to address to me on the appointment of Samuel Bishop to the office of

collector of New Haven . . . The right of our fellow citizens to represent to the public functionaries their opinion on proceedings interesting to them is unquestionably a constitutional right, often useful, sometimes necessary, and will always be respectfully acknowledged by me.

## GOVERNMENT ACKNOWLEDGES A VOICE

In acknowledging a voice, former Federal Trade Commissioner Lowell B. Mason wrote this reply, which was exhibited in the original *Plain Letters:*

Thank you for your letter of June 18 stating the reasons for maintaining the present status of Section 2 (c) of the Robinson–Patman Act.

They are the usual arguments in favor of this law, but you have expressed them so well, so carefully and in such an open and friendly manner that I confess not only admiration for your presentation, but complete agreement with many of your points.

There is, however, more to the problem than either you or I have covered. With your leave, I shall search out in a later note some of the pros and cons of this most interesting subject which we might consider together.

June has been a heavy month for me, so I expect to take a short vacation, what Walt Whitman described as the "white spaces in life." You will hear from me the latter part of July.

## BUSINESS ACKNOWLEDGES A VOICE

Your suggestion on the problems of rerouting and reissuing tickets has a lot of merit. These are problems not only for us but for the entire industry; and for that reason we are arranging to have your proposal brought before the Air Traffic Conference Committee presently working on the problem.

We recently received a similar proposal from one of our air travel plan subscribers who felt that it would be a good idea to leave off the fare until completion of the travel. The total could then be computed and the Company billed accordingly. A survey was made and it was learned that the majority of subscribers wanted fare information on tickets at the time of issuance. Otherwise the card holders would have no figures to enter on their expense reports after completing their trips.

Since the entire matter is now under study your suggestion is particularly timely. Thank you for your interest and your courtesy in writing us.


## LETTERS TO CHILDREN

Young Americans frequently write government departments and well-known business organizations, especially those departments and companies engaged in activities that fire the imagination of the youthful. The vice-president of one company commented that "theme writing" was one of their activities, meaning that his company answered letters from children requesting facts about the science of his business. The literature sent in response to these requests usually goes out with a simple and inspiring letter.

The tone for a letter to a young child may be captured from this one by Abraham Lincoln:

> Your friend, Leroy C. Driggs, tells me you are a very earnest friend of mine, for which please allow me to thank you. You and those of your age are to take charge of this country when we older ones shall have gone; and I am glad to learn that you already take so lively an interest in what just now so deeply concerns us.

A few years ago, as an assignment in his general science class, a fourteen-year-old boy asked Cleo F. Craig, then president of Atlantic

Telephone and Telegraph Company, these questions: "Why should I go to school?" and "What benefits will I get out of it?" In reply Mr. Craig wrote this thoughtful and simple letter:

*I was pleased and complimented to have you write to me. The two questions you ask—"Why should I go to school?" and "What benefits will I get out of it?"—are two of the most important questions in the world. I have thought about them often, but I have never tried to put my thoughts down in black and white—especially for a young person to read. Of course, it has been quite a while since I have been in school—as you think of it—but really I still go to school every day. School is just a name for a place where we learn things, and each day I keep on learning—or at least I hope I do.*

*We go to school so that we shall grow up to be useful and happy people. When we think of school, we think of learning things which will help us make a living and support a family. That, of course, is important, and each of us must learn to read and write and do mathematics, and develop other skills which will be tools in our hands as we go through life. But to me that is not the most important. School, or to call it by a broader term, "education," should teach us how to live, how to be happy, how to be useful. That is what really makes life worth living.*

*A good education gives us understanding, and understanding tends to make us like each other, which after all is the real secret of happiness. Many of the bad things in this world come from ignorance and misunderstanding. We must understand one another and the world around us. And this understanding comes best from familiarity with the thoughts and acts of the world's greatest and noblest men and women. We study history and literature and science to become familiar with what these great men and women have thought and done. We study these people so that we can understand what made them great; so that in turn we can make the world a better* place because we have lived. They are the inspiration for us to do our very best.

You ought to remember too that school is not just the class-room. It is the football and baseball field, the gym, the tennis court—everywhere you go with your friends. You are learning every minute and what you are learning is important. In these games as in your studies, you will learn perseverance, concentration, and also the art of being a good sport—a thoughtful friend.

Add all of these things together and you have a good schooling, a well-rounded education, which will make each day all through your life happier and will bring happiness to all around you. That is why we go to school.

I'm afraid that I have not said this as I should like to, but I hope it will give you something from which you can start your own thinking. Your teacher must be a very wise person to have suggested this question for your study. I am grateful to you for giving me the opportunity of thinking about these things again and for bringing back to my mind my own school days and the many fine teachers I was privileged to study under.

Please tell your family that we are proud to have them as share owners of this Company. I hope that you, too, will be one some day.


INVITATIONS

DINNER AT THE WHITE HOUSE

Winthrop Rockefeller, John L. Lewis, Bishop Fulton J. Sheen, Rabbi Abba H. Silver, movie director Darryl Zanuck and several hundred others have received this informal letter inviting them to one of President Eisenhower's famous stag dinners:

I wonder if it would be convenient for you to come to an in-formal stag dinner . . . I suggest that we meet at the White

House about half-past seven, have a reasonably early dinner and devote the evening to general chat. While I am hopeful that you can attend, I realize that you already may have engagements which would interfere. If so, I assure you of my complete understanding. I shall probably wear a dinner coat but a business suit will be entirely appropriate.

With warmest personal regards,

DWIGHT D. EISENHOWER

#### DINNER HONORING A BUSINESS OR PROFESSIONAL ASSOCIATE

With this explicit letter Henry L. Nelson, once editor of *Harper's Weekly*, invited Hamilton W. Mabie to a dinner in Mabie's honor:

It gives me great pleasure to invite you, in the name of a committee of your friends, to a dinner in your honor to be given at a date most convenient to you. I have reserved three evenings at the University Club, April 26, 28 and 29, but as the earliest of these will interfere with your lectures at Baltimore, I wish to leave the matter to you. Perhaps you would prefer even a later date than April 29, although I rather hope not, since I must be in Williamstown on May 3, and expect to be away several days.

The other members of the committee are Frank Stetson, W. D. Howells, Henry van Dyke, Andrew Carnegie and W. H. Mallory.

#### BUSINESS AT LUNCH

Having just heard that you will be in New York City during the week of September 14 I hasten to get you committed to a luncheon on any day of that week most convenient for you. I know what a hectic schedule you'll be having, and I hope I *can entice you by promising to lunch at your favorite restaurant. Let me know what day suits you best. I'll ask C. M. B—— and R. I. C—— to join us so we can once again probe your suggestions about the X—— bond issue.*

### INVITATION TO BUSINESS

*We are now planning an advertising campaign to introduce a new product in this country and Canada. Would you like to talk it over and suggest what your firm might do for us?*

*You would oblige me if you could call at my office between 2 and 4 P.M. next Tuesday, September 15. Please notify me if this is convenient. If it isn't, perhaps we can set another date. Thank you.*

### ACCEPTING WITH ENTHUSIASM

When Ambassador Walter Hines Page gave England's Archbishop of York a letter of introduction to Theodore Roosevelt, he at the same time wrote Roosevelt to inform him of the Archbishop's impending visit to this country. The vigorous Roosevelt replied with typical enthusiasm and a word of praise for the Ambassador:

*I am very much pleased with you letter, and as soon as the Archbishop arrives he will be addressed by me with all his titles, and I will get him to lunch with me or dine with me or do anything else he wishes. I shall do it for his own sake, and still more, my dear fellow, I shall do it for the sake of the Ambassador who has represented America in London during these trying years as no other Ambassador has ever represented us, with the exception of Charles Francis Adams during the Civil War.*

## INTRODUCTIONS AND RECOMMENDATIONS

Clarence King, geologist and mining expert, was renowned for his wit. When Ruskin offered him the choice of two Turner water colors he replied, "One good Turner deserves another," and took both of them. The same good humor is found in this letter introducing Thomas Sturgis to Horace F. Cutter:

> Life is so short and uncertain that I find myself in haste for you and my friend Mr. Thomas Sturgis, who will "serve this notice" on you, to know each other. I have felt it a privilege to know in you the intimate companion of Socrates. My friend who is like yourself somewhat divided between the hot pursuit of modern things and the contemplation of the too-much-forgotten glories of the past, will be I know a welcome acquaintance to my dear philosopher, my valued anachronism, my friend of the book and the owl. Perhaps the dust still lingers on some solitary glass cylinder known only to you in the secret recesses of the Union Club cellar, and that you will draw out the cork and my friend at the same time.

Letters of introduction are rare nowadays, but many of us are called on to write letters of recommendation which are akin to introductions. Here is an example of a to-the-point and convincing recommendation:

> I understand that Mr. W—— G—— J—— is an applicant for admission as a transfer student to your school.
> Mr. J—— has been employed by us as a messenger since September 19, 1958. During that time he has applied himself intelligently and conscientiously to his duties. He is highly regarded by our customers and our staff; and as one of a group of 135 serving in the same capacity he is outstanding in every respect.

*I am writing this letter, of course, at Mr. J——'s request, but I can say honestly that I am glad to do so. I hope that he is successful in his efforts to gain admission to your school.*

## SALES LETTERS

Usually written by professionals nowadays, sales letters are calculated to appeal to the reader's wants. Most of them are classified more properly as advertising than as letters. But here are two examples composed to conform to the style of personal letters rather than ads. In each of these letters the appeal is to the reader's want for security.

*Did you know that your estate may be subject to a mortgage that you did not sign?*

*Whether your estate is passed under your will or by gifts and trusts during your lifetime, there will be certain taxes which must be paid to the State and Federal Government in cash. These taxes are generally the largest single item of expense in an estate. Through proper planning you can often arrange your estate to save your heirs substantial tax expense.*

*Now, particularly, husbands and wives should carefully consider the revision of the Wills and Trusts to secure the tax savings permitted under the Revenue Act of 1948. To enjoy the benefits of the act you must meet the legal requirements.*

*Why not call or phone me that I may arrange an interview with one of our trust officers? He will be pleased to explain these tax matters to you, and I feel that the interview may result in real savings for you and your family.*

*Have you ever thought how easily your vacation might be ruined if you "trust to luck" and carry your travel fund around with you in cash? You wouldn't have to take a very long trip, either, to be seriously inconvenienced by loss of cash.*

As a reminder to TRAVEL CAREFREE this year, I am enclosing a pamphlet on our Travelers Cheques. You will notice that the cost is small—only 75¢ for each $100. When you plan your next trip, make a mental note to stop in here at the branch for those blue-and-gold aids to worry-free travel. They are your financial passports—anytime, anywhere!

The ad-style letter is designed to attract the reader's attention, often with bright colors, pictures and gimmicks. You may have received one of those brilliant pink letters from *Life* magazine with a window in the back of the envelope displaying a number of pennies —one of them real—and enticing you to open the envelope with the message that every word inside is worth a penny. The letter begins:

DEAR READER,—
Every word in this letter is worth a penny to you!
For there are just three hundred and eighty-four words in this invitation to subscribe to LIFE magazine for thirty-one issues for only three dollars and ninety-one cents.
That's just about three-quarters of a year of LIFE—a $7.75 newstand value at a saving of $3.84—25¢-a-copy LIFE for only 12½¢ a week! . . .

In another letter we find the *Ladies' Home Journal* appealing to a woman's passion for bargains.

DEAR READER:
Every woman loves a bargain . . . and that's why we want to tell you all about this special money-saving offer for LADIES' HOME JOURNAL of
22 SPARKLING ISSUES FOR ONLY $3.85 . . .

## GOOD-WILL LETTERS

### TO AN EMPLOYEE ON A SERVICE ANNIVERSARY

Many executives write notes congratulating employees on an anniversary of service with the company. Warm and inspiring words are the secret of the better letters in this category.

> My secretary just reminded me that you will soon observe your twentieth anniversary with our company.
>
> To many of our associates twenty years must seem a long time. But to those of us who have shared these years time is a meaningless measure. And this little note is not so much to congratulate you on a milestone as to express my thankfulness for the willingness with which you keep moving forward and up.
>
> For those years ahead, my very best wishes!

### WELCOMING A NEW SHARE OWNER

With this letter President Robert B. Semple of Wyandotte Chemicals Corporation welcomes a new share owner and invites suggestions:

> The management of Wyandotte Chemicals Corporation welcomes you as a share owner.
>
> In April, July and October we shall send you interim reports on the sales and earnings progress of the Company. Sometime after the first of the year annual reports not only covering Wyandotte's performance for the year but also stating to some degree its plans for the future, will be sent to you.
>
> Wyandotte is a basic producer of many products for industry. Our industrial chemicals find their way into literally hundreds of products you use each day, such as glass, paper, soap, rayon

and plastics, to mention a few. Bulk materials such as cement, coke and limestone find their way into other basic industries. We are also, through our J. B. Ford Division, a major producer of cleaning products for business and industry. Among these are materials for cleaning metals, railroad cars, locomotives and airplanes; products that assure sanitation wherever food and beverages are prepared or served; floor and wall washing cleaners; germicides; detergents, sours, sizes and bleaches for commercial laundries.

As you become better acquainted with our product fields we know you will recognize the broad service Wyandotte provides.

My associates in the management join me in inviting you to let us have any suggestions you may have for the betterment of the company.

### REMEMBERING AN OLD CUSTOMER ON AN ACCOUNT ANNIVERSARY

We are sharing an anniversary today.

The occasion? Today marks the tenth year since you opened your account with us. It's an important day to us and, we hope, to you too.

One of the nicest features of being in business is the opportunity to serve customers over a number of years. It makes us happy to know that we are rendering a service which continues to merit your approval year after year.

You may be sure we will make every effort to maintain and improve our service so that we may celebrate many more anniversaries together.

### BIDDING FOR THE BUSINESS OF A NEWCOMER

Welcome to Sacramento!

We understand that you and your family plan to reside

here, and we know you will find Sacramento a pleasant and friendly place in which to live and work.

If there is anything we can do to help you in getting started, please come in and let us know. Our business requires us to keep closely informed on local conditions and we may be able to help you in a number of ways.

If you require our services we should welcome the opportunity to include you among our customers.

CONGRATULATIONS ON A SPEECH

When Woodrow Wilson made a speech that won Franklin K. Lane's hearty approval, Lane wrote this enthusiastic letter:

That was a bully speech, a corker! You may have made a better speech in your life but I never have heard of it. Other Presidents may have made better speeches, but I have never heard of them. It was simply great because it was the proper blend of philosophy and practicality . . . You know this country, and every country, wants a man to lead it of whom it is proud, not just because of his talent but because of his personality—that which is as indefinable as charm in a woman. And I want to see your personality known to the American people, just as well as we know it who sit around the Cabinet table. Your speech glows with it, and that is why it gives me so much joy that I can't help writing you as enthusiastically as I do.

CONGRATULATIONS ON ELECTION AS A COMPANY OFFICER

My morning paper tells me that you have been elected Senior Vice-President and Director of ———. Congratulations, old man! It's a wise company management you have when it comes to picking the right man for the job.

*Your success is assured, so I'll simply make the wish that our paths cross soon.*

## CONGRATULATIONS ON ELECTION TO A CIVIC OFFICE

*I was pleased to learn of your recent election to the Board of Governors of the —— Chamber of Commerce. This is an important honor and a reflection of your active participation in civic affairs.*

*Congratulations—hearty and sincere!*

## WORD OF SYMPATHY

*We who had the privilege of being closely associated with your husband fully realize how fine he was and what a loss the community has sustained by his death.*

*He will be missed greatly by all of us who valued his counsel and enjoyed his friendship.*

*I wish to express to you the deepest sympathy of my associates and myself.*

The next letter is said to be one of the most widely read in American history—Lincoln's letter to Mrs. Bixby on the loss of her five sons in the Civil War:

*I have been shown in the files of the War Department a statement of the Adjutant General of Massachusetts that you are the mother of five sons who have died gloriously on the field of battle. I feel how weak and fruitless must be any word of mine which should attempt to beguile you from the grief of a loss so overwhelming. But I cannot refrain from tendering you the consolation that may be found in the thanks of the republic they died to save. I pray that our Heavenly Father* may assuage the anguish of your bereavement, and leave you only the cherished memory of the loved and lost, and the solemn pride that must be yours to have laid so costly a sacrifice upon the altar of freedom.

Compare Lincoln's letter with this coldly impersonal letter said to have been written by the Kaiser Wilhelm to a mother on the loss of nine sons in World War I:

His Majesty the Kaiser hears that you have sacrificed nine sons in defense of the Fatherland in the present war. His Majesty is immensely gratified at the fact, and in recognition is pleased to send you his photograph with frame and autograph signature.

OIL ON TROUBLED WATERS

To allay General Meade's surprise and vexation at Lincoln's show of disappointment when General Robert E. Lee's Army escaped, Major General Halleck offered these words of reassurance:

I take this method of writing you a few words which I could not well communicate in any other way. Your fight at Gettysburg met with universal approbation of all military men here. You handled your troops in that battle as well, if not better, than any general has handled his army during the war. You brought all your forces into action at the right time and place, which no commander of the Army of the Potomac has done before. You may well be proud of that battle. The President's order of proclamation of July 4th showed how much he appreciated your success.

And now a few words in regard to subsequent events. You should not have been surprised or vexed at the President's disappointment at the escape of Lee's army. He had examined into all the details of sending you reinforcements to satisfy himself that every man who could possibly be spared from other places had been sent to your army. He thought that Lee's defeat was so certain that he felt no little impatience at his unexpected escape. I have no doubt, General, that you felt the disappointment as keenly as any one else. Such things sometimes occur to us without any fault of our own. Take it altogether, your short campaign has proved your superior generalship, and you merit, as you will receive, the confidence of the Government and the gratitude of the country. I need not assure you, General, that I have lost none of the confidence which I felt in you when I recommended you for the command.


## APOLOGY

### FDR TO WENDELL WILLKIE

As an apology for a news leak, Franklin D. Roosevelt wrote this personal letter to Wendell Willkie, his opponent in the Presidential campaign:

A most unfortunate thing happened at my Press Conference on Friday. I had written you on July thirteenth, just as I was leaving for my trip to Hawaii and Alaska, a purely personal note telling you I hoped much to see you on a non-campaign subject sometime after I got back. Quite frankly when I was asked—in a series of questions about foreign affairs—whether I had written you to invite you to Washington, I said "No." That afternoon Steve Early said to me "Are you sure you did not write to Wendell Willkie?" And it flashed into my mind then that I had written you before I left.

The interesting thing is how word of my note to you got out to the Press. I have been trying to find out where the leak was down here, as I regarded it as a purely personal note between you and me. As far as I can remember I said nothing about it to anybody, though it is possible that I told Leo Crowley that I was going to ask you if we could talk the subject over. I am awfully sorry that there was any leak on a silly thing like this, but I still hope that at your convenience—there is no immediate hurry—you will stop in and see me if you are in Washington or run up to Hyde Park if you prefer. . . .

## GARDEN-VARIETY APOLOGY

Apologies are to be offered, too, for the more prosaic mishaps of everyday business. A customer doused with coffee got this note of apology:

Few things are more aggravating than having coffee or food spilled on a person's clothes. According to a report I have received you were subject to this aggravation while we were serving you.

Please have the garment renovated by a reputable cleaning establishment, and send me the bill. Our reimbursement check will be forwarded immediately.

Thank you for helping us make this adjustment. We look forward to serving you often in the future.

A customer who received an undeserved notice that his account was past-due got this note of apology:

Normally when we send a customer a notice that his account is past due we hopefully anticipate that he will receive it, read it, and heed it. But I just discovered that we sent you a notice last week that I hope you didn't receive or—if you did—that you paid no attention whatever to it.

Your account is not past-due, Mr. S——. The fact is, we owe

you $18.75 for overpayment instead of your owing us. Shall we send you our check or would you like to apply this credit on a future purchase?

Please forgive us for what must seem to be carelessness, but which I assure you is not typical of our usual practices in this office.


## COLLECTION: THE ART OF PERSUASION

Every company that extends credit is bound to write collection letters. Many businessmen consider the collection letter one of the most difficult to write. Unlike most letter writers the credit man has not one but two audiences for his letters, neither of which is likely to applaud even his best efforts. Before him is a touchy group of slow-paying customers, while on the sidelines stand the company's sales force, understandably jealous guardians of customer appeasement. With management looking over his shoulder for results, the credit man is expected to produce letters that will exhort dollars and at the same time avoid driving customers to other suppliers. This is a task that demands practice of the art of persuasion.

Long-winded letters extolling the virtues of honesty and threatening the damnations of ruined credit are as rare these days as business letters written in longhand. The modern and resultful collection letter is short and tactful like those exhibited here.


### FIRST REMINDERS

Printed notices rather than conventional letters are widely used as first reminders of past-due accounts. This is a sensible practice, but the flippancy of some of the notices may strike you, as it does many others, as ill-advised. There is nothing funny about unpaid obligations. The attempt to make light of the matter with pictures of a short-skirted girl pawing through a file cabinet and saying

"Tucked your bill away?" may seem to put an intelligent customer in the class with morons.

A simple dignity is favored by most companies for past-due notices, as:

*DID IT GO ASTRAY . . .*
*the reminder we sent you that your account with us is overdue . . . or was there something wrong with our statement? If the latter, please let us know at once.*
*Otherwise, if you haven't already done so, won't you send us a check right away?*

Time-minded Hamilton Watch Company writes this unusual and appealing letter:

3:30 P.M. *Hamilton Watch TIME*
*January 29, 1959*

*Gentlemen,—TIME is a very important item to everyone— for you and me it has added significance because it is part of our business.*

*The unit of TIME I must mention to you today is not minutes or hours, but can best be measured in weeks and months. Do you realize that it has been over a month since we last received a payment on your account?*

*The past-due balance remains $——. The TIME to send us a check is now. Thank you for your TIMELY co-operation.*

Time is also the theme of the next letter, with which another manufacturer appeals for payment:

*As a sales-minded and progressive retailer, you fully account for the hours of your day, even before you open your doors in the morning.*

*I am sure you wanted to respond to our reminders, but it's* easy to understand why you might not have found time. You are aware of the importance of keeping your account up to date, however; and you will want to spend a few minutes with it now.

If you have some questions, please let us know and we'll be happy to supply any information needed. If, as we believe, your figures agree with ours, you'll want to send us your check for $289.60 now.

You will note the positive approach in these letters. The face-saving approach is also a commonly employed technique of successful collectors, as:

We realize that unforeseen circumstances sometimes make it difficult to meet bills when they fall due. So if you have been put to some unexpected expense that makes it impossible for you to send us a check on your unpaid balance, please let us know when we may expect it.

You will find us more than willing to co-operate with you in every way we can. But do let us hear from you right away.

HOLDING ORDERS

Your customers have come to recognize your store as their neighborhood headquarters for ———.

Certainly you want to maintain a complete inventory from which they might make their selections while shopping in your store. You wouldn't want to lose a single possible sale just because you might be lacking a particular color or size.

Your most recent order is being held awaiting payment of the overdue balance on your account. I would like to rush this order to you, and I will see that it is handled promptly just as soon as your check is received.

A self-addressed envelope is enclosed. Why not slip your payment inside and mail it today?

PRESSING FOR A FRIENDLY SETTLEMENT

When his assistants were unsuccessful in their collection efforts, a credit manager tried this appeal:

> Your account has been referred to me with the recommendation that it be closed and the balance now due placed with our attorneys for collection.
>
> It would be a shame to terminate our business relations in this unsatisfactory manner, and I just can't bring myself to believe that it is not possible to obtain your co-operation.
>
> We had confidence in your willingness and ability to pay when we extended this credit. We still have confidence in your good intentions.
>
> Won't you please put forth whatever special effort is needed to send us your check today? Better still, telegraph payment today collect . . . at my expense. I have asked that action be withheld 24 hours pending your telegram.
>
> I'm counting on you.

The next two letters are an amusing twist on a serious effort to settle an account. A finance company sent this last-ditch plea for payment:

> For one year now we have tried fruitlessly to secure the balance on your account. We have brought judgment against you, we have endeavored to appeal to your sense of shame and to your sense of justice. Now we shall make one last appeal— this time to your sense of sportsmanship. This is our last offer. We herewith agree to forget one half of your balance of $200 if you will be sporting enough to do something about the other half. We challenge your sense of fair play as a last resort. Will you meet us half way?

To this appeal came the reply:

> You ask me if I am a sport. I am. You've made me a sporting proposition that no sporting man can turn down. I hereby agree to meet you half way. You forget one half of that bill—I'll forget the other half!

## REPORT BY LETTER

As a young lawyer in Boston around the turn of the century, Owen D. Young, later Board Chairman of General Electric, must have been influenced by the fine letter writers of Boston's then famed State Street. Mr. Young is one of the best of our contemporary business writers. In a letter to Dr. Rufus Jones of Haverford College, Pennsylvania, the versatile Young proved himself an educator as well as an industrial giant by this report of his views.

> In my views the objective of an American college should be to assist a student:
> 1. To develop his character.
> 2. To stimulate his intuitions and emotions.
> 3. To discover his mental aptitude and to train it.
> 4. To learn enough about an organized machinery of society to apply his gifts effectively.
> 5. To acquire skill in communications with others. That means language both oral and written and manners, too.
>
> I think I have stated these objectives in order of their importance. The first two items seem to me largely neglected. In the third item too much emphasis is put on training and too little on discovery. In the fourth, too much stress is put on the selfish satisfaction of the individual and too little on his obligations to society. The fifth must be a suitable carrier for the kind of load which is to be put upon it; that is to say, if the man operates in a field of science, clearness and accuracy are essential. If in the field of politics and literature, style must be added.

Now I know that this is all so general that it may seem like a mere set of platitudes, but it is not so in my mind. A very complete course on obligations should be developed. I do not mean a sermon or a set of them, but practical instructions on what is expected of a man of character and why. The extent to which the whole world must rely upon it—how states, especially democracies, must have it—how it is more important to credit and currencies than the gold which is back of them— this will give you a glimpse of the kind of thing that is in my mind. We teach men to rely so much on their minds alone that the thousand and one subconscious nervous reactions become dwarfed in process of education. Our emotions suffer too from our science and mathematics and our fashionable scientific methods of dealing with history, art and literature. There is not enough of human contacts and understanding of human emotions.

## GOOD RESULTS FROM PLAIN LETTERS

The Veterans Administration under the leadership of dynamic Administrator Sumner G. Whittier is making an all-out effort to revolutionize its style of letter writing. Clerks, stenographers, supervisors and directors alike are participating in training courses based on the 4-S principles of plain letters. The campaign is promoted by newsletters, bulletin board announcements, and other publicity methods. In this enthusiastic circular letter Mr. Whittier proves his own skill in the use of simple and inspiring words:

To My Fellow Letterwriters:

Many of you are already aware of my keen interest in good letters—good "4-S" letters: short, simple, strong and sincere!
I am pleased at the way 4-S training is sweeping VA. I am proud, too, that VA is known as a leader in correspondence

*improvement. It's a wonderful reputation to have. And it's worth enhancing. You have my fullest support in your efforts to make VA letter writing the promptest, friendliest, best in the world.*

*Think of the warm pleasure it brings to a veteran, a widow, a dependent—to receive a warm, helpful letter from his or her Government! A letter that can be understood! When I see file drawers full of records I see faces, not cards. The faces of men, women and children. I hope you do, too. Genuine service to those who served means writing, thinking, and doing for those folks in an understanding manner.*

*We must be patient with each other as we learn to write better. Many letters, of course, will have to be rewritten— some perhaps several times—to sharpen our 4-S skills. But I know I can count on you to face these irritations with patience, with understanding, and with the will to work together toward better letters. Let's write our way into the hearts and hopes of the millions we serve.*

The VA drive for 4-S letters is paying off. Such pomposities as "non-compensable evaluation of service-connected disability" are giving way to humanness and informality. Witness this simple and human reply to a veteran who had vented his wrath over a lapsed insurance notice sent him in error:

*You are right! We are wrong! Your policy did not lapse.*
*You did send us $15.80 on July 21. We made a mistake and posted it as $7.90. Thank you for telling us about the error.*
*Premiums are paid through October 31. The next premium of $7.90 is due November 1, 1958.*

The grateful veteran receiving the above letter came back with:

*Thanks for your letter.*
*I'm sorry I blew my top. We all make mistakes, but not all*

*of us will admit it. It's nice to find a government agency that doesn't try to cover up with eight-cylinder words.*

*Here's my check for $7.90 for November.*


## BEFORE YOU SAY NO . . .

One of the most delightful series of letters to be published in recent years is reprinted here by permission of *National Review.* I think we can all learn a lesson in letter writing from the enterprising young businessman and his wise elders who wrote this engaging correspondence.

*March 7, 1958*

DEAR MRS. HEATH:

*I wish to ask you a great favor. My brother David goes to Cranwell and he says they go easier on brothers, so I might have a chance to get in even though my grades aren't so terribly good. But I need three letters of recommendation and I have one from a priest and one from a nun and my father says he thinks the third one better be from someone who is not a priest or a nun. You are not a priest or a nun but yet you know me intamitely from me having delivered your paper even that bad day right after Christmas when their was no school and the Times boy didn't deliver his customers, and from those Catholic Christmas cards you always buy, and from the jack lantern pumpkins I helped you carve three years in a row, and the Easter Eggs, and a lot of other things. (Like the time I picked up John when he broke his arm and taught Priscilla how to ride a two-wheeler.)*

*Before you say no, I did break the trampoline but I didn't honestly know how heavy I was, because I grew very suddenly and the only reason I was always on the roof was because of my gliders which you said I could get if they were on the roof, and the time you wouldn't let me come in your back yard for three*

weeks that time, Catholic Word of Honor, John started it and
it was not my fault because Scout's Honor, I only gave John the
most compleatly gentle kind of tap so he would go home so
Georgie Cunningham wouldn't beat him up, because you know
how Georgie is when he get's mad. Because John threw a mud
ball at him on his bycicle. Not that you were wrong, but that
I'm explaning now, because you were so mad then you wouldn't
give me a chance to explane, because John got their first and he
fed you a lot of garbage. But I still like John, he is a fine young
boy, he has been well brought up by his Mother.

But even if sometimes you don't get along with me too well,
I always think of you as my "Oldest Friend" so I hope you will
do me this great favor of writing me a letter of recommendation.

Thanking you for your trouble,

Respectfully yours,<br>
PETER BAILEY-GATES

P.S. Thank you for the pennies of which I already had the
1926 San Francisco mint but I did not have the 1921 Denver.
Do you have a 1905 Indian Head, I will pay one nickel, clear
profit of four (4) ¢?

March 7, 1958

DEAR PETER:

I would be glad to write you a letter of recommendation to
Cranwell, and I am very flattered that you asked me. Of course,
I will have to tell the Truth, the Whole Truth and Nothing But
the Truth, so I hope nobody will be careless enough to allow
my letter to fall into the hands of the police. I can't tell you
how much I would miss you if you had to spend the next ten
years in a reformatory.

Respectably yours,<br>
MRS. H.

P.S. No, I haven't got a 1905 Indian Head, which saddens me
very much, but what saddens me more is the fact that even after

three years' acquaintanceship you don't know me well enough to realize that I also know that this particular penny is worth $6.00! You and your 4¢ profit—hah! I've told you and told you about my high I.Q. Don't you believe me? However, just to show you I bear no grudge, I will give you my duplicate of the 1911 no mint mark—for free yet!

Respectably yours,<br>Mrs. H.

P.P.S. Don't worry about my letter. I will bet you one dollar (from me) to one doughnut (from you) that you will get into Cranwell—not because you're such a hot-shot, you understand, but because if I'm crazy enough to like you, your priest and your nun are probably suffering from the same form of insanity. On the other hand, they may know you even better than I do, God help them!

Respectably yours,<br>Mrs. H.

March 9, 1958

To Whom It May Concern:

Peter Bailey-Gates has been in and out of my house almost daily for the past three years—by "almost," I mean those short sentences of exile which I have been unkind enough to impose upon Peter—and in that time I have come to know him very well indeed: as friend, paper boy, fellow penny-collector, and as combined decorator, waiter and entertainer at my younger children's birthday parties.

I have found Peter to be unfailingly good-humored, well-mannered and considerate—all of which qualities stand him in good stead in his relations with the public, which are many and varied. I am sure that no boy in New England, much less West Hartford, has been engaged in so many intricate business enterprises as Peter Bailey-Gates. I have bought, hired, subscribed

to, invested in, paid and been paid interest on fully a dozen of
his ventures in the last three years—not even counting his
snow-shoveling, leaf-raking, apple-picking and garbage-can-toting,
for which my own young sons are recruited. Peter's financial sense
is, however, no deterrent to his feeling for what is fitting and
proper: when he washed the car of the 70-year-old spinster who
lives nearby, for instance, he was careful to explain (lest I should
find out, I suppose!) that he had refused payment only because
she had "no man to make money for her"; again, when he asked
me to take an ad in his projected Colony Road News and I was
so irreverent as to reserve two inches of space for the slogan
"HOORAY FOR MRS. HEATH," Peter offered to refund my dollar
because he had caused my ad to appear as "COMPLIMENTS OF A
FRIEND." I must, however, state categorically that Peter has
faithfully and conscientiously fulfilled his share of every and
any contract between us, whatever it may have been. (And the
fact that one or two of these contracts have been rather clearer
to Peter than to me, has been indignantly attributed by my own
children to my habit of doing jigsaw puzzles, reading, watching
television programs and saying "Uh-hunh" simultaneously, when
I should have been listening. My husband affirms this judgment.)

Lest my young friend sound barely lower than the angels, I
must add that his fertile imagination combined with his 13-
year-old sense of humor have led, on occasion, to my addressing
him with "harsh words and unkind"—("You know perfectly well
that when I told you last Tuesday you could climb upon the
roof to get your glider, I didn't mean you could buy ten more
gliders and aim them at the—and by the way, I hope you didn't
buy them with the lottery money for the bicycle horn—when are
you going to have that lottery, anyway? I bought those tickets
six weeks ago!" And much more.) These irrational, if predictable
crises of the adult world leave Peter possibly repentant,
probably remorseful, but certainly unruffled. He is more sophisticated today than three years ago, when, at the age of ten,

he frequently urged me not to get my liver in a quiver. Today, when Peter and I have what he refers to as "a difference of opinion," he retires with complete equanimity to his own back yard until such time as my ill-humor subsides. My change of mood is apparently picked up by Peter's extra-sensory perception within the hour, for whenever I decide that the time has come for forgiving and forgetting, he appears at my front door within fifteen minutes, to assure me he has forgiven and forgotten. By way of proof (or penance?) he then resumes without rancor his status as our daily visitor.

Needless to say, our friendship is steadfast.

ALOISE BUCKLEY HEATH
(Mrs. Benjamin Heath)

March 15, 1958

CRANWELL PREPARATORY SCHOOL
Office of the Principal

Mrs. Benjamin Wild Heath
29 Colony Road
West Hartford, Connecticut
DEAR MRS. HEATH:

I am very grateful to you for your detailed and colorful description of Peter Bailey-Gates.

Many of Peter's accomplishments can be put to good use at School. Leaf-raking and snow-shoveling are part of the punitive curriculum. Endowed with all the energy which you describe, I am sure that Peter will be an early candidate for demerits.

We will try to keep pace with Peter. What substitute we will have when the occasion arises for Peter to "retire to his own back yard" we will try to figure out during the year.

Sincerely yours,
CHARLES E. BURKE, S.J.
(Rev.) Charles E. Burke, S.J.
Principal

March 15, 1958

Dear Mimi and Dad:

Please excuse the paper, for I'm in study hall, and since something happened tonight, which made me feel pretty proud of my little (little? Ha Ha) brother Peter, I thought I'd tell you about it, unless you already know, This has also changed practically my entire attitude toward Father Burke who has practically never been known to crack a smile in the memory of the oldest graduate.

Not more than five minutes ago, during the break between study hall hours, Father Burke called me and showed me a letter which Mrs. Heath had written to him about Peter. It described Peter to a tee. All of the letter was praiseworthy about him, and had been written just about Peter and nothing else. Father Burke was astonished and asked me if it was all true, and I told him it was, and he said in that case PETER GETS IN!! . . .

Say hello to the little kids for me please, and tell them "Big Dave" will be home soon.

Love and prayers,
YOUR SON DAVID

Dear Pete—Boy, does Mrs. Heath sure have your number. Father Burke said he can hardly wait to get you up here to knock it out of you. Love and kisses.                    DAVE

# APPENDIX

APPENDIX

TEST YOUR L.Q.*

To take this test you need copies of ten of your letters. Preferably these letters should be selected from a group of twenty-five to fifty collected for the purpose as suggested in Chapter 1. Select a few short ones, a few long ones, and a few of average length, to a total of ten. Don't try to pick out the ones you think are good or bad. Try to get a fair sampling.

Before beginning the test, estimate the total number of words in the ten letters selected. Then count the number of sentences in the letters. You need not make a big project of word counting. An estimate is good enough. It can be had by counting the number of words in a typical line of typing, multiplying by the number of lines in the body of the letters, and reducing the result by 5 per cent to allow for partial lines. Don't bother with headings and closes.

Take your time. The more time you take the more thorough the test will be. The test is designed to help you discover your shortcomings and do something about them. Often it will be necessary to refer to parts of this book to refresh your memory on a subject. This you can easily do, because each question is followed by a reference to the proper page number. It is especially important to go back to the text for more information about parts B, C, and D.

### A. Have Your Letters the Modern Look?

Take one letter at a time and examine it for the answer to each of the following questions. If the answer is Yes, make a check mark in the column opposite the question. Do this for each of the ten letters.

1. Is the letter neatly typed and spaced with the appearance of being framed on the page? (Pages 190–9)    YES (√)

2. Are the paragraphs short with none longer than ten lines? (Page 74)

* letter-writing quotient

3. Are the words in the body of the letter unabbrevi-   YES (√)
ated, except such words as *Mr., Mrs., Jr., Sr., Dr.,* etc.?
(Page 202)

4. Is the letter free of misspelled words? (Page 168)

5. Have you used commas only where needed for sense
or a "breath"? (Pages 172–80)

6. Did you ask a direct question when appropriate and
conversational? (Page 105)

7. Have you used an occasional contraction (*wouldn't,
isn't, I'm, we'll,* etc.) where appropriate? (Page 104)

8. Is the letter free of Latin words (*per, annum, diem,*
and so on) that can be replaced by English? (Page 99)

9. Is the letter free of old-fashioned letter language
such as *enclosed herewith, kindly advise,* and *duly noted?*
(For other examples see page 99.)

10. Did you avoid beginning the letter with *reference
is made, this is in reply, replying to your letter, this is to
inform you,* and so on? (Page 119)

TOTAL "YES" ANSWERS _____

Add the check marks and divide by 10. For example, if you have
68 "yes" answers, your score is 68 divided by 10, or 6.8. The highest
score you can make on part A is 10.

SCORE _____

### B. *Are Your Letters Wordy?*

Underscore words of the following classes in each of the ten letters:

1. Roundabout prepositional phrases such as *in the amount of,
in reference to, in regard to* and *with respect to.* (For other examples
see pages 30–1.)

2. Paddings such as *attention is called, we should like to point out,*
and *our records show.* (For other examples see pages 41–4.)

3. Adjectives and adverbs that add nothing to the meaning,
tone or color of the letter. (Page 36)

4. Words of overlapping meaning as *on* in *continued on* and
*back* in *return back.* (For other examples see pages 39–41.)

5. Relative pronouns that add nothing to the sense and smooth-

ness of the sentence, as which in the invoice which you requested and that in the question that is doubtful [doubtful question]. (For other examples see pages 37–8.)

6. Words needlessly repeating or paraphrasing what the reader said in his letter. (Pages 20–3)

7. Words supplying details the reader can supply for himself. (Pages 24–6)

8. Any other words that can be left out without affecting the meaning or tone of the letter.

TOTAL WORDS IN THE LETTERS _____

TOTAL WORDS UNDERSCORED _____

Count the total excess words (underscored) and divide by the total number of words in the letters. For example, if you have 320 excess words and there are 1,700 words in the ten letters, your wordiness rate is 18.8 per cent (320 divided by 1,700). Score as follows: If your rate is 5 per cent or less, score 30. If your rate is higher than 5 per cent, reduce the score of 30 by 1 point for each 1 per cent above 5. For example, score 29 for 6 per cent, 28 for 7 per cent, 24 for 11 per cent, 14 for 21 per cent, and so on. If the wordiness rate is 30 per cent you don't score. If it is more than 30 per cent you score a minus 1 for each 1 per cent above 30. Thus if the rate is 35 per cent, your score is minus 5.

SCORE _____

## C. Are Your Letters Stiff?

Circle words of the following classes in each letter:

1. Big words for which you might have used little ones, including heavy connectives like however, therefore and accordingly; technical terms that may not be understood by the reader; and anglicized Latin for which you might have used idiom—delinquent instead of past-due, continue instead of keep up, and so on. (For other examples see pages 52–62.)

2. Abstractions that can be replaced with concrete, specific (picture) words. (Pages 78–81)

3. Passive verbs where active verbs would be more natural and stronger. (Pages 81–3)

4. Nouns that could have been verbs, as *make a decision* instead of *decide, held a meeting* instead of *met,* and so on. (For other examples see pages 34–6.)

5. Impersonal words when you might have chosen personal ones, as *an applicant* instead of *you, this company* instead of *we,* and *the above-mentioned* instead of *Mr. Jones.* (Pages 100–3)

TOTAL CIRCLES _____

Count the circles. (Don't count the number of words in the circles.) Each circle counts 2. Multiply the number of circles by 2, and divide the result by the number of words in the letters. For example, you would get a rating of 9.4 for 80 circles in 1,700 words (80 times 2 divided by 1,700). A rating of 5 per cent or less is excellent. Score 20. Reduce the score by 1 point for each 1 per cent above 5: 19 points for 6 per cent, 18 points for 7 per cent, 15 points for 10 per cent, and so on. If the rating is 20 per cent, you don't score. Score 1 minus point for each 1 per cent above 20. Thus, a rating of 22 per cent would mean scoring a minus 2.

SCORE _____

## D. Are Your Letters Dynamic and Friendly?

Take one letter at a time and examine it for the answer to each of the following questions. If the answer is Yes, make a check mark in the column opposite the question. If the question is not applicable to the letter, check a "yes" answer.

1. Did you answer the reader's question straightaway, YES (√) and then explain or give other information as required? (Pages 122–4)

2. Did you accentuate the positive? (Pages 83–7)

3. Is the letter well organized with the big idea built into the spot where it will be most convincing and most likely to capture the reader's attention? (Pages 118, 129–31)

4. Do you admit mistakes? Save face for the reader? (Pages 106–7, 111–12)

5. Is the letter calculated to appeal to your reader's interests and wants? (Pages 87–92)

TOTAL "YES" ANSWERS _____

Add the "yes" answers in all the letters, divide by 10 and multiply by 6. For example, 40 affirmative answers will give you a score of 24 (40 divided by 10 and multiplied by 6). The highest possible score is 30.

SCORE _____

### E. Did You Give Your Reader One Thought or a Few Related Thoughts at a Time?

Divide the total number of words in the ten letters by the total number of sentences to get your average sentence length.

AVERAGE SENTENCE LENGTH _____

Score as follows:

| Average sentence length | Score |
|---|---|
| 22 words or less | 5 points |
| 22–24 words | 4 points |
| 25–27 words | 3 points |
| 28–30 words | 2 points |
| 31–33 words | 1 point |
| 34 words | none |

If your average sentence length is more than 34 words, score 1 minus point for each word above 34. For example, if your sentences average 37 words, your score would be minus 3.

SCORE _____

### F. Are Your Letters Grammatical?

Take one letter at a time and examine it for errors in grammar that might offend the reader. If you find any such errors, put a box around them. At the same time, take note of grammar that might be improved in future dictation, even though it is not offensive. (See Chapter 7.)

Score 5 points if you discover no embarrassing errors. Reduce this score by 1 point for each such error discovered. If you have more than 5 errors, score 1 minus point for each error above 5.

SCORE _____

### INTERPRETING YOUR SCORE

The total points possible on the six parts of this test are 100, but "100" is not to be taken as a measure of perfection. Chances are no two people would come up with exactly the same score on the same letters. But if you have answered each question carefully, checking the text of this book for guidance, you can make a fair appraisal of your letters.

If your total score is 90 or above, you may be in a class with top professional letter writers. If your total score is between 80 and 90 you can consider your letters very good, perhaps excellent. For a first test, 70 to 80 is good; 60 to 70 is fair.

Your score on the first test isn't too important. The important thing is the discovery of your shortcomings. You can now see just where you need to make improvements. Study the part of the book that can help you. After several weeks take another test to see how much you have improved. You need not take the entire test each time. Take only those parts covering your particular shortcomings.

## THE WATCH LIST

Watch for the words and phrases listed here. Some are over-worked, pompous or awkward. A few are ungrammatical. Many are longer than they need be. Page references are given for those subjects discussed in greater detail in other parts of this book.

ABOUT, AT. Avoid the superfluous *about* or *at* in sentences like this: *He will arrive at about 3 o'clock.* Use *at* or *about*, but not both.

ABOVE MENTIONED, ABOVE NAMED, ABOVE REFERENCED. These may be useful for printed letters, but the proper names add a personal touch and should be used in typed letters. (Pages 100–1)

ABSOLUTELY. Combined with words like *accurate, perfect*, and *certain*, this adverb is uncalled for. (Page 40)

ACCEDE TO. *Grant a request* is more natural than *accede to a request.*

ACCOMPANIED WITH. The preposition *with* will usually express the same idea as *accompanied with*. If *accompanied* is used, the preferred idiom is *accompanied by* instead of *accompanied with*. (Page 157)

ACCOMPLISH is overworked. Try *do.*

ACCORDINGLY. Instead of this heavy connective, try *so*. (Page 72)

ACKNOWLEDGMENT might be reserved for describing a letter notifying the reader that his inquiry has been received and will be answered later. When a letter is answered, *reply* or *answer* is more descriptive.

ACQUAINT. Instead of *acquainting* the reader with facts, why not *tell* or *inform* him?

ACQUIRE. *Buy* is sharper than *acquire* when the word is used in that sense. *To get* or *to gain* will often replace *acquire* for general purposes.

ADDITIONALLY is another heavy connective. Try *and, too, also* and *besides*. (Page 72)

ADVANCE PLANNING. Planning is always in advance. Say *planning*. (Page 40)

ADVISE. *Tell, inform* and *say* are fresher words for letters. *You are advised* is padding, as is the old-fashioned *kindly be advised*.

AFFECT, EFFECT. *Affect* is always a verb meaning to modify or influence. *Effect* may be a verb or noun. As a verb it means accomplish or bring about; as a noun, outcome or result. Both *affect* and *effect* are overworked in letters.

AFFIX YOUR SIGNATURE. Pompous. Say *sign the paper, check, form*, etc. (Page 54)

AFFORD AN OPPORTUNITY is usually just a roundabout way of saying *allow*.

AFOREMENTIONED. It's just as easy to repeat the name or use a pronoun as it is to say *aforementioned*. (Pages 100–1)

ALL AROUND. Say *all-round* in the sense of all-round clerk.

ALL OF. *Of* is uncalled for in phrases like *all (of) the workers* and *all (of) the profits*.

ALL READY, ALREADY. *All ready* is an adjective phrase correctly used in this sentence: *When the hour came, they were all ready.* *Already* is an adverb that oftener than not can be omitted: *We have (already) finished the job.*

ALONG THE LINES OF usually equals *like*. Oftentimes superfluous. Say *management research* instead of *research along the lines of management*.

ALTERNATIVE, CHOICE. In a strict sense *alternative* refers to two only; *choice* to two or more. The *alternative* expresses the same idea as the longer phrase *the only other alternative*.

AMONG, BETWEEN. Strictly, *between* refers to two only; *among* to more than two. (Page 151)

AMOUNT, NUMBER. *Amount* is a sum total; *number* in this relation denotes a quantity of units. Preferably, then, you have a large *number* (not *amount*) of errors.

ANGLE. *From every angle* is overworked. Often the idea is more accurately expressed by *entirely* or *in every way*.

ANTICIPATE means to foresee or prevent by prior action. *Expect* is a stronger word to imply the likelihood of a happening. Thus, the collector who says *we shall expect your payment* writes a stronger sentence than he who says *we anticipate your payment.*

ANXIOUS. Why give your sentence the unpleasant suggestion of anxiety when you mean eagerness? Say *we are eager* [not *anxious*] *to see your plan.*

ANY. You don't need to follow superlatives with *any*, as *Our products are the best of any.* Also, if you want to make the grammarian happy, you will use *other* in a comparative statement following *any*, as *That car is smoother than any other on the market* instead of *than any on the market.*

APPARENTLY is a hedger to be used only when necessary. (Page 84)

APPEAR suggests that which is visible. So a woman *appears* to be young, but *seems* to be intelligent.

APPRECIATE YOUR INFORMING US is a clumsy way of saying *Please write us* or *Please tell us.*

APPRISE. Stuffy. Why not *tell?*

APPROXIMATELY. Overworked. Use *about* sometimes.

APT in its strict meaning suggests predisposition. A tactless person is *apt* to write a blunt letter, but delayed replies are *likely* (in preference to *apt*) to damage public relations.

ARRANGE TO is frequently superfluous, as in *arrange to inform us.* Say *inform us.*

AS, THAN. Don't make a preposition out of *as* in a sentence like this: *He is as old as me.* Write *as I.* Similarly, don't write *He is older than me.* Say *than I.* (Pages 151–2)

AS FROM. *As from November 1 the product will be withdrawn from the market* is crude. Omit *as from.* When a preposition is needed, use *from, since* or *after* instead of *as from.* For example, *We've kept records since January 1* instead of *We've kept records as from January 1.*

AS OF THIS DATE equals *today.* (Page 30)

AS TO WHETHER can usually be expressed as *whether*.

AS YOU KNOW. If the reader knows what you are about to say, why tell him? (Page 24)

ASCERTAIN is often used when *learn* would do the job. Reserve *ascertain* for getting across the idea that there is effort involved. (Page 60)

ASSEMBLED TOGETHER. *Assembled* is enough. (Page 40)

ASSISTANCE. Let's have more *help* and *aid* and less *assistance*.

AT—

    —ALL TIMES equals *always*.

    —AN EARLY DATE equals *soon*.

    —THE DUE DATE equals *when due*.

    —THE PRESENT TIME equals *now*.

    —THE TIME OF equals *when*.

    —THIS TIME equals *now*.

    —YOUR EARLIEST CONVENIENCE. Do you mean this? That time may never come.

ATTACHED—

    —HERETO    Worn-out letter language. *Attached* or *enclosed* is enough.

    —HEREWITH

    —PLEASE FIND

ATTENTION IS CALLED. Avoid calling attention to your statements with expressions like *attention is called, attention is invited,* and *I would like to call your attention to the fact*. Let your words speak for themselves. (Page 42)

BASIC FUNDAMENTALS. Omit *basic*. (Page 40)

BASIS FOR. *For* often does the job of *as a basis for*. Example: *Get the facts needed (as a basis) for the report*.

BEG TO ADVISE. Dead language. (Page 98)

BETWEEN YOU AND I, though frequently heard in speech, should be avoided in writing. Say *between you and me*. Similarly, say *between us supervisors* instead of *between we supervisors*. (Page 151)

BIANNUAL, BIENNIAL. *Biannual*, like *semiannual*, means twice a year. *Biennial* means every two years.

BIMONTHLY means every two months. *Semimonthly* is used to express twice monthly.

BY—

—MEANS OF equals *by* or *with*.

—REASON OF equals *because of, through* or *by*.

—WAY OF usually equals *to* or *for*.

(Pages 30–1)

CAN, MAY. *Can* suggests ability; *may*, possibilty or permission. Although you need not be fussy about the distinction in all cases, it is polite to use *may* when asking permission, as *May we show you our latest model?* (Page 152)

CARBON COPY. In referring to a carbon copy of a letter, *copy* is sufficient. (Page 40)

CHARACTER is an abstract word that can often be avoided. Instead of *His work is of a high-grade character*, say *His work is high-grade.*

CHOICE. See *Alternative.*

CLAIM. *You say* is more pleasing to the reader than *you claim.*

COGNIZANCE. Avoid this big word both in its legal meaning of jurisdiction and its common meaning of *heed* or *notice*. Instead of saying *not under the cognizance of this department*, be specific, as: *This department does not audit travel vouchers.* Instead of *having cognizance of a fact*, try *aware of a fact.*

COMMENCE. *Start* and *begin* are stout words.

COMMITMENT. Don't forget *promise.*

COMMUNICATE, COMMUNICATION. Avoid these words when you can be specific, replacing *communicate* with *write, wire* or *phone,* and *communication* with *letter, wire* or *phone call.*

COMPLIANCE, COMPLIES. The phrase *in compliance with your request* is needlessly formal. *As you requested* is better for a friendly letter. *Meets requirements* or *meets the needs* takes the weight off *complies with requirements.*

CONCLUDE. *Close a letter* is better than *conclude a letter.*

CONSEQUENTLY. Use *so* sometimes. (Page 72)

CONSIDERABLE. Use only as an adjective and then use sparingly.

*This is important* is better than *this is a matter of considerable importance.*

CONSIDERED OPINION. Forget this one.

CO-OPERATE TOGETHER. Co-operate suggests togetherness. (Page 40)

CORRESPONDENCE. When referring to one letter, say *letter*. Use *correspondence* only for variety in expressing the idea of an exchange of letters or a body of letters.

CONTINUOUSLY, CONTINUALLY. *Continuously* means without interruption; *continually*, intermittently or at frequent intervals. If the distinction is unimportant there is no cause to be precise.

COULDN'T HARDLY is a double negative to be avoided. Say *could hardly*. (Page 164)

CREDIT ACCOMMODATION. It goes without saying that credit is an accommodation.

CURRENTLY PREVAILING. *Prevailing* is sufficient.

DATA may be used as a singular or a plural noun. (Page 159) Why not use *facts* when that word expresses the same meaning?

DATE. Instead of *this date*, say *today*; instead of *under date of*, say *on*.

DEGREE. *A degree of improvement has been noted by our company* is jargon for *We have noted improvement.*

DELINQUENT. Prefer *past due* in the sense of a delinquent account.

DEMONSTRATES. *Shows* is a good plain word for this one.

DESIRE. *If you wish* or *if you want* is usually better than *if you desire.*

DETERMINE. Overworked. Try *decide* or *find out.*

DEVELOP. Avoid this word in the sense of *happen, find out* or *take place.*

DIFFERENT is superfluous in *Six (different) plans were discussed.* The preferred idiom is *different from* rather than *different than.* (Page 154)

DUE TO THE FACT THAT is a roundabout way of saying *because.* (On use of *due to* as a prepositional phrase, see page 155.)

DURING THE TIME equals *while*.

EACH, EVERY. You can't get "between" an *each* or an *every*, so avoid expressions like *between each payday*. Say *between paydays*. (Pages 155-6)

EARLIEST PRACTICABLE DATE. Heavy. Be specific if you can.

EFFECT. See *Affect*.

EFFECTUATE. A pompous way of saying *bring about*. (Page 61)

EMPLOYED is overworked in the sense of *used*. Instead of *We are employing every tool*, why not *We are using every tool?*

EMPLOYMENT. *Jobs* and *work* have equal dignity.

ENCLOSED—

    —HEREWITH

    —PLEASE FIND    *Enclosed* will do.

    —WITH THIS LETTER

ENCOUNTER DIFFICULTY can be expressed as *find hard* or *have trouble*. Instead of *Let us know if you encounter difficulty collecting the account*, why not *Let us know if you have trouble?*

ENDEAVOR TO ASCERTAIN, high-sounding phrase through it is, simply means *try to find out*.

EQUALLY AS GOOD. Omit the *as*.

EQUIVALENT is seldom better than *equal*. (Page 61)

EVERY. See *Each*.

EXERCISE CARE is a stuffy way of saying *be careful*.

EXPEDITE, though not so popular in recent years, still shows up where the little words *hurry* or *hasten* might be used. Do you know that the Latin from which *expedite* derives means "to free one caught by the foot"?

EXPERIENCE HAS INDICATED THAT. Try *we have learned*.

FACILITATE means *make easy*, but it makes hard reading for some people. (Page 61)

FACT. *Due to the fact that* is a roundabout way of saying *because*.

FARTHER, FURTHER. In strict usage *farther* suggests distance; *further* denotes quantity or degree. You go *farther* away; you hear nothing *further*. (Page 156)

FAVOR. Does anybody use *favor* nowadays in the sense of a *letter*? Don't. It's old-fashioned.

FEWER, LESS. *Fewer* is for numbers; *less* is for quantities or amounts. Write *fewer* pages and use *less* ink. (Page 156)

FILED FOR FUTURE REFERENCE. Meaningless.

FIRST is both an adjective and adverb. Don't say *firstly*.

FOLLOWING is now widely used in the sense of *after*, but it is preferable to say *he retired after* [not *following*] *an outstanding career*. (Page 157)

FINALIZE, FINALIZATION. We don't need to manufacture words like these when we have *end, conclude* and *complete*.

FOR—
   —THE MONTH OF JULY equals *for July*.
   —THE PURPOSE OF equals *for*.
   —THE REASON THAT equals *because, since, as*.
   —YOUR INFORMATION is padding.

FORMER, LATTER. Don't make your reader look back for the antecedents of these words. Repeat the name. (Page 157)

FORWARD is sometimes used when *send* is better, as *forward* [*send*] *the merchandise C.O.D.*

FULLEST POSSIBLE EXTENT is padding. *Fully* expresses the idea.

FURNISH. One of the most overworked words in letters. Why not *give the facts* instead of *furnish the facts*?

FURTHER. See *Farther*.

FURTHERMORE. Lighten the sentence with a little connective like *too, again*, or *also*. (Page 72)

HAVEN'T BUT. A double negative. Say *have but*. (Page 164)

HEREIN, HERETO, HEREWITH. Legal style to be avoided in letters.

HOWEVER. *But* and *yet* will often replace this heavy connective. (Page 72)

IF AND WHEN. One or the other—not both. Make it *if* for the conditional; *when* for a certainty.

IMPLEMENT. *Carry out* is good idiom. (Pages 57–9)

IMPLY, INFER. When the other fellow *implies*, you may *infer*—and vice versa. To *imply* is to *hint* or *suggest*; to *infer* is to *derive a* meaning or draw a conclusion from a statement or a set of facts. So you might say to your correspondent (regarding a statement of his): *You imply* [not *infer*] *that you wish to sell the bonds;* or *I infer* [not *imply*] *that you wish to sell the bonds.* Or you might say (concerning your own statements) *I do not mean to imply* [not *infer*] *that you should sell the bonds.*

IN. Most of the roundabout prepositional phrases (*in the event of, in the amount of, in reference to,* etc.) begin with *in.* Boil them down to single prepositions (*if, for, about,* etc). (Page 31)

INADVERTENCY. You can't hide an error behind this word. (Pages 106–7)

INASMUCH AS. Heavy. Say *as, because* or *since.*

INCLINED TO SAY. Just say it.

INDICATE is overworked. Try *show.*

INDORSE ON THE BACK OF THE CHECK. *Indorse the check* is enough. (Page 40)

INFORM. Use *tell* oftener. *You are informed* is padding. Avoid the use of *informing* with an infinitive: *We are asking* [not *informing*] *our salesman to meet you in Detroit.*

INITIAL is overworked, but *first* isn't.

INITIATE is no more impressive than *begin.*

INSTRUMENTS. Avoid this stuffy word when you mean *papers.*

INSURE is a good word, but in the sense of *make sure* it is overworked.

INTERPOSE NO OBJECTION. A favorite government abstraction. Be specific with *I approve;* or if you're just being a good fellow in going along with something you don't like, you might say *I won't stand in the way.* (Pages 61–2)

IT, ITS, IT'S. Avoid impersonal passives such as *it is believed* and *it is recognized.* Say *I* [we] *believe* or *I* [we] *recognize.* (Page 83) *Its* is the possessive of *it. It's* is a contraction of *it is.* (Page 158)

JURISDICTION. See *Cognizance.*

KIND, SORT. Use in the singular if you want to be grammatical. Avoid *kind of a* and *sort of a,* and refer to a class of objects as *kind of machine* and *sort of trap.* (Page 158)

KINDLY. Prefer *please* to *kindly*, saying *please reply* instead of *kindly reply*. *Kindly be advised* is dead language. (Page 99)

LAST, LATEST. Prefer *last* in the sense of final; *latest* in the sense of most recent: *the last page of a book; the latest* [not *last*] *book on the subject.*

LATTER. See *Former.*

LAY, LIE. *Lie* in the meaning of recline never takes the form of *laid.* For the past tense of *lie*, say *he lay* (or *was lying*) *on the floor*— not *he laid on the floor. Lay* in the meaning of placing never takes the form of *lie.* Say *He laid the paper on the desk*, or *Lay the paper on the desk.* (Page 159)

LEAST is used when more than two persons or things are mentioned. Use *less* when only two: *He is the less* [not *least*] *forceful of the two speakers.*

LENGTH OF TIME is usually a circumlocution. Instead of *Let us know the length of time you will be away* say *Let us know how long you'll be away.*

LENGTHY is a good word to describe a tediously long letter. *Long* is better for the two-page letter that sticks to what is worth saying.

LESS. See *Fewer* and *Least.*

LIABLE. Avoid *liable* in the sense of *likely. The consumer is likely* [not *liable*] *to be cautious.*

LIEU OF. Why not *in place of* instead of *in lieu of?*

LIKE. Grammarians say *like* should not be used to introduce a clause of comparison. *He wrote as* [not *like*] *he spoke.* (Page 159)

LIQUIDATE. Try *pay off* if that is the idea. (Pages 57–9)

LOCALITY. *Place* is usually better.

LOCATE. In the sense of looking for, it is better to say *find a file* than *locate a file.*

MATERIALIZE. A big word that can usually be replaced by *happen, occur* or *come about.* (Page 61)

MAY. See *Can.*

MEANS in the sense of *resources* is always plural. In the sense of *means to an end* it may be singular or plural.

MEETS WITH OUR APPROVAL is a roundabout way of saying we approve. (Pages 34–6)

MISPOSTED IN ERROR. Say misposted. (Page 40)

MODIFICATION. Try change. (Page 61)

MORE OR LESS. Delete more or less in a sentence like this: We are (more or less) inclined to favor . . .

MOREOVER. Another heavy connective to watch. Try besides, too and also. And how about what's more? (Page 72)

MYSELF. This is a reflexive pronoun properly used in referring back to I. I will do it myself, but he selected Joe and me [not myself]. (Pages 163–4)

NEAR. Say not nearly enough instead of not near enough.

NECESSARY is sometimes used when need would be sharper, as: It is not necessary for you instead of You need not.

NEGLIGIBLE AMOUNT. Overworked. Try small amount.

NEVERTHELESS. Still, yet and just the same are lighter. (Page 72)

NOMINAL means in name and, by implication, small. Why not say small?

NOTED. It will be noted is padding. If you need an emphatic, simply say Note.

NOTIFICATION is a big word for notice. (Page 61)

NOTWITHSTANDING THE FACT THAT equals although or even though.

NUMBER. Treat a number as a plural noun and the number as a singular noun: a number were but the number was. (Page 153)

OBLIGATION can be debt.

OF EVEN DATE equals today.

ON is superfluous in stating days and dates: He arrived Tuesday [not on Tuesday].

ON—

—A FEW OCCASIONS equals occasionally.

—THE BASIS OF usually equals by.

—THE PART OF equals by, among, for.

(For other roundabout prepositional phrases see pages 30–1.)

ONE. Omit one in sentences like this: This error is not the first (one).

OPTIMUM is Latin for *best*. Let's stick to English. (Page 99)

OUR MR. *Our Mr. Jones* smacks of commercialese. Say *Mr. Jones* or *Mr. Jones of our company.*

OUT is uncalled for in phrases like *lose out* and *start out. He started (out) as a messenger.*

OVER is preferably avoided in the sense of *more than* when referring to a number. *He found more than* [not *over*] *a dozen errors in the letter.*

OVER-ALL. Beware of this overworked word. Often it adds nothing to the meaning of the sentence, as: *Caution is the (over-all) trend among buyers.*

OVER THE SIGNATURE OF is a formal way of saying *signed by.*

PAMPHLET. Don't say *little pamphlet.* The suffix *-let* on words like *pamphlet, booklet* and *leaflet* means small or little.

PART. *Our mistake* is better than *a mistake on our part.*

PARTICIPATE is a common word, but *take part* is a good way of saying the same thing.

PARTY. Why use *party* when you mean *person?*

PAST. *Last year* should be preferred to *past year* when speaking of the preceding year.

PER. Avoid the Latin *per annum* and *per diem.* Say *a year* and *a day* or *by the year and day.* (Page 99)

PHOTOSTATIC COPIES. *Photostats* is now generally accepted.

PORTION. *Part of the time,* not *portion of the time.*

POSSESS. Why not *have?*

PRACTICABLE, PRACTICAL. A *practicable suggestion* can theoretically be carried out, but a *practical suggestion* can actually be carried out.

PREDECEASE is used as a euphemism. Euphemisms are not as tone-invoking as you might think. Nobody will be shocked by *die before.*

PREVENTIVE is better than the irregular doublet *preventative.*

PREVIOUS TO, PRIOR TO. Why not *before?* (Page 166)

PRINCIPAL, PRINCIPLE. These words are sometimes used incorrectly. *Principal* as a noun means head or chief, as well as capital sum. The adjective *principal* means highest or best in rank or importance. *Principle*, always a noun, means truth, belief, policy, conviction or general theory. Thus, a *principal purpose* and an *accepted principle*.

PROCESS OF PREPARATION makes the act no more important than *being prepared*.

PROCURE is often used when *get* or *buy* would serve.

PROMULGATE. A big word for *issue*.

PROVIDED, PROVIDING. Reserve *provided* for formal stipulations, as: *We agree to build a plant in your city provided*. . . . *If* will replace *provided* for simple conditions, as: *We will make a down payment of $3,000 if he agrees to sell*. Avoid the use of *providing* in the sense of *if* or *provided*. (Pages 166–7)

PURCHASE. Use *buy* oftener.

PURSUANT TO YOUR REQUEST is needlessly formal. Say *as you requested*. (Page 99)

RARELY EVER, SELDOM EVER. *Ever* is unwanted here. *He rarely (ever) speaks unless spoken to; we seldom (ever) fail*.

QUESTION. *There is no question but that* is a circumlocution for *unquestionably*.

REASON IS BECAUSE. Omit *because*.

RECENT DATE. Unbusinesslike. Omit or give the specific date.

REGARDING. Overworked. Little words wear better, so use *about* oftener.

REMUNERATION. The tax collector's word for *pay*.

RENDER. Often superfluous, as *We will render assistance in any way we can*, when *We will help in any way we can* would be neater.

RESPECTING, like *regarding*, is overworked. Here again you can vary with little words like *about* and *in*.

RETURN BACK. Say *return*. (Page 40)

REVIEW OF RECORDS. Expressions like *Review of our records fails to disclose* and *Our records show* can be dispensed with. (Page 43)

SAME. Drop *same* from your letter vocabulary in this usage: *Please sign and return same*. Repeat the word to which *same* refers or use a pronoun, as *Sign the form*, or *Sign it*.

SAID. Avoid this word in phrases such as *the said date* or *the said mortgage*. Use a pronoun or repeat the date or title. (Page 99)

SAY. The reader doesn't need to be told that you are saying something. Avoid paddings like *will say, would say, wish to say*, and so on. (Page 42)

SECURE. Although generally used in the sense of *get, take* and *obtain*, this word adds needless weight to the sentence.

SELDOM EVER. See *Rarely ever.*

SET, SIT. *Set* in the meaning of *set the typewriter on the desk* never takes the form of *sit. Sit* in the meaning of *she sits at this desk* never takes the form of *set.* Past tense of *sit* is *sat* or *was sitting.* (Page 168)

SOME. *Somewhat, a little* or *rather* is preferable to *some* in sentences like this: *His letters are somewhat* [not *some*] *better.*

SORT. See *Kind.*

SPOUSE. Unless you are quoting a law, why use this word in preference to *husband* or *wife?*

STANDPOINT. Watch this one. It encourages wordiness, as *I see no advantage in selling the stock from the standpoint of taxes,* when you might say *I see no tax advantage in selling the stock.*

STATE is more formal than *say.*

STILL REMAINS. Omit *still.* (Page 41)

SUBSEQUENT TO equals *after.*

TAKE THE LIBERTY OF. This phrase and its companion *take the opportunity of* are overworked and seldom effective.

TENDER. Commercialese. Instead of *tendering* payments and apologies, simply *make* them.

TERMINATED. *Ended* is just as final.

THAN. See *As.*

THANKING YOU IN ADVANCE. *Thank you* or *Thanks* is the modern way of saying the same thing.

THAT, WHICH. Use *that* to introduce a restrictive clause required to complete your meaning, as *This is the house that Jack built.* Use *which* to introduce a clause that can be left out without materially changing the meaning of the sentence, as *The Dallas plant, which we opened in January, is now operating full time.* (Pages 169–70)

THIS—

—IS TO INFORM YOU. Padding. Omit.

—IS TO ACKNOWLEDGE AND THANK YOU. *Thank you* is enough.

TO THE EFFECT THAT. Usually a circumlocution, as *your argument to the effect that* for *your argument that.*

TRANSMITTED. What's wrong with *sent?*

UNDER DATE OF equals *on.*

UNDER SEPARATE COVER. A detail the reader can usually supply for himself. If not, say *separately.* (Page 99)

UNDERSIGNED is you, the signer of the letter. Refer to yourself in human terms, *I* or *me.* (Page 99)

UNTIL SUCH TIME AS. Try *when* or *until.*

UP TO THE PRESENT WRITING is *up to now.*

UTILIZATION is an inflated word for *use.*

VERY is redundant in phrases like *very complete.* Use *very* sparingly. When used in excess it becomes obtrusive. (Page 37)

VISITATION is the organization man's word for *visit.* (Page 53)

WERE. The subjunctive *were* is generally considered a must in *if I were you.* Don't write *if I was you.* (Page 169)

WHICH. See *That.*

WHILE serves its best purpose in expressing time, as: *He worked while I slept. Although* is stronger than *while* in a sentence like this: *Although* [*while*] *he works hard, he accomplishes little.*

WISH TO ADVISE, WISH TO APOLOGIZE. Do it without wishing.

WITH—

—REFERENCE TO. Try *about* or *on.*

—REGARD TO. Try *about* or *in.*

WORTH WHILE. *While* is superfluous in *It is worth* (*while*) *noting.*

## FORMS OF ADDRESS

Certain conventions are usually followed in addressing high-ranking government officials and dignitaries with whom the writer is not personally acquainted. Some preferred forms of address are shown here.

UNITED STATES GOVERNMENT OFFICIALS

### The President

| | |
|---|---|
| The President | The Honorable *full name* |
| The White House | The White House |
| Washington 25, D. C. | Washington 25, D. C. |

*or*

| | |
|---|---|
| My dear Mr. President: | My dear President *last name*: |
| *or* | *or* |
| Sir: | My dear Mr. President: |

### The Vice-President

The Vice-President
*or*
The President of the Senate
United States Senate
Washington 25, D. C.

*or*

The Honorable *full name*
Vice-President of the United
States
Washington 25, D. C.

My dear Mr. Vice-President:
*or*
Sir:

My dear Mr. *last name*:
*or*
My dear Mr. Vice-President:

## Cabinet Members

The Secretary of *department* or
or
The Attorney General of the
United States
or
The Postmaster General of the
United States
Washington 25, D. C.

My dear Mr. Secretary:
or
My dear Mr. Attorney General:
or
My dear Mr. Postmaster General:
or
My dear Sir (or Madam):

Honorable *full name*
Secretary of *department*
or
Attorney General of the United
States
or
Postmaster General of the
United States
Washington 25, D. C.

Dear Mr. (Mrs. or Miss) *last
name:*
or
Dear Mr. (or Madam) Secretary:
or
Dear Mr. Attorney General:
or
Dear Mr. Postmaster General:

## Heads of Independent Agencies

The Administrator of *service* or
*agency*
Washington 25, D. C.

My dear Sir:
or
Sir:

Honorable *full name*
or
Mr. *full name*
Administrator of *agency*
Washington 25, D. C.

Dear Mr. (Mrs. or Miss) *last
name:*

Similarly to a director and a commissioner.

MEMBERS OF THE CONGRESS OF THE UNITED STATES

*Senator*
Honorable *full name*
United States Senate
Washington 25, D. C.

Dear Senator *last name:*
or
Dear Senator:

*Representative*
Honorable *full name*
House of Representatives
Washington 25, D. C.

Dear Congressman *last name:*
or
Dear Mr. (Mrs. or Miss) *last name:*
or
Dear Congressman:

STATE GOVERNMENT OFFICIALS

Governor

The Governor of *state*     or
*Capital city, State*

My dear Sir:
or
Sir:

Honorable *full name*
Governor of *State*
*Capital city, State*

Dear Governor *last name:*
or
Dear Governor:

Similarly to a lieutenant governor.

## Heads of Departments

Secretary of department
or
The State Treasurer
or
The Attorney General
State of name of state
Capital city, State

Dear Sir:

or

Honorable full name
or
Mr. (Mrs. or Miss) full name
Secretary of department
or
State Treasurer
or
Attorney General
State of name of state
Capital city, State

Dear Mr. (Mrs. or Miss) last name:
or
Dear Sir (or Madam):

MEMBERS OF THE STATE LEGISLATURE

### Senators

Senator from district
The State of name of state
Capital city, State

Dear Sir:
or
Dear Madam:

or

Honorable full name
or
Mr. (Mrs. or Miss) full name
The State Senate
Capital city, State

Dear Mr. (Mrs. or Miss) last name:
or
Dear Senator:

*Representatives, Assemblymen and Delegates*

Representative from *district*   or
or
Assemblyman from *district*
or
Delegate from *district*
House of Representatives
   (Delegates or State Assembly)
*Capital city, State*


Dear Sir:
or
Dear Madam:

Honorable *full name*
or
Mr. (Mrs. or Miss) *full name*
Representative (Assemblyman or
   Delegate) from *district*
House of Representatives
   (Delegates or State Assembly)
*Capital city, State*


Dear Mr. (Mrs. or Miss) *last
   name:*

## MAYOR

The Mayor of *city*   or
City Hall
*City, State*


Dear Mr. Mayor:
or
Dear Sir (or Madam):

Honorable *full name*
or
Mr. (Mrs. or Miss) *full name*
Mayor of the City of *name of city*
City Hall
*City, State*


Dear Mayor *last name:*
or
Dear Mayor:

## JUDICIARY

### Chief Justice of the United States

The Chief Justice    or    The Honorable *full name*
The Supreme Court          Chief Justice of the Supreme
Washington 25, D. C.        Court
                                 Washington 25, D. C.

My dear Mr. Chief Justice:
        or          My dear Mr. Chief Justice:
Sir:

### Associate Justice of the Supreme Court of the United States

Mr. Justice *full name*    or    The Honorable *full name*
The Supreme Court          Justice, Supreme Court of the
Washington 25, D. C.        United States
                                 Washington 25, D. C.

My dear Mr. Justice *last name:*
      or        My dear Mr. Justice *last name:*
My dear Mr. Justice:            or
                               My dear Mr. Justice:

### Judge of U. S. District Court      Judge of a State Court

Honorable *full name*           Honorable *full name*
United States District Judge    Chief Justice (Presiding Judge or
*District*                      Associate Judge) of *court*
*Address*                    *Address*

Dear Judge *last name:*         Dear Chief Justice *last name:*
     or                    or
Sir:                          Sir:

## SCHOOL OFFICIALS

### President of a University or College

Full name, Ph.D.        or     Dr. full name
President, college or university    President, college or university
Address                 Address

My dear President last name:    Dear Dr. last name:
        or                      or
Sir:                    Dear President last name:

### Dean

Dean full name     or    Dr. (Mr., Mrs. or Miss) full
College or university          name
Address                 Dean of the College of college
                        University
Dear Dean last name:        Address
        or
Dear Dean:              Dear Dr. last name:
                            or
                        Dear Dean last name:
                            or
                        Dear Mr. (Mrs. or Miss) last
                            name:

## Superintendent of Schools

Superintendent full name   or
School or schools
Address

Dear Mr. (Mrs. or Miss) last
name:

Dr. (Mr. Mrs., or Miss) full
name
Superintendent of school or
schools
Address

Dear Dr. last name:
or
Dear Mr. (Mrs. or Miss) last
name:

### Roman Catholic

#### The Pope
His Holiness, the Pope
Vatican City
Rome, Italy

Your Holiness:

#### Cardinal
His Eminence first name
Cardinal last name
Archbishop of . . .
Address

Your Eminence:
or
My dear Cardinal last name:

#### Archbishop
The Most Reverend full name,
D.D.
Archbishop of . . .
Address

Your Excellency:
or
My dear Archbishop:
Similarly to a bishop.

#### Monsignor
The Right Reverend Monsignor
full name
Address

My dear Monsignor:
or
Monsignor:

*Priest*

Reverend Father *full name*
*Address*

Dear Father:
            or
Dear Father *name:*
            or
Reverend Sir:

*Heads of Colleges,
Universities and Seminaries*

The President of *name of*    or
    *school*
*Address*
Dear Father:

Similarly to a chancellor.

*Mother Superior*

The Reverend Mother Superior
Order
*Address*

My dear Reverend Mother:

*Member of a Brotherhood*

Brother *full name*
*Address*

Dear Brother *name:*
            or
Dear Brother:

The Very Reverend *full name*
President, *name of school*
*Address*

Very Reverend dear Father:

*Sister*

Sister *name*
Order
*Address*

Dear Sister *name:*
            or
Dear Sister:

## Protestant

### Episcopal Bishop
The Right Reverend full name
Bishop of State
Address

My dear Bishop last name:
or
Right Reverend Sir:

### Methodist Bishop
The Reverend Dr. full name
Methodist Bishop
Address

My dear Bishop last name:
or
Reverend and Dear Sir:

### Ministers
The Reverend (or Reverend Dr.)
full name
Address

My dear Mr. (or Dr.) last name:
or
Reverend and Dear Sir:

### Jewish Rabbi

The Rabbi of name of
synagogue
Address

My dear Rabbi:

or     Rabbi full name
or
Dr. full name
Address

My dear Rabbi last name:
or
My dear Dr. last name:

298

## BIBLIOGRAPHY

BERNSTEIN, THEODORE: *Watch Your Language.* Great Neck, New York: Channel Press, 1958.

FLESCH, RUDOLF: *The Art of Readable Writing.* New York: Harper and Brothers, 1949.

FOWLER, H. W. AND F. G.: *The King's English.* New York: Oxford University Press, 1931.

GOWERS, SIR ERNEST: *Plain Words: Their ABC.* New York: Alfred A. Knopf, Inc., 1955.

HUTCHINSON, LOIS: *Standard Handbook for Secretaries.* New York: McGraw-Hill Book Company, 1950.

MAYO, LUCY GRAVES: *Communication Handbook for Secretaries.* New York: McGraw-Hill Book Company, 1958.

NICHOLSON, MARGARET: *American-English Usage.* New York: Oxford University Press, 1957.

PERRIN, PORTER G.: *Writer's Guide and Index to English.* Chicago: Scott, Foresman and Co., 1950.

QUILLER-COUCH, SIR ARTHUR: *On the Art of Writing.* New York: G. P. Putnam's Sons, 1916.

STEBBINS, HAL: *Copy Capsules.* New York: McGraw-Hill Book Company, 1957.

*Webster's New International Dictionary.* 2nd ed. Springfield, Mass.: G. & C. Merriam Co., 1957.

WHITFORD, HAROLD C. AND DIXSON, ROBERT J.: *Handbook of American Idioms and Idiomatic Usage.* New York: Regents Publishing Co., 1953.

# Index

verbs, agreement with subject, 150
    efficiency of, 34–6
    used as nouns, *see* Possessives
      and the Verbal Noun,
      165–6
    vigor of, 81–3
verbosity in
    adjectives and adverbs, 36–7
    nouns, 34–6
    overlapping meaning, 39–41
    prepositions, 30–3
    relative pronouns, 37–8
very, used superfluously, 37, 287
vocabulary, 7

we and I, good usage of, 103
welcome, letters of, 245–6
which, distinguished from that,
    169–70
    superfluous, 37–8
who, misuse of, 170
    superfluous, 37–8
whom, misuse of, 170
will, *see* shall, 167
wish to say, 42
worth while, 287

you, important word, 90, 101

## ABOUT THE AUTHOR

MONA SHEPPARD studied English literature and creative writing at the University of Alabama. When she went to work for the U.S. Government, she was quickly impressed by the millions of letters written in all government offices in pure and unintelligible federalese, more commonly known as "gobbledygook." The "plain letters" she started writing almost cost her her job—they were too simple—but it was not long before Miss Sheppard became the number-one government consultant on letter writing. In 1955 her pamphlet Plain Letters, which was the nucleus of this book, was published by the U.S. Government Printing Office and became one of their all-time best sellers. It has reached the desks of over 500,000 federal employees, as well as businessmen and women everywhere. The U.S. Government honored her that same year with the Distinguished Service Award.

Miss Sheppard has subsequently advised numerous large business organizations on simplifying their correspondence. At present she is carrying on her campaign for "plain letters" as vice-president of Leahy and Company, a management-consultant firm.